PENGUIN BOOKS

# THE GREAT UNRAVELLING

'If you want an American liberal economist who will knock the right-wingers down so they *stay* down, then turn to Paul Krugman' *Independent on Sunday*

'Krugman's columns have become the most searing indictment around of "corporate misbehaviour on an epic scale" . . . witty, sceptical and brave but always compellingly lucid and entertainingly well-informed . . . He is a constant breath of fresh air. More power to his pen' *Herald*

'While the rest of the media leads the cheers, it's up to Krugman to explain how Bush is looting the economy' *Rolling Stone*

'Bush's greatest critic and a hero of the left . . . He is all the more despised by Republicans because his analysis has largely been right' *New Statesman*

'The most vociferous and effective critic of the Bush White House' *Guardian*

'The White House's most significant and penetrating domestic critic . . . His columns are a "must read"' *The Times Higher Education Supplement*

'The unofficial opposition to the Bush administration' *Independent*

'Essential reading . . . the columnist every Democrat in the country feels they need to read – and every Bush republican loves to hate' *Washington Monthly*

Krugman has been called 'the most important political columnist in America' by the *Washington Monthly*, 'the most celebrated economist of his generation' by the *Economist* and named Columnist of the Year by *Editor and Publisher* magazine. He teaches at Princeton University. He writes a twice-weekly column in *The New York Times*, on which this book is partly based.

*The*
# GREAT
# UNRAVELLING
*From boom to bust in three*
*scandalous years*

## PAUL KRUGMAN

PENGUIN BOOKS

PENGUIN BOOKS

Published by the Penguin Group
Penguin Books Ltd, 80 Strand, London WC2R 0RL, England
Penguin Group (USA), Inc., 375 Hudson Street, New York, New York 10014, USA
Penguin Books Australia Ltd, 250 Camberwell Road, Camberwell, Victoria 3124, Australia
Penguin Books Canada Ltd, 10 Alcorn Avenue, Toronto, Ontario, Canada M4V 3B2
Penguin Books India (P) Ltd, 11 Community Centre, Panchsheel Park, New Delhi – 110 017, India
Penguin Group (NZ), cnr Airborne and Rosedale Roads, Albany, Auckland 1310, New Zealand
Penguin Books (South Africa) (Pty) Ltd, 24 Sturdee Avenue, Rosebank 2196, South Africa

Penguin Books Ltd, Registered Offices: 80 Strand, London WC2R 0RL, England

www.penguin.com

First published in the United States of America by W. W. Norton and Co., 2003
First published in Great Britain by Allen Lane 2003
Published in Penguin Books with new material 2004

3

Copyright © Paul Krugman, 2003, 2004

Printed in England by Clays Ltd, St Ives plc

*To Robin*

# CONTENTS

# ACKNOWLEDGMENTS

**WRITING A COLUMN,** especially in difficult times, is a task best not done alone. Luckily, I've had enormous help.

First, thanks to all the crucial people at *The New York Times*. Howell Raines and Arthur Sulzberger offered me the job, and persuaded me that it was worth doing; they were right. (And thank God for *The New York Times*'s belief in the principle of a free press, and its willingness to stand by its writers.) Gail Collins watches over me now, and has given me consistently good advice.

Even more important than the bosses, of course, are the people you work with. Most of these columns were copyedited by Steve Pickering, a legend at the *Times* who has recently gone to a well-earned retirement. If you've never done this sort of thing, it's hard to realize how important a copy editor's job is. True, some of it consists of "you're one line over, what can we cut?" But when Steve—or Linda Cohn, or Sue Kirby, who also did magnificent work on these columns—says, "I didn't quite understand what you said here," it's a gentle way of telling you that you need to do some serious revision.

Many thanks also to the team at Norton: Drake McFeely, who has shepherded this author's career over the years; Bob Weil, whose enthusiasm drove this project to completion; and Ann

Adelman, another invaluable copy editor. Oh, and Eve Lazovitz, who gently kept my logistics from spinning out of control. I'd also like to thank Barbara Monteiro of Monteiro and Company, who organized the publicity and the book tour for the hardcover edition, for making a cause out of this book and making an extraordinary effort on its—and my—behalf.

Most of all, my wife, Robin Wells, has been more than a support; she reads every column in draft and is an integral part of the writing process. This is as much her book as mine.

# Introduction
# to the
# Paperback Edition

I FINALIZED THE INTRODUCTION to the hardcover edition of *The Great Unravelling* on April 10, 2003—the day after Baghdad fell to U.S. forces. I'm writing this exactly one year later, as a bloody insurrection is sweeping Iraq. This paperback edition contains three new chapters, consisting of columns written over the course of that year.

In the original introduction, reprinted in this volume, I went out on a limb. I wasn't just extremely critical of the Bush administration at a moment of triumph, when TV screens were showing, over and over again, scenes of the toppling of Saddam's statue. I went beyond criticism of specific policies to argue that the Bush administration poses a challenge to America as we know it, that Bush represents a "revolutionary power" that aims at a transformation of American politics. And the radicalism of this movement, I argued, extends across both domestic and foreign policy. In saying this I was also saying that much of the public and most of the media were missing the real story of what was happening in America.

This brought the predictable charge that I was overreacting.

Gerard Baker of *The Financial Times*—who like many commentators seems disturbed by any suggestion that what's happening in America is more than politics as usual—wrote that I was going into "emotive and rather solitary territory. . . . Surely independent observers can draw a contrast between Bush's economics and his national security strategy."

Since I wrote that introduction, a year has passed, and I've written another year's worth of columns. The introduction to Part VI, which contains a selection of those columns, explains where they fit in. Here, let me talk about what a year's experience says about the proposition that a radical movement now occupies the corridors of power.

## War and terror

The dominant story of the past year has, of course, been the Iraq war and its place in the fight against terror. The conventional wisdom, a year ago, was that the war was a necessary defensive action—Saddam was concealing weapons of mass destruction, and supporting terrorism. Even critics of the administration's domestic policies rallied behind the war. Economic policies, they said, were one thing, national security another.

But opponents of the war argued that the Iraqi threat was being deliberately exaggerated to justify a war the Bush administration wanted for other reasons. Some of us reached this conclusion in part because we believed that one couldn't draw a contrast between Bush's economic policy and his national security policy. Both, we argued, reflected the priorities of an administration with a radical political agenda.

The war's opponents were right about the exaggeration of the Iraqi threat. After a year of occupation, we know that

Saddam didn't have an active nuclear program, which would have been the only justifiable reason for a pre-emptive war. He wasn't even concealing chemical weapons from the much-maligned U.N. inspectors. And no evidence has surfaced of any significant connection between Saddam and Al Qaeda, let alone the links to 9/11 repeatedly implied by administration officials.

But were the critics right to question the administration's motives? Or was the exaggeration of the threat from Saddam simply a failure of intelligence? Well, we now know that administration officials repeatedly made claims that weren't supported by the intelligence they had, and in some cases—like the claim that Saddam had purchased uranium from Niger—were flatly contradicted by intelligence reports. And accounts by Paul O'Neill, the former Treasury secretary, and by Richard Clarke, the former head of counterterrorism, confirm what the critics suspected: administration insiders wanted an Iraq war from Bush's first day in office, and saw 9/11 as their opportunity to launch that war.

Maybe General Anthony Zinni, who supported Bush in the 2000 election and served as his Middle East envoy, said it best. In September 2003, speaking to Marine and Navy officers about the war in Iraq, he referred to his generation's experience in Vietnam, "where we heard the garbage and the lies, and saw the sacrifice. I ask you, is it happening again?"

And it has also become clear over the past year that the administration diverted resources from the pursuit of Al Qaeda—the people who actually attacked us—to pursue the war it wanted to fight, in Iraq. There was a direct diversion of military and intelligence resources; for example, Arabic-speaking special forces units were diverted from Afghanistan to Iraq, to be replaced with Spanish speakers. There was also a general loss of focus. And the great fear of the war's original opponents—that occupation of Iraq would fuel anti-Americanism, and serve as a great recruiting device for terrorist groups—has come true.

Five months before the war began, I worried about possible parallels with the Spanish-American War, in a column titled "White Man's Burden" (p. 388). " . . . Quick conventional military victory is not necessarily the end of the story . . . a clean, high-tech war against Spain somehow turned into an extremely dirty war against the Filipino resistance. . . ." Sadly, my worries were justified. Iraq is in chaos as I write, as the guerrilla war against U.S. forces has exploded into an open uprising, and radical Shiites have joined angry Sunnis. I don't know how events will finally turn out, but right now it seems as if the misgivings of war skeptics are being borne out in full.

My main point here, however, is not that the Iraq war seems to be turning into a debacle. It is that those of us who questioned the administration's motives, who believed that it was less interested in national security than in promoting its radical political agenda, have—to our great dismay—found ample evidence to support our concerns.

## Dollars and cents

Before the Iraq war, Republican strategists made no secret of their intent to use the glow of military victory to push through their domestic agenda. And so they did. After the fall of Baghdad—but before the difficulties and expense of postwar occupation were fully apparent to the public—the administration pushed through another big tax cut, which became law in June 2003.

The 2003 tax cut demonstrated in an unambiguous way the

radicalism of Bush administration economic policy. In 2001 one could have argued that administration officials actually believed they could cut taxes while pursuing an agenda of "compassionate conservatism." But in 2003 the administration did something no previous government in the United States— or anywhere else, as far as I can tell—has done: it cut taxes in the face of a war. Wars are expensive, and governments usually raise taxes to pay for them. Furthermore, the U.S. government was deep in deficit even before the Iraq war. And even aside from the money, what about the symbolism? Wars are traditionally a time for shared sacrifice; it's unheard of to cut taxes for the wealthy while soldiers are dying to protect us.

How can the extraordinary decision to slash the government's revenues at a time of fiscal need, and to shower benefits on the wealthy in a time of war, be explained? By understanding the administration's radical political agenda. It's now clear that the Bush administration is engaged in the strategy known on the right as "starve the beast": push through tax cuts that deprive the government of the revenue it needs, then use deficits as an excuse to cut popular social programs. Thanks in large part to the Bush tax cuts, we now face the prospect of huge, ultimately unsustainable budget deficits as far as the eye can see, unless there is either a sharp increase in taxes or major cutbacks in Social Security and Medicare. And major cutbacks in those programs are the policy's goal.

One can see the bait and switch clearly by following the statements of Alan Greenspan, who has used his position and reputation to further the "starve the beast" program. In 2001 I accused Greenspan of partisanship when he urged Congress to cut taxes to reduce an excessive budget surplus. Three years later, in the face of huge budget deficits, he proved me right:

rather than admit that his position was mistaken, he argued that the tax cuts should be preserved, and that long-run deficits should be controlled by reducing Social Security benefits.

Like the Iraq war, the administration's economic policy has gone badly. Tax cuts for the wealthy haven't produced much economic payoff; despite some signs of life in the labor market, Bush will end this presidential term with the worst job record since Herbert Hoover, even while piling up record debt. As in the case of the Iraq war, however, my main point isn't the policy debacle. It's that events over the past year have demonstrated that in economic policy as in national security, those of us who questioned the administration's motives and honesty, who accused it of promoting a radical agenda on false pretenses, have had our suspicions confirmed.

## *Abuses of power*

In the original introduction to this book I argued that because we are now ruled by a radical movement, the usual rules of politics no longer apply. Our current leaders, I suggested, are prepared to abuse their power in pursuit of their political goals. Such a claim was greeted, understandably, with some disbelief and derision. But the past year has given us some evidence of just how far the right is willing to go.

Over the past year we've seen abuse after abuse, from the Texas redistricting—an unprecedented move that may have given the Republicans a lock on the House of Representatives— to the suppression of scientific evidence against administration environmental policies, to the smearing of Richard Clarke, the former counterterrorism chief. When Paul O'Neill spoke out about what he had seen, the Treasury Department immediately threatened to prosecute him, suggesting that he might have revealed classified information. And the administration has stonewalled investigations into its record, from the Cheney energy task force to the 9/11 commission.

The ruthlessness of the administration reached its height— so far—when officials outed Valerie Plame, the wife of administration critic Joseph Wilson, as a covert CIA operative. Bush seemed curiously uninterested in finding who was responsible for the leak; a few months after the incident, when the subject seemed to have died down, one White House official boasted, "We have let the earthmovers roll in over this one." The investigation seems to have picked up steam again, but we have yet to see where that investigation leads.

Equally disturbing, in a different way, has been the ongoing effort to create a cult of personality around Bush. The infamous "Mission Accomplished" carrier landing, while ludicrous, was also chilling. Elderly friends, refugees from central Europe, described it as a Leni Riefenstahl moment. They weren't saying that Bush is the equivalent of Hitler; but they were saying that the personal glorification of the president as military hero, aside from its fakeness, wasn't what they expected to see happening in America. And while the administration would just as soon forget the business with the flight suit, the cult of personality continues, with heroic photos of the president adorning even the most unlikely government documents; as I explain in one of the new columns collected here, the 2005 budget contained no fewer than twenty-seven glamorous pictures of the commander in chief.

Behind these visible episodes of abuse of power lies a drive by the right to consolidate its political dominance without precedent in American history. Grover Norquist, one of the Republican party's most important power brokers, famously declared that he wants to shrink the government "down to the size where we can drown it in the bathtub." In April 2004 he told *The New Yorker* how he proposes to accomplish that: "One of the steps for getting there is a permanent Republican government, in the sense of fifty-five Republican senators and a thirty-vote margin in the House and a Republican president for twenty years in a row." The drive to achieve that dominance includes efforts to dominate and bully the media; to secure an overwhelming dominance in campaign finance, not just by raising lots of money, but by threatening businesses that support the other side with retribution; and repeated efforts to shout down any criticism as unpatriotic.

How far will the drive to ensure political dominance go? Let me put it this way: nothing on the American political scene scares me as much as the shift to electronic voting machines that leave no paper trail. Maybe the people who, in a supposed drive to root out felons, prevented thousands of eligible voters from voting in Florida in 2000, who redistricted Texas, not to reflect a new census but simply to gain political advantage, who boasted about letting the earthmovers roll in over the Plame affair, would refuse to engage in high-tech ballot-box stuffing. Do you want to bet your democracy on it?

## *A great revulsion?*

As far as I can tell, nothing in the introduction to the hardcover rings false a year later. Back then I declared that when it came to administration actions the alarmists had been right, every time; that rule still holds. A year later, it's clear that a revolutionary power has indeed taken over Congress and the White House.

My hope, a year ago, was of a great revulsion: "a moment in which the American people look at what is happening, realize how their good will and patriotism have been abused, and put a stop" to the drive of the radical right. As I write this, there are signs that this revulsion may be happening: facts are coming out, scandals are breaking into the open, hard questions are being asked. But not enough people understand, yet, what is being done in their name.

This edition will come out in the middle of an election—one that, we can safely predict, will be the meanest and dirtiest in living memory. My hope is that this book will help some people understand what's really at stake.

# PREFACE

**METAPHORS CAN BE TRICKY THINGS,** but Manhattan's "debt clock" is as good as they come.

A public-spirited businessman installed the clock in 1989, hoping to shame politicians into acting responsibly. Huge numerals counted off the ever-rising national debt—ever-rising because each year the federal government spent far more than it took in, and was forced to borrow the difference. But in the late 1990s a funny thing happened: the government's tax take soared along with the stock market, and those mammoth budget deficits first shrank, then turned into record surpluses. In September 2000, the owner of the clock pulled the plug.

In July 2002, with the nation once again facing deficits as far as the eye could see, he turned it back on.

There's much more to recent American history than the way the federal government declared victory in its long struggle against deficits, only to see the red ink quickly return. But as the budget went, so went many other indicators of our national well-being. In the early 1990s we were a depressed nation, economically, socially, and politically: a best-selling book of the era was titled *America: What Went Wrong*. By the end of the decade we had, it seemed, pulled ourselves together. The economy was booming, jobs were plentiful, and millions of people were getting rich. Budget deficits had given way to record surpluses. The long crime wave that began in the 1960s came to an end; major cities were suddenly, amazingly, safer than they had been for many decades. The future seemed almost incredibly bright.

Then the good times stopped rolling. By 2003, the fabric of our economy—and, perhaps, of our political system and our society—seemed once again to be unraveling. The nation was gripped by anxiety, with polls showing a majority of the public feeling that the country was headed in the wrong direction.

This book is, first of all, a chronicle of the years when it all went wrong, again—when the heady optimism of the late 1990s gave way to renewed gloom. It's also an attempt to explain the how and why: how it was possible for a country with so much going for it to go downhill so fast, and why our leaders made such bad decisions. For this is, in large part, a story about leadership—incredibly bad leadership, in the private sector and in the corridors of power. And yes, it is in particular an indictment of George W. Bush. Helen Thomas, the veteran White House correspondent, has called Mr. Bush "the worst president in all of American history." I'm not sure about that—he has some stiff competition. But the really terrible presidents of the past led a nation in which presidential incompetence and malfeasance mattered far less either to the nation or to the world than it does today.

Most of this book consists of columns that I wrote for *The New York Times* between January 2000 and January 2003. I hope that readers will find that the sum is more than the whole of its parts—that taken together these columns tell a coherent story. I'll talk shortly about how I came to write those columns. But first, let's recall the background.

## *The dreary years*

During the late 1990s, as everything seemed to be going right—as jobs proliferated, stocks soared, budgets moved into surplus, and even the crime rate plunged—the dreary mood of the decade's early years faded from memory. By 2000, few people remembered the national funk that prevailed in 1992. Yet that funk is essential background to what came later.

If you are one of those people who thinks that national greatness is defined by military success (and such people are running the country right now), the nation's foul mood in 1992 may seem puzzling. Militarily, America was on top of the world. Communism had collapsed. A war in the Persian Gulf that many had feared would become another Vietnam turned instead into a spectacular demonstration of American military prowess. We had already become what we remain today, the world's one and only superpower.

But glory doesn't pay the bills. A tag line of the time—drawing attention to the contrast between American stagnation and the seemingly relentless rise of Japan—said, "The Cold War is over. Japan won." Whether or not you bought the thesis that America was the victim of unfair Japanese competition (it wasn't), it was a time of national disillusionment.

Though Japan wasn't the villain some people imagined—and it was soon to experience economic setbacks that are a cautionary tale for all of us—America's economic woes were real enough. True, by 1992 statisticians had declared the recession of 1990–91 over. But in 1991–92 it was still a "jobless recovery"—that is, a period in which GDP grows but unemployment continues to rise. As far as ordinary Americans were concerned, it was a continuing recession. Nor were things all that great for workers who managed to keep their jobs: the real wage of the typical worker had been stagnant or falling for almost 20 years. Traditional industries like autos and steel, in which ordinary workers could earn good wages, seemed to be in steady decline. Poverty was rising, not falling—more than 20 percent of children were living below the poverty line, the highest percentage since 1964.

Popular culture reflected a deep sense of disillusionment. Among the big movies of the early 90s were *Falling Apart*, about a laid-off worker who erupts in rage, *Grand Canyon*, about the menace of crime, and *Rising Sun*, about American decline and the rise of Japan.

What about the promise of new technology? In the early 1990s, this seemed like a promise broken. For sure, new technology was all around us—but it didn't seem to be delivering much in the way of results. More and more workers were equipped with computers, every office had a fax machine, cell phones and e-mail were starting to become widespread, but none of it seemed to pay off in employment or higher living standards. One prominent economist—he would later be a notable American triumphalist—told me privately that he regarded high tech as "high bull——."

Above all, the American people were disillusioned with their leaders, private and public. Every airport bookstore featured rows of volumes with samurai warriors on their covers, promising to teach readers the secrets of Japanese management; the point was not just that the Japanese seemingly knew how to run modern corporations, but that the people running American companies seemingly didn't. All the latest gadgets seemed to come from Japan; not only had "made in the U.S.A." ceased to be a guarantee of quality, many consumers had come to distrust domestic products. CEOs of major corporations were mocked as bumbling, overpaid incompetents—when President George Bush took auto company executives to Japan to demand economic concessions, the affair turned into a public relations disaster.

The loss of respect extended to our politicians. The most remarkable thing about the 1992 election wasn't that Bush lost. It was that H. Ross Perot, a candidate completely out of the mainstream, took 19 percent of the vote. In a nation where third parties have never flourished, that was a huge vote of no confidence in conventional political leaders.

In short, it wasn't the best of times—and many observers expected things to keep getting worse. Yet over the next eight years the nation would experience an amazing economic and social turnaround.

## *The good years*

It took quite a while before people realized that things had really turned for the better. You might say that pessimism had become a national habit. As late as the winter of 1995–96, despite a steadily falling unemployment rate, the newspapers were full of alarmist headlines about job loss and downsizing. In the 1996 presidential campaign, Bob Dole's economists attacked the Clinton administration for what they claimed was a sluggish, below-par economic recovery. Less partisan economists knew better, but they remained cautious, having seen too many false dawns. Yet eventually the evidence became too strong to deny: the U.S. economy really was on the mend. And so, it began to seem, was our society.

Given our current state of renewed disillusionment, it's tempting to dismiss everything that went right in the Clinton years as a mirage. Indeed, the manic optimism of the late 90s got ahead of the reality. But the nation's real achievements were spectacular.

First and foremost for the lives of most people, by the end of the 90s jobs were plentiful—more plentiful than they had been for decades. Between 1992 and 2000, U.S. companies added 32 million workers to their payrolls, driving the unemployment rate to a 30-year low. Full employment meant jobs, and a chance of escape, for families that had been caught in the poverty trap: poverty rates fell sharply, for the first time since the 1960s. Partly as a consequence, social indicators like crime rates showed spectacular improvement: by the end of the 90s, New York City was as safe as it had been in the mid-1960s.

If job growth was impressive, the increase in productivity— the amount produced per worker—was even more impressive. In the 1970s and 1980s, low productivity growth—barely 1 percent per year—was the greatest failing of the U.S. economy. Poor productivity performance was the most important reason why living standards stagnated for typical American families: an economy without productivity growth can't deliver a sustained rise in wages. But during the 1990s productivity took off; by decade's end it was rising faster than ever before in American history, and wages had ended their long stagnation.

Why did productivity surge? The main answer, probably, was that information technology had come of age: all those computers and networks were finally showing what they could do. But business leaders, understandably, took much of the credit. As Japan faltered, American business regained its confidence, and American businessmen became heroes. It was the age of the CEO as superstar. And if those superstars took home supersized paychecks, why not? America, it seemed, had devised a system in which big incentives produced big results.

Then there was the stock market. At the end of 1992 the Dow

was at 3,500; by 2000 it had zoomed past 10,000. And yet Dow investors felt like losers: they had missed out on the really big gains, as tech stocks made many people instant millionaires. Not since 1929, and maybe not even then, had quick wealth seemed so attainable. And authoritative-sounding voices assured us that there was more to come, that the Dow would soon reach 36,000.

There were stock market skeptics; I was one of them. (I also had some initial doubts about the U.S. productivity miracle. By 2000 I was a believer, but I still thought stock prices were way out of line.) And those of us who followed foreign economies also worried a bit about what would happen when the stock market rediscovered the law of gravity. There were some undeniable similarities between the U.S. economy in the late 90s and Japan's "bubble economy" a decade earlier—and after Japan's stock market bubble collapsed, the seemingly unstoppable Japanese economy fell into a profound funk, which has continued to this day.

Yet the 90s had given us reason for optimism, even if the bubble burst. For the problems of Japan had been exacerbated by poor leadership—and the economic leadership of the United States was exceptionally good.

In the early years of the Clinton administration this wasn't clear to everyone. I myself was a pretty harsh critic of the new president's economic team, in the days before the ascendancy of Robert Rubin was fully established. But by decade's end "Rubinomics" was triumphant. First, Bill Clinton dared to raise taxes to help close the budget deficit—an action that was doubly brave. His predecessor, George Bush, had been vilified for his own tax increase (though even Ronald Reagan had retracted part of his own tax cut); and conservatives predicted that the Clinton tax increase would sink the economy. Nonetheless, he did the right thing—and got a booming economy and a budget surplus as his reward.

Moreover, Washington proved itself flexible and effective in dealing with crises. When the Mexican peso plunged in 1995, the administration—again braving harsh criticism from the right—came to our neighbor's rescue. Then an even bigger financial crisis erupted in Asia. In the fall of 1998 the crisis spread to the United States, as Russia's default on its debt led to the downfall of Long-Term Capital Management, a huge hedge fund. Financial markets briefly seized up: borrowing and lending came to a virtual halt. I was at a meeting in which one Fed official briefed us on the situation; when asked what we could do, he replied, "Pray." Yet Rubin, together with Alan Greenspan, managed to exude a sense of calm—remember what it was like when people actually admired the Treasury secretary? And the markets recovered. Early in 1999 the cover of *Time* featured Federal Reserve Chairman Alan Greenspan, Treasury Secretary Robert Rubin, and Deputy Treasury Secretary Larry Summers, whom it dubbed—cornily, but with considerable justification—the "committee to save the world."

At the beginning of the new millennium, then, it seemed that the United States was blessed with mature, skillful economic leaders, who in a pinch would do what had to be done. They would insist on responsible fiscal policies; they would act quickly and effectively to prevent a repeat of the jobless recovery of the early 90s, let alone a slide into Japanese-style stagnation. Even those of us who considered ourselves pessimists were basically optimists: we thought that bullish investors might face a rude awakening, but that it would all have a happy ending.

# America: What went wrong?

The satirical weekly *The Onion* describes itself as "America's finest news source"—and for the last few years that has been the literal truth. The mock news story for January 18, 2001, reported a speech in which President-elect George W. Bush declared, "Our long national nightmare of peace and prosperity is over." And so it has turned out.

What happened to the good years? For many people, the great emotional turning point—the moment when their dreams of security were shattered—was September 11, 2001. But for me the turn was slower and broader than that.

I don't mean to belittle the horror. But anyone who followed Middle Eastern events knew that the United States was a terrorist target. You may remember that at first everyone assumed that the 1995 bombing in Oklahoma City involved Muslims. Experts on terrorism warned us repeatedly over the years that there would someday be a major attack on U.S. soil—though the sheer size of the mass murder on September 11 was a shock. We knew there were people out there who wanted to hurt us; it wasn't that much of a surprise when they finally scored a hit.

The real surprise was the failure of leadership, private and public, right here at home.

Some people realized that there were business excesses in the 1990s, though they had a hard time getting themselves heard. But the extent and brazenness of the excesses was greater than anyone realized. The bull market, we learned too late, both encouraged and concealed corporate misbehavior on an epic scale. Who could have imagined that famous companies, lauded in business schools as the very models of a major modern corporation, would turn out to be little more than Ponzi schemes? (Actually, some people did say that, but they were dismissed as cranks.)

Even more troubling was the revelation that our political system was far less mature than we thought, that the responsible leadership we had come to take for granted had been a sort of accident. In the 2000 campaign, George W. Bush offered a tax plan and a Social Security plan that were obviously, blatantly based on bogus arithmetic. Yet the media focused on the politics of personality, and avoided explaining the issues. Meanwhile, Alan Greenspan turned out not to be who we thought he was: the stern advocate of austerity and fiscal discipline when a Democrat was in office became an apologist and enabler for irresponsible tax cuts, even in the face of soaring deficits, once the White House had changed hands.

Moreover, the new team showed neither the long-run responsibility nor the short-term flexibility of its predecessors. The original Bush economic plan involved big, long-run tax cuts that phased in only gradually. By 2002 it was clear that this plan had it backwards. Like his father, Bush was presiding over a "jobless recovery"—that is, an economy that was growing, but too slowly to provide new jobs, so that most people found their lives getting worse. This economy badly needed a short-term boost, not a long-run tax cut. And the spectacular deterioration of the budget meant that long-run tax cuts were no longer remotely affordable. Yet Bush's aides continued to insist that their program, formulated back in 1999 at the height of the bubble, was exactly the right solution for the economy's current difficulties. And in early 2003, when they finally seemed to realize that something more was needed, the new "stimulus" plan was practically a clone of the original plan: hardly anything to stimulate the economy now, but lots of long-term tax cuts, mainly for the rich.

More ominously, it gradually became clear that something deeper than mere bad economic ideology was at work. The bigger story was America's political sea change, the central theme of this book's Introduction.

## Why me?

I began writing for *The New York Times* in January 2000. Neither I nor *The Times* knew what I was getting into.

I was and am an economics professor by trade. International financial crises were one of my main specialties, and I spent much of the 1990s tracking and commenting on disasters abroad. Some of my work consisted of what I call "Greek-letter" economics, abstruse papers for the professional journals. But I also wrote about global economic issues for a wider audience. By 1998 I had two regular monthly columns, one in *Fortune* and one in the online magazine *Slate*; some of those columns are included in this collection.

In the summer of 1999 *The New York Times* contacted me about writing for the paper's Op-Ed page. Howell Raines, then the paper's editorial page editor, felt that in an age when, more than ever, the business of America was business, *The Times* needed to broaden its Op-Ed commentary beyond the traditional focus on foreign affairs and domestic politics. I was brought on in the expectation that I would write about the vagaries of the new economy, the impacts of globalization, and bad policies in other countries. I didn't expect to spend a lot of time on domestic politics, since everyone assumed that American policy would remain sensible and responsible.

I have tried, as best I can, to cover economics and business. As you'll see, some of the columns in this book are straight economic analyses, without a political edge. But as events unfolded, politics inevitably intruded. More and more, I found myself speaking very uncomfortable truth to power.

Why me?

These days I often find myself accused of being a knee-jerk liberal, even a socialist. But just a few years ago the real knee-jerk liberals didn't like me at all—one magazine even devoted a cover story to an attack on me for my pro-capitalist views, and I still have the angry letter Ralph Nader sent me when I criticized his attacks on globalization. If I have ended up more often than not writing pieces that attack the right wing, it's because the right wing now rules—and rules badly. It's not just that the policies are bad and irresponsible; our leaders lie about what they are up to.

I began pointing out the outrageous dishonesty of the Bush administration long before most of the rest of the punditocracy. Why did I see what others failed to see? One reason is that as a trained economist I wasn't even for a minute tempted to fall into the he-said-she-said style of reporting, under which opposing claims by politicians are given equal credence regardless of the facts. I did my own arithmetic—or, where necessary, got hold of real economists who could educate me on the subjects I wrote about—and quickly realized that we were dealing with world-class mendacity, right here in the U.S.A. I wasn't entirely alone in this: one thing I've noticed the last few years is that business reporters, who know a bogus number when they see one, have often accused our leaders of outrageous mendacity even while political pundits celebrate those leaders for their supposed sterling character. But the writings of business reporters necessarily have a narrow focus, and rarely affect political commentary. With a wider brief, and a spot on the Op-Ed page, I attracted a lot more attention.

I have also been willing to see things differently, and report on what I see, because I'm not properly socialized. The commentariat mainly consists of people who live in Washington and go to the same dinner parties. This in itself foments group-think; at any given moment there is a story line that shapes journalists' perceptions. Until September 11 this story line had it that George W. Bush was dumb but honest; after September 11 the new story was that he was a tough-minded hero, all determination and moral clarity, "Texas Ranger to the world." (Yes, one prominent pundit actually wrote that.) The over-whelming evidence that neither of these pictures bore any resemblance to reality was simply brushed aside.

But I'm not part of the gang—I work from central New Jersey, and continue to live the life of a college professor—so I never bought into the shared assumptions. Moreover, I couldn't be bullied in the usual ways. The stock in trade of most journalists is inside information—leaks from highly placed sources, up-close-and-personal interviews with the powerful. This leaves them vulnerable: they can be seduced with offers of special access, threatened with the career-destroying prospect that they will be frozen out. But I rely almost entirely on numbers and analyses that are in the public domain; I don't need to be in the good graces of top officials, so I also have no need to display the deference that characterizes many journalists.

Whatever the reason, I have spent much of the last three years providing a picture of the world that differs greatly from the vision of most other mainstream pundits. (Web-based commentators have done yeoman duty—but they don't land on a million doorsteps twice a week.) One of the columns in this book is titled "An Alternate Reality"; that about captures it. At a time when most pundits were celebrating the bold vision, skill, and moral clarity of our leaders, I saw confusion, ineffectuality, and dishonesty. It wasn't a popular point of view, especially in the early months after September 11. But have I been right? Read the book and decide for yourself.

## About this book

I've tried to make this book more than a chronological sequence of columns. There is, of course, an element of chronology; each column was written on a particular date, and my views on some subjects have evolved, as new facts have come to light. But the columns are grouped according to major themes, and within each theme into "chapters" that focus on a particular subject. I've also added an Introduction that sets the political stage, and further additional material at the beginning of each thematic section, to put the columns into a broader perspective.

The columns begin with the rise and fall of America's stock market bubble, with all that went with it. As the pieces here show, I was always a stock market skeptic—though not, as you will see, skeptical enough. My focus on troubled economies abroad prepared me for the possibility that the United States would suffer serious economic difficulties once the bubble burst—though here again I initially understated the risks. What nobody realized was how thoroughly corrupted the U.S. corporate system had become; like everyone else, I played catch-up here.

The book turns next to the federal budget and the fate of Social Security. It's the story of a debt foretold. From the beginning it was obvious to me that George W. Bush's plans didn't add up, that he and his people were simply lying about all the important numbers, and that their plans would dissipate the budget surplus. It has played out just as I feared, but sooner and more forcefully than I expected. As I write these words, the administration has just conceded that the $230 billion surplus it inherited has been converted into a $300 billion deficit—and you know that's an underestimate.

How was such a misstep possible? In Part III, I go beyond economics pure and simple, trying to understand what has gone wrong with American politics. It seems to me now that many reasonable people, liberals and conservatives alike, still don't get it—as I explain in these columns, the real world of politics is much tougher and uglier than the picture most of us carry in our heads.

The last few years didn't just shake my faith in our political system; they were also a reminder that free markets, while often a very good thing, can sometimes go very badly wrong. Part IV describes some of the shocking failures of the market system in the last few years, from the California energy crisis to the catastrophe in Argentina.

Of course, there's more to the world, even the world of economics, than the ups and downs of the United States. The book concludes with a wider view—a look at the global economy, and at the tools we use to understand it.

This is not, I'm sorry to say, a happy book. It's mainly about economic disappointment, bad leadership, and the lies of the powerful. Don't despair: nothing has gone wrong in America that can't be repaired. But the first step in that repair job is understanding where and how the system got broken.

*The*
## GREAT
## UNRAVELLING

# INTRODUCTION

## *A Revolutionary Power*

**A LOT HAS HAPPENED** these past three years—stock market decline and business scandal, energy crisis and environmental backsliding, budget deficits and recession, terrorism and troubled alliances, and now, finally, war. I've written about all these things, mainly from an economic point of view. But as I explained in the Preface, to talk about economics requires, more and more, that one write about politics. And there's a political story that runs through much of what has happened to this country lately—the story of the rise and growing dominance of a radical political movement, right here in the U.S.A.

I'm talking, of course, about America's radical right—a movement that now effectively controls the White House, Congress, much of the judiciary, and a good slice of the media. The dominance of that movement changes everything: old rules about politics and policy no longer apply. In this Introduction I want to offer an overview of that rise, and the difference it makes.

### *A political sea change*

Most people have been slow to realize just how awesome a sea change has taken place in the domestic political scene. During the 2000 election, many people thought that nothing much was

3

at stake; during the first two years of the Bush administration, many pundits insisted that the radically conservative bent of that administration was only a temporary maneuver, that Bush would tack back to the center after solidifying his base. And the public still has little sense of how radical our leading politicians really are. A striking example: in the fall of 2001, when focus groups were asked to react to Republican proposals for a retroactive corporate tax cut—the proposal described in my column "The One-Eyed Man" in chapter 10—members of the focus groups literally refused to believe the group leaders' description of the policy.

For reasons described in the Preface, I was ahead of the curve in realizing that something radical was happening. As a professional economist, I was in a position to appreciate the disconnect between official claims and reality; as a media outsider I wasn't part of the Washington culture, in which it's considered bad form to suggest that leading politicians have ulterior motives that bear little resemblance to their stated goals. But looking at the wreckage, I realize that I, too, didn't understand how far things would go.

To take the most straightforward example: In 2001, even many liberals thought that one shouldn't make too much fuss about Bush's fiscal irresponsibility. The tax cut isn't a good idea, they said, but it isn't all that important. But by 2003, we saw the unprecedented spectacle of an administration proposing huge additional tax cuts not just in the face of record deficits, but in the middle of a war. ("Nothing is more important in the face of a war than cutting taxes," declared House majority leader Tom DeLay.)

Another example: those who suggested that Republicans would exploit September 11 for political advantage were widely denounced for undermining national unity. Yet they did—

4

indeed, during the 2002 election campaign Republican supporters ran ads linking Democratic senator Tom Daschle with Saddam Hussein.

What is happening, and why have most people been so slow to come to grips with the reality? Just before putting this book to bed, I discovered a volume that describes the situation almost perfectly. It's not a new book by a liberal, writing about contemporary America; it's an old book by, of all people, Henry Kissinger, about nineteenth-century diplomacy.

## A revolutionary power

Back in 1957, Henry Kissinger—then a brilliant, iconoclastic young Harvard scholar, with his eventual career as cynical political manipulator and, later, as crony capitalist still far in the future—published his doctoral dissertation, *A World Restored*. One wouldn't think that a book about the diplomatic efforts of Metternich and Castlereagh is relevant to U.S. politics in the twenty-first century. But the first three pages of Kissinger's book sent chills down my spine, because they seem all too relevant to current events.

In those first few pages, Kissinger describes the problems confronting a heretofore stable diplomatic system when it is faced with a "revolutionary power"—a power that does not accept that system's legitimacy. Since the book is about the reconstruction of Europe after the battle of Waterloo, the revolutionary power he had in mind was the France of Robespierre and Napoleon, though he clearly if implicitly drew parallels with the failure of diplomacy to effectively confront totalitarian regimes in the 1930s. (Note: drawing parallels does not mean claiming moral equivalence.) It seems clear to me that one should regard America's right-wing movement—which now in effect controls the administration, both houses of Congress, much of the judiciary, and a good slice of the media—as a revolutionary power in Kissinger's sense. That is, it is a movement whose leaders do not accept the legitimacy of our current political system.

Am I overstating the case? In fact, there's ample evidence that key elements of the coalition that now runs the country believe that some long-established American political and social institutions should not, in principle, exist—and do not accept the rules that the rest of us have taken for granted.

Consider, for example, the welfare state as we know it—New Deal programs like Social Security and unemployment insurance, Great Society programs like Medicare. If you read the literature emanating from the Heritage Foundation, which drives the Bush administration's economic ideology, you discover a very radical agenda: Heritage doesn't just want to scale back New Deal and Great Society programs, it regards the very existence of those programs as a violation of basic principles.

Or consider foreign policy. Since World War II the United States has built its foreign policy around international institutions, and has tried to make it clear that it is not an old-fashioned imperialist power, which uses military force as it sees fit. But if you follow the foreign policy views of the neoconservative intellectuals who fomented the war with Iraq, you learn that they have contempt for all that—Richard Perle, chairman of a key Pentagon advisory board, dismissed the "liberal conceit of safety through international law administered by international institutions." They aren't hesitant about the use of force; one prominent thinker close to the administration, Michael Ledeen of the American Enterprise Institute, declared that "we are a warlike people and we love war." The idea that war in Iraq is just a pilot project for a series of splendid little wars seemed, at first, a leftist fantasy—but many people close to the administration have made it clear that they regard this war as only a beginning, and a senior State Department official, John Bolton, told Israeli officials that after Iraq the United States would "deal with" Syria, Iran, and North Korea.

Nor is even that the whole story. The separation of church and state is one of the fundamental principles of the U.S. Constitution. But Tom DeLay, the House majority leader, has told constituents that he is in office to promote a "biblical worldview"—and that his relentless pursuit of Bill Clinton was motivated by Clinton's failure to share that view. (DeLay has also denounced the teaching of evolution in schools, going so far as to blame that teaching for the Columbine school shootings.)

There's even some question about whether the people running the country accept the idea that legitimacy flows from the democratic process. Paul Gigot of *The Wall Street Journal* famously praised the "bourgeois riot" in which violent protestors shut down a vote recount in Miami. (The rioters, it was later revealed, weren't angry citizens; they were paid political operatives.) Meanwhile, according to his close friend Don Evans, now the secretary of commerce, George W. Bush believes that he was called by God to lead the nation. Perhaps this explains why the disputed election of 2000 didn't seem to inspire any caution or humility on the part of the victors. Consider Justice Antonin Scalia's response to a student who asked how he felt making the Supreme Court decision that threw the election to Bush. Was it agonizing? Did Scalia worry about the consequences? No: "It was a wonderful feeling," he declared.

Suppose, for a moment, that you took the picture I have just painted seriously. You would conclude that the people now in charge really don't like America as it is. If you combine their apparent agendas, the goal would seem to be something like this: a country that basically has no social safety net at home, which relies mainly on military force to enforce its will abroad, in which schools don't teach evolution but do teach religion and—possibly—in which elections are only a formality.

Yet those who take the hard-line rightists now in power at their word, and suggest that they may really attempt to realize such a radical goal, are usually accused of being "shrill," of going over the top. Surely, says the conventional wisdom, we should discount the rhetoric: the goals of the right are more limited than this picture suggests. Or are they?

Back to Kissinger. His description of the baffled response of established powers in the face of a revolutionary challenge works equally well as an account of how the American political and media establishment has responded to the radicalism of the Bush administration over the past two years:

> Lulled by a period of stability which had seemed permanent, they find it nearly impossible to take at face value the assertion of the revolutionary power that it means to smash the existing framework. The defenders of the status quo therefore tend to begin by treating the revolutionary power as if its protestations were merely tactical; as if it really accepted the existing legitimacy but overstated its case for bargaining purposes; as if it were motivated by specific grievances to be assuaged by limited concessions. Those who warn against the danger in time are considered alarmists; those who counsel adaptation to circumstance are considered balanced and sane. . . . But it is the essence of a revolutionary power that it possesses the courage of its convictions, that it is willing, indeed eager, to push its principles to their ultimate conclusion.

As I said, this passage sent chills down my spine, because it explains so well the otherwise baffling process by which the administration has been able to push radical policies through, with remarkably little scrutiny or effective opposition. To elaborate, let me talk about two big examples: the tax cuts of 2001, and the Iraq war of 2003.

## Tax cuts and war

War and economic policy seem, on the surface, to have little in common—and in normal times they play very differently on the political scene. Yet there was a striking similarity between the selling of Bush's tax cuts and the selling of his Iraq war.

Chapters 5 and 6 tell the story of the 2001 tax cut; let me give a preview. Candidate Bush introduced his original tax-cut proposal in 1999 to solidify his right-wing credentials, and fend off a Republican primary challenge from Steve Forbes. Anyone familiar with recent political history knew that Forbes represented a wing of the Republican party that always wants more tax cuts for the rich, regardless of economic circumstances. After all, Republican leaders in Congress tried to pass big tax cuts every year during the 1990s, through good times and bad times, deficit and surplus. A clear-eyed assessment should have been that Bush had signed on to that position, and thus that his goals were very radical—as they have turned out to be. As Dan Altman of *The New York Times* points out, if you take the administration's tax proposals as a group, they effectively achieve a longstanding goal of the radical right: an end to all taxes on income from capital, moving us to a system in which only wages are taxed—a system, if you like, in which earned income is taxed but unearned income is not.

The point is that on the matter of taxes the right had more or less declared its intention to—as Kissinger put it—"smash the existing framework," in this case the framework of the American tax system as we know it. Yet the American political and media establishment couldn't believe that Bush would really try to achieve that goal. Despite the evident radicalism of the people behind the Bush policy, moderates convinced themselves that Bush's aims were limited, and that he could be appeased with a limited victory. Furthermore, unwilling to admit Bush's radical goals, moderates accepted at face value his administration's ever-shifting rationales for its unchanging policy. At first, tax cuts were about returning an excessive surplus to the people—and many Democratic senators, alas, voted for the 2001 tax cut on that basis. Then, as the surplus vanished, tax cuts were about providing short-run economic stimulus. Then, as it became clear that they weren't serving that purpose, tax cuts were about promoting long-run growth. Even now, many well-meaning politicians and journalists find it hard to face up to the truth.

But what about the war?

People who followed debates over foreign policy knew that an important faction of the right was as determined to have a war in the Middle East as another faction was to cut taxes. Back in 1992, Paul Wolfowitz, then undersecretary of defense (and now deputy secretary) tried to make what is now known as the "Bush doctrine" our official defense posture: the document he wrote called for intervention in Iraq, and the legitimization of preemptive attacks on other countries. Dick Cheney, then secretary of defense, initially endorsed that view. He backed off in the face of public protest, but he and a number of other people now in key administration positions continued to agitate for an Iraq war, and the adoption of preemption as a regular policy, through the 1990s.

Given this background, it was or should have been obvious that the proposed invasion of Iraq, like the tax cut, wasn't really a response to current events (in this case September 11); it was part of a preexisting and much more radical agenda. Yet as in the case of the tax cut, the political and media establishment couldn't bring itself to accept that the right actually meant to pursue the goals it had declared. Instead, most people accepted as sincere the ever-shifting ostensible rationales offered by the Bush administration. A war with Iraq was at first justified by alleged ties between Saddam Hussein and Al Qaeda. When no evidence was found for that link, despite intense efforts, the issue became Saddam's alleged nuclear program. (The administration deliberately blurred the issue by stretching the term "weapons of mass destruction" to include chemical weapons—but poison gas isn't really in the same category, and never posed a serious threat to the United States. What scared the public were visions of a mushroom cloud.) Concerns about such a program helped convince many moderates that a war with Iraq was a good idea, and Congress gave Bush a green light to proceed with a war.

Eventually, the case for believing in an Iraqi nuclear program was discredited. One of the two key pieces of evidence, Iraq's purchase of aluminum tubes, turned out to be a misinterpretation: the tubes weren't suitable for their alleged purpose, uranium enrichment. The other key piece, documents allegedly showing Iraqi purchases of uranium from Niger, were revealed to be inept forgeries. But by then, Bush was pushing the idea that America, by installing a democratic government in Iraq, would generate a wave of democratization across the region—an idealistic goal that, once again, drew support from many well-meaning moderates. Only once the war was well underway did James Woolsey, widely believed to be in line for a top post in the occupation government, declare the war in Iraq to be the start of a "fourth world war" (with the Cold War as number three), a conflict that would involve Syria and Iran as well as Iraq.

There's a pattern here; in fact, pretty much the same story can be told about energy policy, environmental policy, health care policy, education policy, and so on. In each case the officials making policy within the Bush administration have a history of highly radical views, which should suggest that the administration itself has radical goals. But in each case the administration has reassured moderates by pretending otherwise—by offering rationales for its policy that don't seem all that radical. And in each case moderates have followed a strategy of appeasement, trying to meet the administration halfway while downplaying both the radicalism of its policies and the trail of broken promises. The young Kissinger had it right: people who have been accustomed to stability can't bring themselves to believe what is happening when faced with a revolutionary power, and are therefore ineffective in opposing it.

I should admit at this point that I am not entirely sure *why* this is happening—why we are now faced with such a radical challenge to our political and social system. Rich people did very well in the 1990s; why this hatred of anything that looks remotely like income redistribution? Corporations have flourished; why this urge to strip away modest environmental regulation? Churches of all denominations have prospered; why this attack on the separation of church and state? American power and influence have never been greater; why this drive to destroy our alliances and embark on military adventures? Nonetheless, it's increasingly clear that the right wants to do all these things. How should those of us who don't agree with its goals respond?

# Rules for reporting

The first step in these times is to understand what's going on. As a part-time journalist, I think of this in terms of rules for reporting—how to tell the story. But they apply equally to any concerned citizen trying to make sense of the news.

## 1. Don't assume that policy proposals make sense in terms of their stated goals

When you're dealing with a revolutionary power, it's important to realize that it knows what it wants, and will make whatever argument advances that goal. So there should be no presumption that the claims it makes on behalf of its actions make any sense in their own terms. As I explain in chapter 7, the Bush plan to privatize Social Security wasn't a dubious or ineffective way to strengthen the system's finances—it had absolutely nothing to do with that stated goal, and would actually have aggravated the system's problems. The tax-cut proposals offered by the Bush administration in early 2003 were billed as a program to accelerate economic growth. Yet when the Congressional Budget Office—whose new head had, just months earlier, worked for the administration—tried to evaluate the growth effects of the proposal, it found little reason to think that they would be significantly positive. On a different front, most independent analysts expected a war with Iraq to increase, not reduce, the risk of terrorist attack.

Journalists find it very hard to deal with blatantly false arguments; by inclination and training, they always try to see two sides to an issue, and find it hard even to conceive that a major political figure is simply lying about the content of his proposals. I hear that several journalists were very angry after I joked in my column that if Bush said that the world was flat, the headline on the news analysis would read "Shape of Earth: Views Differ"—each of the angry journalists thought I was making fun of him.

To be fair, when one is dealing with ordinary political movements, it makes sense to presume that their policy proposals, right or wrong, are made in good faith. But when one is dealing with a revolutionary movement, a movement that does not accept the legitimacy of the existing system, there's no reason to make that presumption. Revolutionary movements, which aren't concerned about the rules of the game, have no compunction about misrepresenting their goals. David Wessel of *The Wall Street Journal* wrote about a White House aide who said one thing on the record and the opposite off the record; when Wessel protested, the aide replied: "Why would I lie? Because that's what I'm supposed to do. Lying to the press doesn't prick anyone's conscience."

## 2. Do some homework to discover the real goals

There was no widely accepted economic theory, left or right, under which the type of tax cuts proposed in early 2003—which would gradually end taxes on capital income, but pump very little money into the economy in the first year—made any sense as a way of creating jobs in the short run. Yet administration officials touted their plan as a job-creation strategy. Were they misinformed? No, not really. Whatever those officials said, economic growth was not their goal.

Moreover, it wasn't hard to figure out what the real goal was. As I pointed out above, radical conservatives have long advocated an end to all taxes on capital—and that's what the administration's proposal would in effect accomplish. So the way to understand the policy was to look at what its architects wanted before they tried to sell their plans to the public.

This is a general principle for understanding what's happening: do some homework to find out what these people *really* want. I'm not talking about deeply hidden motives; usually the true goal is in the public domain. You just have to look at what the people pushing the policy said before they were trying to sell it to the broader public. When you learn that the official now in charge of forest policy is a former timber industry lobbyist, you can surmise that the "healthy forests" initiative, under which logging companies will be allowed to cut down more trees, isn't about preventing forest fires. When you learn that the House majority leader has said that his purpose in office is to promote a "biblical worldview," you can surmise that "faith-based" initiatives aren't mainly about delivering social services more effectively. When you learn that the architects of the Iraq war have wanted to topple Saddam Hussein for a decade, you can surmise that the war has nothing to do with responding to September 11.

Again, this is hard for journalists to deal with: they don't want to sound like crazy conspiracy theorists. But there's nothing crazy about ferreting out the real goals of the right wing; on the contrary, it's unrealistic to pretend that there *isn't* a sort of conspiracy here, albeit one whose organization and goals are pretty much out in the open.

## 3. *Don't assume that the usual rules of politics apply*

Washington has long had a routine for scandal. Some awkward facts come out about an official, and the press begins playing up the story; soon the official is quietly urged to resign, and life goes on.

So, when various Bush administration officials began to have problems, people expected the same story line—but it didn't happen. Stephen Griles, a coal industry lobbyist who was appointed deputy interior secretary, intervened in an energy exploration dispute on behalf of a former client; he's still there. Thomas White, a former Enron executive, was appointed secretary of the Army; then his division of Enron was revealed to have been a source of phantom profits—but he's still there. Richard Perle, chairman of the Defense Policy Advisory Board, was revealed to have business dealings that raised strong questions about conflict of interest—but he took only a token demotion, from chairman to member, and is still there. And both the president and vice president have, of course, brushed off concerns about their distinctly questionable business careers.

Why don't the usual rules apply? Because a revolutionary power, which does not regard the existing system as legitimate, doesn't feel obliged to play by the rules. Are there hints of scandal regarding administration personnel? No matter: Fox News, *The Washington Times*, and *The New York Post* won't follow up on the story—instead they'll harass other media outlets if they try to make it an issue. Are there complaints about how homeland security is being handled? A sudden rash of terror alerts will drown out the story. "But they wouldn't do that!" protest reasonable people—and a normal regime wouldn't. But we're not dealing with a normal regime here, we're dealing with a revolutionary power.

## 4. Expect a revolutionary power to respond to criticism by attacking

A revolutionary power, which doesn't accept the legitimacy of the existing system, also doesn't accept the right of others to criticize its actions. Anyone who raises questions can expect a no-holds-barred counterattack.

There was a spectacular example in April 2003. John Kerry, among the front-runners for the next Democratic presidential nomination, told an audience that "What we need now is not just a regime change in Saddam Hussein and Iraq, but we need a regime change in the United States." By the normal standards of political rhetoric—including wartime—this wasn't unusual. For example, in the 1944 election—that is, at the height of World War II, with millions of American servicemen slugging it out on multiple fronts, Thomas E. Dewey campaigned by calling Franklin Roosevelt a "tired old man." As far as I know, nobody considered that treasonous. After all, you can't have free elections if you can't criticize the incumbent—and wasn't freedom what we were fighting for?

The tradition of tolerance for criticism, even in times of war, has continued. For example, Tom DeLay was harshly critical of President Bill Clinton during the 1999 campaign in Kosovo, blaming Clinton for civilian deaths and urging a halt to the campaign. Some eyebrows were raised, but DeLay's career wasn't harmed.

Now that a revolutionary power holds the White House, however, the rules have changed. "Senator Kerry crossed a grave line when he dared to suggest the replacement of America's commander-in-chief at a time when America is at war," declared the chairman of the Republican National Committee, and dozens of Republican politicians piled on, questioning Kerry's patriotism. (It so happens that Kerry is a decorated Vietnam veteran.)

Kerry's experience was only the latest in a series of episodes in which those who question or criticize the administration are demonized, their ethics questioned, their careers destroyed if possible. As I mentioned, the Republican party ran ads linking Tom Daschle, the Democratic Senate leader, to Saddam Hussein; it successfully questioned the patriotism of Senator Max Cleland, who lost three limbs in Vietnam.

All this was to be expected. The Bush administration has become notorious for its intolerance for dissent, even from those who are mostly on its side. According to *The Washington Post*, "GOP lawmakers and lobbyists say the tactics the Bush administration uses on friends and allies have been uniquely fierce and vindictive." To some extent this may reflect Bush family values; but it's also what you would expect from a revolutionary power. Here's a bit more from Kissinger: "The distinguishing feature of a revolutionary power is not that it feels threatened . . . *but that nothing can reassure it* (Kissinger's emphasis). Only absolute security—the neutralization of the opponent—is considered a sufficient guarantee."

## 5. *Don't think that there's a limit to a revolutionary power's objectives*

When the tax cut of 2001 was introduced, many moderates downplayed its significance, calling it a modest reversal of tax increases in the 1990s; even if they didn't approve, they thought that it wasn't such a bad idea to let Bush have what he wanted. When the budget projections used to justify the tax cut proved wildly overoptimistic, moderates urged the administration to reconsider its plans, believing that it might listen and seek a compromise. The administration responded by pushing for even more tax cuts—and senators who had voted for the first round of tax cuts had a hard time explaining why they were opposed to more of the same.

Only now is respectable opinion beginning to acknowledge that the administration's real goal, all along, was to eliminate taxation of capital income and sharply reduce if not eliminate the progressivity of the tax system—and that the initial appeasement by moderates removed the main obstacle toward that goal. Moreover, I'm not even sure that zero taxes on capital and a flat tax on wages mark the limits of the administration's ambitions. Poll taxes, anyone?

Similarly, quite a few moderates supported a war on Iraq—as a special case to deal with a dangerous, brutal dictator. But it has become increasingly clear that the administration's inner circle views the Iraq war as only a start on the "Bush doctrine," in which U.S. power will be used aggressively in much of the world. And having given in on the first step, moderates find it hard to explain why they don't support the overthrow of other dictators. Pax Americana, here we come.

There must be limits somewhere to what the right will actually attempt to accomplish. It may move us to a tax system in which poor people pay a higher share of their income than rich people, but it won't take us to a system where rich people actually pay less than poor people—or will it? It may go on from Iraq to Syria and Iran, but it won't start threatening already democratic countries with military force—or will it? I don't know where the right's agenda stops, but I have learned never to assume that it can be appeased through limited concessions. Pundits who predict moderation on the part of the Bush administration, on any issue, have been consistently wrong. Kissinger again: "It is the essence of a revolutionary power that it possesses the courage of its convictions, that it is willing, indeed eager, to push its principles to their ultimate conclusion."

So that's the way it is. I suspect that many readers, despite everything that has happened, will find it an alarmist picture. As Kissinger wrote, "Those who warn against the danger are considered alarmists; those who counsel adaptation to circumstance are considered balanced and sane." But so far the alarmists have been right, every time. What can we do?

## The great revulsion

A growing number of people are starting to realize just how serious the situation is. Maybe Andy Rooney of CBS's *60 Minutes* put it best: "The only real good news will be when this terrible time in American history is over."

What can bring that real good news closer?

To hope for a turnaround, you have to believe that most Americans don't really support the right's agenda—that the country as a whole is more generous, more tolerant, and less militaristic than the people now running it. And I think that's true—but for the right's success in obscuring its aims, and wrapping itself in the flag, I believe that most Americans would strongly oppose the direction this country is going.

I have a vision—maybe just a hope—of a great revulsion: a moment in which the American people look at what is happening, realize how their good will and patriotism have been abused, and put a stop to this drive to destroy much of what is best in our country. How and when this moment will come, I don't know. But one thing is clear: it cannot happen unless we all make an effort to see and report the truth about what is happening.

## Part One

# BUBBLE TROUBLE

REMEMBER what it was like—when it seemed as if the laws of business gravity had been repealed? Smart young people were dropping out of college and becoming multimillionaires on the spot. Companies you never heard of were suddenly worth $20 billion, and were using their ultra-valuable stock to take control of businesses that had existed for generations. Anyone who owned shares—especially tech stocks—had won the lottery. Anyone who didn't felt a sense of loss, even shame. "What did you do in the bull market, Daddy?" asked my fellow *Times* columnist Maureen Dowd.

Some people will tell you that the stock market boom of the 90s lies at the root of all our current troubles—that we are now paying the price for the bubble years. Although there's a grain of truth to that view, it's far from the whole story. As we'll see later in this book, long-run trends—growing economic and political polarization, the rising influence of a highly organized right wing—also helped set the stage for our present malaise. Specific events—above all, September 11, a crisis made for exploitation—also played an important role. And much of what has gone wrong reflects the character of the man in the White

House. Still, you can't understand where we are today without recalling the illusions and excesses of the 90s. So this part of the book is about irrational exuberance and its consequences.

One puzzle is why so few people raised red flags as the Dow shot past 10,000 and the Nasdaq past 5,000. There were strong indications that stock prices were way, way out of line: standard measures of stock valuation, like the price-earnings ratio, were far into what is normally considered the danger zone. And there were skeptics during the years of the surging market; I was one of them. Yet clever men in expensive suits invented all kinds of rationales for the market's ascent. Chapter 1 contains some of my attempts—going back to my pre–*New York Times* days—to demolish those rationales, and also to explain why normally sensible people got caught up in the frenzy.

Those who were skeptical about stock prices weren't just worried that investors would lose money when the market regained touch with reality; they were concerned about collateral damage to the real economy. History contains some ominous lessons: the stock market bubble of the 1920s was followed by the crash of 1929, and *that* was followed by the Great Depression. Fortunately, the United States hasn't had to deal with a serious financial crisis since the 1930s, but other countries have had more recent experiences—and I know a fair bit about them.

As an academic economist, I have been something of an ambulance chaser: much of my research has focused on economies in trouble, from Indonesia to Japan. As a result, I knew, even before our bubble burst, that our experience in the 1930s was normal: a loss of financial confidence after a bull market often leads to a crisis in the real economy. Many economists were quite sure that it couldn't happen here, that the

U.S. economy was immune to similar ills; I wasn't. In chapter 2 I talk about economic crises abroad, and their lessons for us.

So how has the United States coped with the end of the bubble years? Even pessimists generally expected our economic leaders—above all, Alan Greenspan, the legendary chairman of the Federal Reserve—to deal effectively with the economic consequences when stock prices returned to earth. But as an economist with an international perspective, I was all too aware of the history of Japan—the economic powerhouse of the world in the 1980s, but also the scene of one of history's great financial bubbles. And Japan's experience was a warning that we shouldn't take a happy ending for granted. When the Japanese stock market fell, that fall was followed by a protracted period of economic stagnation that continues to this day. In other words, even a highly advanced country with sophisticated leadership can stumble badly. And so it has turned out in the United States, which has experienced at least a touch of Japanese-style malaise. Chapter 3 chronicles the slide of the U.S. economy into recession, and its tentative, inadequate return to growth. (The usual term for growth too slow to reduce the unemployment rate is a "jobless recovery," but I've always thought the old term "growth recession" makes the point even better.) It also chronicles my growing sense of disillusion with U.S. economic policy, as Greenspan's efforts proved inadequate and the Bush administration doggedly refused to take the problem seriously.

Part of the reason the aftermath of the 90s has been so troubled is that much more went wrong than a temporary overvaluation of stocks. In an era of ever-rising stock prices hardly anyone noticed, but in the cold clear light of the morning after we can see that by the turn of the millennium something was very rotten in the state of American capitalism. On this issue I was no more perceptive than anyone else: during the bull market years some people did send me letters claiming that major corporations were cooking their books, but—to my great regret—I ignored them. However, when Enron—the most celebrated company of its time, lauded as the very model of a modern business enterprise—blew up, I immediately saw the implications: if such a famous and celebrated company could have been a Ponzi scheme, it was very unlikely that the rest of U.S. business was squeaky clean. In fact, it quickly became clear, the bubble years were both the cause and effect of an epidemic of corporate malfeasance.

Chapter 4 follows up on that revelation: it describes the motives for and techniques of business fraud. It also tells a story that many people don't want to hear, the extent to which our current political leadership is part of the problem. For it is a simple fact that George W. Bush and Dick Cheney got rich through pretty much the same tricks, albeit on a smaller scale, as those that enriched executives at Enron and other scandal-ridden corporations. That's part of a larger story: at a time when we really need another Franklin Roosevelt, we are instead led by men who are part of the problem. More on that later in the book.

## CHAPTER 1

# *Irrational Exuberance*

## SEVEN HABITS OF
## HIGHLY DEFECTIVE INVESTORS

Fortune, *December 29, 1997*

I like the theory of efficient financial markets as much as anyone. I don't begrudge Robert Merton and Myron Scholes the Nobel Prize they just received for showing how that theory can help you price complex financial instruments. But unless you spent the past five months in a Tibetan monastery, you must have noticed that markets have been behaving pretty strangely of late. As recently as June the "miracle" economies of Southeast Asia could do no wrong—investors cheerfully put billions into local stock markets. By October those same investors were in full flight; after all, everyone could see how corrupt and badly managed those economies were. When the IMF and the World Bank held their September meeting in Hong Kong, everyone congratulated the hosts on their economic policies, which had insulated them from the turmoil to the south and maintained prosperity through the handover to China. A month later Hong Kong had not only crashed but had briefly brought Brazil and much of the rest of the world down with it.

What is the market up to? Well, I recently had a chance to listen to the market, or at least a fairly large part of it, when I attended a meeting of money managers. Collectively they control several hundred billion dollars, so when they talked, I listened. Mainly I wanted to know why such smart men and women—and they must be smart because if they aren't smart, why are they rich?—do such foolish things. Here's what I learned: the seven habits that help produce the anything-but-efficient markets that rule the world:

1. Think short term. A few people in that meeting tried to talk about the long term—about what kind of earnings growth U.S. corporations might be able to achieve over the next five years. This sort of thing was brushed aside as too academic. But wait: Any economist will tell you that even a short-term investor should look at the long run. This year's stock price depends on this year's earnings plus what people think the price will be next year. But next year's price will depend on next year's earnings plus what people next year expect the price to be the following year. . . . Today's price, then, should take into account earnings prospects well into the future. Try telling that to the practitioners.

2. Be greedy. Many of the people kept talking about how they expected a final "meltup" in prices before the big correction and how they planned to ride the market up for awhile longer. Well, maybe they were right, but if you really think stocks are overvalued, how confident should you be about your ability to time the inevitable plunge? Trying to get those extra few percent could be a very expensive proposition.

3. Believe in the greater fool. Several money managers argued that Asian markets have been oversold, but that one shouldn't buy in until those markets start to turn around—just as others argued that the U.S. market is overvalued, but they

didn't plan to sell until the market started to weaken. The obvious question was, If it becomes clear to you that the market has turned around, won't it be clear to everyone else? Implicitly, they all seemed to believe that the strategy was safe, because there is always someone else dense enough not to notice until it really is too late.

4. Run with the herd. You might have expected that a group of investors would have been interested to hear contrarian views from someone who suggested that the U.S. is on the verge of serious inflationary problems, or that Japan is poised for a rapid economic recovery, or that the European Monetary Union is going to fail—which would have offered a nice challenge to conventional wisdom. But no: The few timid contrarians were ridiculed. The group apparently wanted conventional wisdom reinforced, not challenged.

5. Overgeneralize. I was amazed to hear the group condemn Japanese companies as uncompetitive, atrociously managed, unable to focus on the bottom line. But surely it can't be true of all Japanese companies; guys who managed to export even at 80 yen to the dollar must have at least a few tricks up their sleeves. And wasn't it only a couple of years ago that Japanese management techniques were the subject of hundreds of adulatory books and articles? They were never really that good, but surely they are better than their current reputation.

6. Be trendy. I came to the meeting expecting to hear a lot about the New Economic Paradigm, which asserts that technology and globalization mean that all the old rules have been repealed, that the inflation-free growth of the past six years will continue indefinitely, that we are at the start of a 20-year boom, etc. That doctrine is basically nonsense, of course—but anyway I quickly determined that it is, as they say in *Buffy the Vampire Slayer*, "so five minutes ago." All the rules have changed again:

Now we stand on the brink of a dreadful epoch of global deflation, and despite its previous track record of engineering recoveries, there is nothing the Fed can do about it. You see, it's a new new economy.

7. Play with other people's money. If, as I said, the people at that meeting were very smart, why did they act in ways that seem so foolish? Part of the answer, I suspect, is that they are employees, not principals; they are trying to make money and careers for themselves. In that position, it is hard to take a long view: In the long run, even if you aren't dead, you probably won't be working in the same place. It is also difficult for someone managing other people's money to take an independent line. To be wrong when everyone else is wrong is not such a terrible thing: You may lose a bonus, but probably not your job. On the other hand, to be wrong when everyone else is right . . . So everyone focuses on the same short-term numbers, tries to ride the trends, and buys the silly economic theory du jour.

Listening to all that money talking made me very nervous. After all, these people can funnel money into a country's markets, then abruptly pull that money out—and create a boom-bust cycle of pretty spectacular proportions. I don't think they can do it to the U.S.—in Greenspan I trust—but I am not 100% sure.

One thing that I am sure of is that the Asian leaders who have been fulminating against the evil machinations of speculators have it wrong. What I saw in that room was not a predatory pack of speculative wolves: It was an extremely dangerous flock of financial sheep.

# THE ICE AGE COMETH

Fortune, *May 25, 1998*

The more I look at the amazing rise of the U.S. stock market, the more I become convinced that we are looking at a mammoth psychological problem. I don't mean mammoth as in "huge" (though maybe that too), but as in "elephant." Let me explain.

If you follow trends in psychology, you know that Freud is out and Darwin is in. The basic idea of "evolutionary psych" is that our brains are exquisitely designed to help us cope with our environment—but unfortunately, the environment they are designed for is the one we evolved and lived in for the past two million years, not the alleged civilization we created just a couple of centuries ago. We are, all of us, hunter-gatherers lost in the big city. And therein, say the theorists, lie the roots of many of our bad habits. Our craving for sweets evolved in a world without ice cream; our interest in gossip evolved in a world without tabloids; our emotional response to music evolved in a world without Celine Dion. And we have investment instincts designed for hunting mammoths, not capital gains.

Imagine the situation back in what ev-psych types call the Ancestral Adaptive Environment. Suppose that two tribes—the Clan of the Cave Bear and its neighbor, the Clan of the Cave Bull—live in close proximity, but traditionally follow different hunting strategies. The Cave Bears tend to hunt rabbits—a safe strategy, since you can be pretty sure of finding a rabbit every day, but one with a limited upside, since a rabbit is only a rabbit. The Cave Bulls, on the other hand, go after mammoths—risky, since you never know when or if you'll find one, but potentially very rewarding, since mammoths are, well, mammoth.

Now suppose that it turns out that for the past year or two the Cave Bulls have been doing very well—making a killing practically every week. After this has gone on for a while, the natural instinct of the Cave Bears is to feel jealous, and to try to share in the good fortune by starting to act like Cave Bulls themselves. The reason this is a natural instinct, of course, is that in the ancestral environment it was entirely appropriate. The kinds of events that would produce a good run of mammoths—favorable weather producing a good crop of grass, migration patterns bringing large numbers of beasts into the district—tended to be persistent, so it was a good idea to emulate whatever strategy had worked in the recent past.

But now transplant our tribes into the world of modern finance, and—at least according to finance theory—those instincts aren't appropriate at all. Efficient markets theory tells us that all the available information about a company is supposed to be already built into its current price, so that any future movement is inherently unpredictable—a random walk. In particular, the fact that people have made big capital gains in the past gives you absolutely no reason to think they will in the future. Rational investors, according to the theory, should treat bygones as bygones: if last year your neighbor made a lot of money in stocks while you unfortunately stayed in cash, that's no reason to get into stocks now. But suppose that, for whatever reason, the market goes up month after month; your MBA-honed intellect may say, "Gosh, those P/Es look pretty unreasonable," but your prehistoric programming is shrieking, "Me want mammoth meat!"—and those instincts are hard to deny.

And those instincts can be self-reinforcing, at least for a while. After all, whereas an increase in the number of people acting like Cave Bulls tended to mean fewer mammoths per hunter, an increase in the number of modern bulls tends to produce even bigger capital gains—as long as the run lasts. Any broker can tell you that in the last few months the market has been rising, despite mediocre earnings news, because of fresh purchases by ever more people distraught about having missed out on previous gains and desperate to get in on the action. Sooner or later the supply of such people will run out; then what?

O.K., O.K., I know that this isn't supposed to happen. Sophisticated investors are supposed to take the long view, and arbitrage away these boom-bust cycles. And maybe, just maybe, the market is where it is because wise and far-seeing people have understood that the New Economy can produce growing profits forever, and that the rise of mutual funds has eliminated the need for old-fashioned risk premia. But my sense is that people who try to take a long view have been driven to the edge of extinction by the sheer scale of recent gains, and that the supposed explanations you now hear of why current prices make sense are rationalizations rather than serious theories.

The whole situation gives me the chills. It could be that I just don't get it, that I'm a Neanderthal too thick-skulled to understand the new era. But if you ask me, I'd say that there's an Ice Age just over the horizon.

# THE PONZI PARADIGM

*March 12, 2000*

Charles Ponzi wasn't the first to try it, but he has joined Dr. Bowdler and Captain Boycott among those whose names will forever be terms of abuse. And the classic scam that bears his name—using money from new investors to pay off old investors, creating the illusion of a successful business—shows no sign of losing its effectiveness.

Robert Shiller's terrific new book, *Irrational Exuberance*, contains a brief primer on how to concoct a Ponzi scheme. The first step is to come up with a plausible-sounding but complicated profit opportunity, one that is difficult to evaluate. Ponzi's purported business involved international postage reply coupons. In a more recent example, Albanian scammers convinced investors that they had a profitable money-laundering business.

From that point on it's all a matter of timing and publicity. An initial group of investors must be pulled in, large enough to attract attention but not too large; then a larger second group, whose investments can be used to pay off the first, a still larger third group, and so on. If all goes well, stories about how much early investors have made will spread, attracting ever more people, and the continuing success of the company will silence or drown out the skeptics.

In the U.S., regulators—who know very well just how effective such scams often are—do their best to stop them before they get started. So you might think that Ponzi schemes are mainly a historical curiosity. But Mr. Shiller is not interested in history for its own sake; he uses Ponzi schemes as a model for something much more important.

Imagine, just hypothetically, that a new set of technologies—technologies that are really, truly, deeply fabulous—has just emerged. And suppose also that a number of companies have been created to exploit these new technologies, in the entirely honest—but very hard to assess—belief that they will eventually be able to earn huge profits. For the time being they earn little if any money; even if they make an accounting profit, they must continually raise more cash to pay for equipment, acquisitions and so on. Still, as the evidence for a true technological revolution mounts, the prices of their stocks keep rising, producing huge capital gains for early investors. And this attracts ever more investors, pushing the prices still higher.

If the process goes on long enough—and there is no reason it cannot go on for years—the doubters will start to look like fools, and the bears will go into hibernation. Everyone (well, almost everyone) may be completely sincere; nonetheless, in effect you get a Ponzi scheme without a Ponzi, a scam with no scammer.

Given the title of Mr. Shiller's book, you can guess the punch line. He makes a powerful case that the soaring stock market of recent years is a huge, accidental Ponzi scheme in progress, one that will come to a very bad end. The book actually focuses on the market broadly defined (most numbers are for the S&P 500), but it reads even better as a tale of the tech stocks. It's a book that I hope many people will read; but I doubt that many will be persuaded.

You see, right now bears have an extra credibility problem. Not long ago many people were skeptical not only about the prospects for today's technology companies but about the importance of the technology itself. (I plead guilty.) And every new statistic showing soaring productivity and earnings growth shows how wrong they were. As a matter of logic you can concede the reality of a technological revolution, even while asserting that the valuations of many technology companies are crazy; but who will listen?

It's also true that savvy investors (at least they seem savvy) are following the Levi Strauss strategy: Let others get caught up in the gold rush, we'll sell them the supplies. It is quite possible that the valuations of companies that sell Internet infrastructure make sense even if those of the dot-coms do not.

Still, as you watch those who missed out on the first few thousand points of the Nasdaq's rise feverishly try to make up for lost time, you have to wonder. Will people 80 years from now talk, without quite knowing where the term comes from, about being bezosified or qualcommed?

# DOW WOW, DOW OW

*February 27, 2000*

Early in his book *Irrational Exuberance*, Robert Shiller—who has done more than any other economist of his generation to document the less rational aspects of financial markets—describes the full-page advertisement that Merrill Lynch ran a year ago, when the Dow Jones industrial average passed 10,000. "Even those with a disciplined long-term approach like ours have to sit back and say 'wow,' " the ad declared. And the accompanying stock market chart bore the caption HUMAN ACHIEVEMENT.

In the year to date, however, blue-chip investors, battered by interest rate fears, have experienced more ow than wow. On Friday the Dow zipped through 10,000 again, this time heading the other way. Will we soon see another chart, with the caption HUMAN FAILURE?

O.K., O.K., the Dow is still more than 50 percent higher than it was in December 1996, when Alan Greenspan tried unsuccessfully to dampen our exuberance. And other stock indices have not felt the Dow's pain: the broader S&P 500 index is still well above its level of a year ago, while the Nasdaq—whose heavy weighting of tech stocks has made it the unofficial bellwether of the "new economy"—keeps setting new records.

But that divergence of fortunes is very much to the point: although the chatter is all about Mr. Greenspan's next move, the question this market really poses is, Who will own the future?

37

The very fame of the Dow tends to make us forget that this is even a question. In Steve Bodow's hilarious 1997 *Slate* article "Dow te ching," one of the koans reads: "The Dow does not exist, yet all things exist within it / O.K., only 30 stocks exist within it / But it seems like a much bigger deal." It is common practice to speak loosely of "the Dow" when we really mean "stock prices in general"—I've done it myself—and many people compound that looseness by talking as if the Dow stocks represented a claim on the future earnings of corporate America. But they don't: if you buy the Dow, you only buy a claim on the future earnings of the companies currently in the index.

That's not a trivial distinction: to be bullish on the Dow you must believe not just that American capitalism will prosper, but that today's corporate giants will share proportionately in that prosperity—not just for the next couple of years, but far into the future. And I mean far. To take an extreme example, the calculation that underlies last year's best seller *Dow 36,000* [by James Glassman and Kevin Hassett] assumes that the earnings of today's Dow companies will grow as fast as overall corporate profits forever; and half of what the authors believe to be fair value comes from projected earnings after the year 2070. (Actually, even then you don't get 36K—more like 20—but never mind.)

So, do you believe that 70 years from now the Dow companies—not the companies that will be in the Dow then, but the companies that are in it right now—will capture the same share of corporate profits that they do today? The investors bidding up the Nasdaq, not to mention those buying into I.P.O.'s, clearly don't. They believe that whatsit.com has a good chance of being tomorrow's Microsoft, and correspondingly that today's General Electric—or even today's Microsoft—may be tomorrow's Sears, Roebuck. To be a serious Dow bull, you must believe that the new economy will belong to old companies; to justify the price of tech stocks, you must believe that the future belongs to the upstarts. Both beliefs can't be right.

Both could, on the other hand, be wrong. Mr. Shiller believes that the whole stock market, not just the Dow, is inflated by a speculative bubble. I'm sympathetic but not entirely convinced. The social and psychological hallmarks of a bubble—like the fact that the TV in my local greasy pizza place is now tuned to CNBC, not ESPN—are plain to see, but so is the spectacular pace of technological progress. I'm not sure that the current value of the Nasdaq is justified, but I'm not sure that it isn't.

In any case, the fall in the Dow is not a verdict on the economy as a whole. As long as we have full employment and low inflation, I say let the blue chips fall where they may.

# MONEY FOR NOTHING?

*May 28, 2000*

Economists don't usually make good speculators, because they think too much. Like the famous if apocryphal professor who refused to pick up a $100 bill, they tend to assume that if there were money to be had, someone would already have taken it.

However, caution that can be a liability on the trading floor is an asset off it. Sometimes the observant do spot opportunities for large, risk-free gain—$100 bills lying in the street—that others have somehow missed. But a wise man doesn't assume that such opportunities will present themselves on a regular basis, and he certainly doesn't use that assumption as a basis for his family budget—or his plan to save Social Security.

It is a fact that historically stocks have been a very good investment. The best-known demonstration of that fact comes from Jeremy Siegel of the University of Pennsylvania, who has pointed out—in his book *Stocks for the Long Run*—that during the 20th century anyone who was willing to buy and hold for long periods would almost always have done better buying stocks than bonds. So there wasn't a tradeoff between risk and return: stocks were just a better investment, period. It turns out that there was a $100 bill lying on the sidewalk (quite a few billion bills, actually) that for some reason nobody picked up.

But many people have misunderstood what that observation means. It doesn't say that there is some natural law guaranteeing that stocks will always be a great investment; it says that historically stocks have been underpriced. Investors weren't willing to pay as much for claims on corporate earnings as they would have if they had properly understood how low the risks were.

And a funny thing happened on the way to the 21st century: the price-earnings ratio—the price of a dollar of corporate earnings—soared. In the period studied by Professor Siegel, prices were on average less than 15 times earnings, and stock investors on average earned a real return of 7 percent. Nowadays the price-earnings ratio is on average more like 30. Is this irrational exuberance, or did investors finally absorb Professor Siegel's lesson? Either way, that $100 bill has now been picked up. If stock investors now have to pay twice as much as they used to for a claim on earnings, and if profits grow in the future as they have in the past, those investors should now expect to earn only half the historical rate of return.

And yet many of those offering plans to reform Social Security—among them, of course, advisers to George W. Bush—insist that stocks are the answer, and that it is safe to assume that stocks will keep on yielding 7 percent forever. And if you try to point out that buying a piece of corporate America is much more expensive than it used to be, they just repeat the mantra that stocks have historically been a great investment. In other words, that $100 bill was there yesterday, so it must still be there, right?

Is the odd susceptibility of first-rate economists to such a naïve fallacy a triumph of wishful thinking over analysis, or a disingenuous bow to political expediency? Recent remarks by Mr. Bush offer evidence of good old-fashioned American disingenuity at work.

In a May 15 speech he asked his listeners to "consider this simple fact: even if a worker chose only the safest investment in the world, an inflation-adjusted U.S. government bond, he or she would receive twice the rate of return of Social Security." That's an amazing fact; it's even more amazing when you realize that the Social Security system invests all its money in, you guessed it, U.S. government bonds. But the explanation—which Mr. Bush's advisers understand very well, even if the governor does not—is that today's workers are not only paying for their own retirement, but also supporting today's retirees. And if you think that's a minor detail—that the question of how to meet existing obligations when workers are allowed to invest their contributions elsewhere is a side issue—let me assure you that I too would have no trouble devising a painless plan to save Social Security, if you let me assume that a large part of the system's obligations would magically disappear.

Or maybe "magic" isn't quite the right word. How about "voodoo"?

# CREATE AND DESTROY

*October 8, 2000*

Hold your horsemen! Last week the market guru James J. Cramer, once famed for his boundless optimism about tech stocks, declared himself, yes, disillusioned with the sector. He detailed his disappointment with the "four horsemen" of tech: Dell, Microsoft, Intel and Cisco.

But in the same week an article in *BusinessWeek Online* also spoke of the "four horsemen of the new economy"—Cisco again, but the others were Oracle, EMC and Sun. Aside from the fact that most people probably have no idea what these companies do (I'm a bit blurry myself), the interesting thing is that while Mr. Cramer's list is dominated by companies associated with PC's, the other list is all about computer networks. And that suggests an interpretation not only of Mr. Cramer's loss of faith but of the broader disillusionment of investors, a disillusionment that has pushed the Nasdaq down more than 20 percent from its summer highs. Think of it as the revenge of Joseph Schumpeter.

In recent years Schumpeter, an Austrian economist who moved to Harvard between the wars, has become a sort of new-economy icon. That status owes something to his early work; the young Schumpeter, writing before World War I, was the first major economist to recognize that continual technological change is part of what capitalism is all about. But most of his modern reputation rests on a single phrase that he introduced

43

late in his career, when he referred in passing to technology as a force of "creative destruction."

One suspects that people in the business world like that phrase mainly for the wrong reasons—because it makes what they do sound a lot more glamorous than it really is, or because it seems to excuse the hardships and injustices that markets often inflict. (It's no accident that Schumpeter is a favorite of right-wing publications like *Forbes*.) But misused as it is, the phrase is still perfect: new technologies do indeed destroy as well as create. In particular, each new technology destroys or at least diminishes the value of old skills and old market positions.

But do investors—and their gurus—really appreciate what that implies? Only a few months ago they clearly didn't. They were (rightly) excited about all the creation going on, but they forgot about the destruction bit. Or maybe they thought that destruction happened only to old-economy companies.

The reason tech companies sometimes have such high ratios of value to earnings is that investors have learned very well the lesson of Microsoft and Intel: that technology markets tend to be winner-takes-all, and a company that gets an early advantage in a new technology may well be able to translate that advantage into a sustained, lucrative monopoly. So investors were willing to pay very high prices for companies with some prospect of becoming the next Microsoft.

The tech slump last spring came when people began to realize that not every tech company is going to be another Microsoft, and also that dominating a market in which nobody is ever going to make any money is no prize. But the winners who had already taken all—companies that had established dominant positions in important markets and were earning real money from those positions—continued to be valued at many times their earnings.

What's happened now is that disappointing earnings at some of those old new-economy companies have reminded investors that creative destruction is not confined to the dinosaurs. A small company with an edge in an exciting technology like fiber optics or wireless networks might well be the next Intel, but Intel itself may be the next I.B.M., a company whose dominance in one technology became a lot less valuable as still newer technologies took center stage.

What does that say about the current tech slump? It cuts both ways. There is a good case to be made that the market reaction is overdone, that investors have allowed disappointing results at old new-economy companies to overshadow the remarkable things still happening in new new-economy companies.

On the other hand, the realization that tech companies are mortal, too, should limit the price that investors are willing to pay even for companies with a very bright near future. The same breathless pace of technological progress that has made it possible for major companies to emerge out of nowhere also means that those companies may have only a brief moment in the sun.

# THE PIZZA PRINCIPLE

*July 9, 2000*

It has always been hard to have a rational discussion about the stock market: hope and fear, greed and envy get in the way. And it's even harder nowadays because politics has entered the mix. Not only do some ideologues believe that to love capitalism is to love its stocks, whatever their price; also, the promise of high stock returns serves the same purpose today that the Laffer curve served 20 years ago. That is, it helps politicians—particularly politicians who want to privatize Social Security—offer visions of sugar plums, of gain without pain.

Still, there is a real debate about the prospects for stock prices, with serious arguments on both sides.

Last year bulls dominated the public discourse, but we have lately been hearing a lot from the sophisticated bears—people like Robert Shiller, the author of *Irrational Exuberance*, or Andrew Smithers and Stephen Wright, co-authors of *Valuing Wall Street*. Their arguments are straightforward: by historical standards, current stock values look way out of line. The price-earnings ratio of the average company is more than twice its historical average; so is "q"—the ratio of the market value of corporations to the value of their underlying assets. And in the past a high P/E or a high q was usually a portent of capital losses to come. So this is certainly a point of view that should be taken seriously.

But will the future be like the past? Sophisticated bulls—

exemplified by Jeremy Siegel, author of the influential 1993 book *Stocks for the Long Run*—point out that stocks have historically been a high-yield, low-risk investment. Indeed, stocks were so good an investment that people should have been willing to pay much higher prices than they did. So valuations that look very high by historical standards might represent not the rise of irrational exuberance but the decline of irrational pessimism. And this, too, is a point of view that should be taken seriously.

It's important, however, to recognize the limits of sophisticated bullishness. The long-run rate of return on stocks tends to be about the same as the "earnings yield"—the price-earnings ratio people usually talk about, only upside down. So even if you believe that stocks aren't particularly risky, this only justifies stock prices high enough so that the earnings yield—and hence the long-run rate of return on stocks—is no higher than the rate of return on safe assets like bonds. And we are already there (actually a bit beyond). So the views of sophisticated bulls do not justify a belief either that stocks are still greatly undervalued, or that today's generously priced stocks will yield investors anything like the rate of return investors got on the undervalued stocks of decades past.

The reason I emphasize this point, of course, is that if you do not understand it you might confuse the sophisticated bulls with those in a third camp—mad bulls?—who do hold one or both of these beliefs.

This is a confusion actively encouraged by the mad bulls themselves. For example, the authors of last year's *Dow 36,000* claimed to base their ideas on the work of Professor Siegel. And there is a sense in which this claim is true. But it is the same sense in which a recipe for pineapple-marshmallow-baloney pizza is based on pizza dough. Yes, the dough is a crucial ingredient; but there are other crucial ingredients, and very questionable ingredients at that.

The sophisticated bulls deserve to be taken seriously; so do the sophisticated bears. The mad bulls don't.

But those are fighting words, and the fight won't be fair. I myself have been angrily accused of inconsistency because I have both criticized the mad bulls and said nice things about Professor Siegel. In other words, "Last year you made fun of pineapple-marshmallow-baloney pizza—but now you say you like pizza after all. Ha! You've changed your position!"

So let me now lay down the pizza principle for stock prices. I like pizza, and so should you—that is, you should take seriously the view that a stock market that looks grossly overvalued by historical standards isn't. But even if you do like pizza, you don't have to accept the baloney some people want you to swallow.

## DAMAGED BY THE DOW

*September 2, 2001*

In late 1999—about the time when George W. Bush first announced his tax-cut plan—I had lunch at a beer-and-pizza joint, the sort of place that has a TV over the bar where the patrons can watch ESPN. But the TV wasn't tuned to ESPN—it was showing CNBC. I thought to myself, "This will end badly." And it has.

The Dow first passed 10,000 in 1999. Although the index briefly dropped below that milestone in early 2000, that decline didn't really count—it was a perverse side-effect of truly irrational exuberance, as investors deserted the boring old Dow for the Nasdaq. Last week, on the other hand, was the real thing: a broad market decline carried the Dow past 10,000 in the wrong direction. The era of the stock-market bubble has now well and truly ended. But what a mess that bubble has left behind!

By now the direct economic impact of the bubble is a familiar story. During the years of booming stock prices, which were closely linked to euphoria about the "new economy," businesses invested frantically, sinking vast sums into information technology. Now, of course, many of those businesses realize that they invested far too much. And the overhang of excess capacity is likely to keep business investment depressed for years.

That's not an encouraging thought. But the direct economic consequences of the bubble are only half the story. The bubble also had a dire effect on our national politics.

After all, it wasn't an accident that the Bush tax plan was proposed just before the bubble popped. There was an intimate relationship between stock-market mania and tax-cut mania, a relationship that ran in both directions.

On one side, in the late 1990's the right-wing media were enthusiastic stock boosters. The editorial page of *The Wall Street Journal*, in particular, was extremely fond of crank theories about stock valuation, as long as they pointed upward. Remember *Dow 36,000*? And anyone who pointed out that such theories rested on fuzzy math, and suggested that the stocks could not be counted on to deliver high returns forever, was clearly a dangerous leftist—after all, the stock market is the purest expression of capitalism, so anyone who doubts that market must be anticapitalist, right?

But the more important causation ran the other way: the stock bubble, alas, provided an environment in which deeply irresponsible policy proposals temporarily looked plausible.

It's important to realize how much of the late lamented budget surplus was the result of the bull market. Tax rates didn't increase between 1994 and 2000, but tax receipts as a share of GDP surged, largely because of the extra taxes paid on all those capital gains. The result was a false sense that there was plenty of money in hand, that big tax cuts would fit comfortably into the budget. And the Bush tax plan was formulated when such delusions were at their height.

Now reality has started to sink in. Unfortunately, though the new realism may have come soon enough to prevent a disaster on Social Security—for Mr. Bush's other signature policy proposal was also based on the delusions of a bubble economy—it has come too late to prevent a disastrous tax cut.

Of course, you might wonder why Mr. Bush himself didn't have second thoughts—why he thought that the exact same tax plan he proposed in the feverish bull-market days of late 1999 was still appropriate in the post-bubble economy of 2001. And his officials surely knew that tax receipts were dropping like a stone even as they were reassuring a docile Congress that everything was just fine.

But one thing we have learned about this administration is that it never responds to altered circumstances by changing its plans; all it does is change the sales pitch. So the tax cut was relabeled as a recession-fighting measure, a task for which it is peculiarly ill-suited. For that matter, the administration hasn't given up on Social Security privatization, either. Now that it can no longer entice people with visions of stock-market sugar-plums, it has decided to scare them with imaginary crises instead.

In any case, immense damage has already been done. The stock-market bubble led to bad political decisions as well as bad business decisions; and we'll be paying the price for many years to come.

# CHAPTER 2

# Portents Abroad

## ASIA: WHAT WENT WRONG?

Fortune, *March 2, 1998*

There is a part of me that is excited, even happy, about Asia's financial crisis. You see, financial disasters are one of my specialties. The very first serious economics paper I ever wrote, more than 20 years ago, was titled "A model of balance-of-payments crises." And so I am a bit like a tornado-chaser who has just caught up with a monster twister. I'm as sorry as anyone about those poor people in the trailer park, but I am also more than a bit thrilled to have the chance to watch this amazing spectacle unfold. I can even offer an excuse for my mixed feelings: You learn a lot more about how the global economy works when something goes wrong than when everything hums along smoothly. And maybe the lessons we learn from this crisis will help us avoid, or at least cope better with, the next one.

So what have we learned from Asia's mess? Speculative attacks on currencies are nothing new, and some of us even warned a couple of years ago that Southeast Asian countries

53

might be at risk. But the scale and depth of this crisis have surprised everyone; this disaster has demonstrated that there are financial dangers undreamt of in our previous philosophy.

By now we have a pretty good idea of what happened to Asia. Think of it, so far, as a play in two acts, the first about reckless behavior and the second about its consequences. What nobody knows yet is how close we are to the end. Is the play almost over, or is there a tragic final act still to follow?

The first act was the story of the bubble. It began, we now think, with bad banking. In all of the countries that are currently in crisis, there was a fuzzy line at best between what was public and what was private; the minister's nephew or the president's son could open a bank and raise money both from the domestic populace and from foreign lenders, with everyone believing that their money was safe because official connections stood behind the institution. Government guarantees on bank deposits are standard practice throughout the world, but normally these guarantees come with strings attached. The owners of banks have to meet capital requirements (that is, put a lot of their own money at risk), restrict themselves to prudent investments, and so on. In Asian countries, however, too many people seem to have been granted privilege without responsibility, allowing them to play a game of "heads I win, tails somebody else loses." And the loans financed highly speculative real estate ventures and wildly overambitious corporate expansions.

The bubble was inflated still further by credulous foreign investors, who were all too eager to put money into faraway countries about which they knew nothing (except that they were thriving). It was also, for a while, self-sustaining: All those irresponsible loans created a boom in real estate and stock markets, which made the balance sheets of banks and their clients look much healthier than they were.

Soon enough, Asia was set up for the second act, the bursting of the bubble. The bursting had to happen sooner or later. At some point it was going to become clear that the Panglossian values Asian markets had placed on assets weren't realistic in this imperfect world, that Asian conglomerates are no better than their Western counterparts at trying to be in every business in every country. But the collapse came sooner rather than later because speculative bubbles are vulnerable to self-fulfilling pessimism: As soon as a significant number of investors begin to wonder whether the bubble will burst, it does.

So Asia went into a downward spiral. As nervous investors began to pull their money out of banks, asset prices plunged. As asset prices fell, it became increasingly doubtful whether governments would really stand behind the deposits and loans that remained, and investors fled all the faster. Foreign investors stampeded for the exits, forcing currency devaluations, which worsened the crisis still more as banks and companies found themselves with assets in devalued baht or rupiah, but with liabilities in lamentably solid dollars.

What actually started this downward spiral? Who cares! Any little thing can set off an avalanche once the conditions are right. Probably the proximate causes were a slump in the semiconductor market and a rise in the dollar-yen exchange rate, but if they hadn't triggered the crisis, something else would have.

Asia's financial implosion is, of course, dragging the real economies down with it. Partly, that is because the collapse of asset values is making people feel poorer, depressing consumer demand; partly it is because low stock prices and high interest rates are depressing investment. But there is also—disturbingly—a supply-side effect. Although runaway banks were the original source of the mess, a functioning banking system remains a crucial lubricant for the economic engine. With banking in some Asian countries effectively paralyzed, that engine is showing signs of seizing up: even companies that should be profitable—like exporters—are finding themselves hamstrung by lack of credit. It is, in short, a terrible but also fascinating spectacle.

Could it get worse? If there is a third act, it will involve the interaction of economics and politics: economic crisis will lead to political instability, instability will lead to capital flight that reinforces the economic crisis, and all heck will break loose. But so far only Indonesia shows even faint signs of such a new vicious circle, and even there most sensible observers think that the risks of really serious unrest have been exaggerated.

I hope they are right. For economic tornado-chasers, Asia's disaster may have been a perfect storm. But anyone who cares seriously about the real people whose livelihoods—and, in some cases, lives—are now at risk can only hope that the storm will soon be over.

# WHY GERMANY KANT KOMPETE

Fortune, *July 19, 1999*

A while back various versions of a fake European Commission document began circulating via e-mail. The memorandum argued that once a common European currency had been established, the obvious next step would be adoption of a common language. Practical considerations dictated that this language be English, with a few improvements. Thus, the memorandum suggested that the superfluous hard "c" be replaced with "k," eliminating one source of konflikt; that in order konfusion to avoid writers the verbs at the end of the sentence put should; and by the end of the memorandum English had been transformed into German.

What gave the joke its edge was, of course, the presumption that the new Europe would be dominated by Germany. Not only is Germany the most populous nation of the European Union, but it has also traditionally had its most powerful economy. Indeed, since the early 1980s, Germany has effectively exercised monetary hegemony over its neighbors; the job of Dutch, Belgian, even French central bankers was simply to follow the Bundesbank's lead. But somehow, when we weren't looking, Germany stopped being the powerhouse of Europe and became its biggest source of weakness.

When did Germany become the economic sick man of Europe? For anyone old enough to remember the '50s and '60s, the very adjective "German" cries out to be followed with the words "economic miracle." As late as the early '90s, German performance still looked pretty good by international standards. But lately almost all the news from Germany has been bad.

Some attribute the problems to missteps by the current government of Gerhard Schröder, which has undermined business confidence with its occasional reversion to traditional socialist rhetoric. But German economic growth was sputtering before Schröder was elected; all he has done is to make a bad situation a bit worse.

Others date the problem to Germany's reunification after the fall of the Berlin Wall. Certainly the unintended effect of that reunification was to turn Germany into Italy without the *dolce vita*. Just as Italy is divided into a prosperous, productive north and a backward south, Germany is now divided between a productive west and a dependent east; and in both cases the aid provided to the backward region strains not only the budget but the society, creating in the recipients a sort of culture of dependency.

Still others date the problem much earlier. It is now 20 years since the German economist Herbert Giersch coined the term "eurosclerosis" to describe how overregulation and a too-generous welfare state undermine efficiency and job creation; and he was thinking of Germany in particular.

But this seems to make the contrast between Germany and the vigorous Anglophone economies a simple left-right matter: free markets vs. the heavy hand of the government. And while there is something to this, anyone who has spent time talking to German economists and officials knows that in some ways they are more conservative—that is, more opposed to activist government—than Americans. Perhaps they don't believe in letting grocers stay open whatever hours they want to, but they do believe in sound money and sound budgets and abhor the idea that the government should lower interest rates or—horrors—devalue the currency to fight unemployment.

Well, here's my theory: The real divide between currently successful economies, like the U.S., and currently troubled ones, like Germany, is not political but philosophical; it's not Karl Marx vs. Adam Smith, it's Immanuel Kant's categorical imperative vs. William James's pragmatism. What the Germans really want is a clear set of principles: rules that specify the nature of truth, the basis of morality, when shops will be open, and what a Deutsche mark is worth. Americans, by contrast, are philosophically and personally sloppy: they go with whatever seems more or less to work. If people want to go shopping at 11 P.M., that's O.K.; if a dollar is sometimes worth 80 yen, sometimes 150, that's also O.K.

Now, the American way doesn't always work better. Even today, Detroit can't or won't make luxury cars to German standards; Amtrak can't or won't provide the precision scheduling that Germans take for granted. America remains remarkably bad at exporting; the sheer quality of some German products, the virtuosity of German engineering, have allowed the country to remain a powerful exporter despite having the world's highest labor costs. And Germany did a better job of resisting the inflationary pressures of the '70s and '80s than we did.

But the world has changed in a way that seems to favor flexibility over discipline. With technology and markets in flux, not everything worth doing is worth doing well; in an environment where deflation is more of a threat than inflation, an obsession with sound money can be a recipe for permanent recession.

And so Germany is in trouble—and with it, the whole project of a more unified Europe. For Germany is supposed to be the economic engine of the new Europe; if it is a drag instead, perhaps the whole train in the wrong direction goes, not so?

# WE'RE NOT JAPAN

*December 27, 2000*

When Lucy tells Charlie Brown that this time she really is going to let him kick that football, you know what's going to happen. When Wile E. Coyote insists that this time he really is going to catch the Road Runner, you know what's going to happen. And when Japanese officials tell you that this time their nation really is on the road to self-sustaining recovery . . .

A new clutch of indicators confirms that, sure enough, Japan's economy is stalling yet again. Business confidence has gone flat, consumer spending is falling, unemployment is rising, deflation is accelerating. And the Nikkei stock index, which was over 20,000 earlier this year, is now oscillating around 14,000.

For Japan, it's the same old story. But with the U.S. economy going through its roughest patch in years, with panicky analysts and self-interested politicians declaring that the sky is falling, maybe it's worth explaining why our story remains very different.

You see, the general rule—the rule to which Japan is the great exception—is that recessions are not a serious problem for large, modern economies. It's not that the forces that cause recessions have been abolished—though every long expansion brings foolish proclamations of the end of business cycles. Rather, the point is that recessionary tendencies can usually be effectively treated with cheap, over-the-counter medication:

cut interest rates a couple of percentage points, provide plenty of liquidity, and call me in the morning.

Or more accurately, call me in six months—or maybe as much as a year. Experience suggests that the Fed can almost always persuade consumers and businesses to spend more by cutting interest rates, but that there's a longish lag between the rate cut and the spending increase. And that's why we're still vulnerable to recessions: now and then the Fed gets behind the curve, failing to recognize a weakening economy until it's too late to prevent a slump. That's what happened in 1990; it may be what's happening now.

Specifically, it's now pretty clear that the Fed went an interest rate hike too far—that while it was right to raise rates in late 1999 and early 2000 to cool off a red-hot economy, that last half-percentage-point increase in May was overkill. Of course, I'm talking with the benefit of hindsight; it seemed like a good idea at the time.

The Fed can and almost surely will reverse that rate hike sometime soon, but the favorable effects of that reversal on spending will take time to materialize. Meanwhile the economy will slow, and could shrink for a couple of quarters, which is the technical definition of a recession. But it should be only a temporary setback—which brings us to the difference between ourselves and Japan.

In Japan, the sky really is falling. Because the interest rate is already very close to zero (it isn't quite zero, because of the Bank of Japan's foolish decision to raise rates back in August— but don't get me started), the slowdown is a sign that the nation's basic economic policies aren't working, and that it is long past time to do something radical. By contrast, our slowdown is just one of those things that happen now and then; it doesn't indicate any fundamental flaws in our economic policy, any need to do anything except cut interest rates.

So what should we be afraid of? The nightmare scenario, which cannot be completely ruled out, is that we will turn out to be more like Japan than we think—that we have just gone through our own version of the infamous "bubble economy," and that we are about to find out that this time cutting interest rates won't do the trick. But at this point that scenario isn't very plausible.

What worries me is not the recession that we may or may not be about to experience; it is the way that our politicians are likely to react to that slowdown. Will they use a mild, easily treated ailment as an excuse to force expensive, dangerous quack remedies down the nation's throat? I am, of course, talking about tax cuts—which won't cure the short-term slowdown, and will undermine our long-run fiscal health.

We don't need to fear a recession; if it does happen, it's something that the Fed can easily cure. What we do need to fear is fear itself: the all-too-likely prospect that the threat of recession will panic us into doing things we will regret for years to come.

# A LEAP IN THE DARK

*July 8, 2001*

In a way, I wish that I had more negative things to say about the Japanese executives and officials I spoke to over the last few days. If the executives had been obviously out of touch with the realities of modern business, if the officials had been obstinate and foolish, it would be easy to dismiss Japan's economic malaise as the product of a deeply flawed social and political system—something that couldn't happen in America.

But by and large the people I talked to seemed well informed and reasonable. In fact, I'd say that the Japanese make far more sense now than they did when their economy was booming. Fifteen years ago, you just couldn't hold a rational discussion; even private-sector economists would refuse to criticize any government policy, no matter how absurd. Now it's possible to have real give-and-take.

And yet I've got a bad feeling about Japan's situation.

If good intentions and enthusiasm were enough to solve macroeconomic problems, economic recovery would be just around the corner. Prime Minister Junichiro Koizumi came into office with an unprecedented popular mandate, which he has used to pursue an ambitious program of "structural reform." And his approval ratings remain sky-high, even though he has explicitly warned that his reforms might produce several years of pain before Japan sees any gain.

But when you ask what the catch phrase "structural reform" really means, doubts start to creep in.

So far, what the phrase seems to mean is mainly two things: forcing banks to write off bad loans and scaling back the huge public works programs that have been used, year after year, to prop up employment. Both steps are entirely justified. Sooner or later, Japanese banks have to get honest in their accounting. And Japan's public works programs have become a source not just of inefficiency but of vast corruption.

But here's the problem: the clear and present danger to Japan's economy is not inefficiency but inadequate demand. That is, the immediate problem is not that Japan fails to get the most out of the resources it employs; it is that it fails to employ the resources it has. And Mr. Koizumi's reforms are all too likely to worsen that immediate problem. When banks foreclose on companies that will never be able to repay their debts, when the government stops building dams and roads the country doesn't need, the direct result will be higher unemployment. In a booming economy, the workers released as firms go bankrupt and public works are canceled would soon find productive jobs elsewhere. But in a persistently depressed economy, those workers will stay unemployed—and because unemployed workers buy fewer goods, the economy will become even more depressed.

So where's the prospect for recovery? I put this question to Heizo Takenaka, the professor and popular pundit who has emerged—through one of those boundary-crossing transformations familiar in America but unheard of in Japan—as the architect of the Koizumi government's economic plan. To his credit, he didn't try to obfuscate the issue: he conceded that his plan is "supply-side"—that is, intended to make Japan's economy more efficient—when the immediate problem that economy faces is "demand-side"—people are spending too little. Nonetheless, he argued that eventually the reforms will help the demand side too. Once consumers realize that the economy's long-term prospects have improved, he asserted, they will open their wallets. And he also argued that further structural reform—mainly deregulation and privatization—would open new business opportunities, and thereby spur investment.

Well, maybe. But the plan does seem like a leap in the dark—radical measures taken because they might work, not because there is solid reason to believe that they will work.

The plan's chances of success would be much greater if it were supported by equally bold action on the part of the Bank of Japan, which controls monetary policy. But the attitude of B.O.J. officials seems to be the reverse of Mr. Koizumi's: they seem unwilling to take actions that probably would work, for fear that they might not.

So will Mr. Koizumi succeed? I hope so, but as I said, I have a bad feeling about this. The implicit slogan of the Koizumi government is "reform or bust." But it is dangerously likely that the actual result will be "reform and bust."

# CHAPTER 3

# Greenspanomics

## DON'T ASK ALAN

*August 6, 2000*

Onstage, the song and dance went perfectly. Offstage, however, George W. Bush's top economic adviser flubbed his lines. On Wednesday *The Financial Times* ran an interview with Lawrence Lindsey in which the former Fed official made much of his relationship with Alan Greenspan, and appeared to claim that Mr. Greenspan endorses Mr. Bush's economic plan. By the next day Mr. Lindsey was furiously back-pedaling, conceding that he had in fact never discussed the plan with the Fed chairman, and further opining that "It's not for Chairman Greenspan to endorse one tax plan or another tax plan, or to endorse one candidate or another."

Presumably Mr. Lindsey—perhaps a bit rattled by analysts at Goldman Sachs and elsewhere who have warned that Mr. Bush's proposed tax cuts will drive up interest rates—was just being sloppy. One hopes that from now on the Republican team will defend its plans on the merits—starting, in the case of Social Security, by explaining what the plan actually is—instead of trying to reassure us that everything is O.K. because Uncle Alan approves. And yet there is something more to this story than Mr. Lindsey's blooper. If you ask me, we're hearing too much these days about Mr. Greenspan's opinions.

Mr. Greenspan, after all, holds a position that must be filled with great discretion, because he has a degree of autonomy that is peculiar in a democratic polity. Neither Congress nor the president can tell Mr. Greenspan what to do: he is a power unto himself.

There are good reasons for that special status. Monetary policy presents politicians with dangerous temptations—for example, to pump up the economy just before an election. To protect themselves from those temptations, even countries where the central bank used to take orders from the finance ministry, like Britain and Japan, have chosen (after hard-learned lessons) to have independent monetary policy boards.

And no central bank has justified its independence as thoroughly as the Fed. Mr. Greenspan has been lucky to preside over an era when everything has gone right with the U.S. economy, but he has made the most of that luck, letting growth rip without reviving inflation. And twice—in 1987 and 1998—he calmed markets at a time when a financial meltdown seemed imminent. It's no surprise that his opinions are sought on many issues.

But here's the problem: if the Fed is to be exempt from normal political control, it must itself be scrupulously nonpolitical, if only for its own sake. Stuff happens: it's a safe bet that one of these years the Fed—perhaps under Mr. Greenspan, perhaps under his successor—will make a big mistake. If it is perceived as an institution that carefully respects its limits, that mistake will be forgiven. But if the Fed chairman has come to be perceived as just another political player, trying to influence policy in areas that have nothing to do with his brief, the cries of "Who elected him?" will be hard to answer.

So I get uneasy when I see Mr. Greenspan weighing in on issues that seem remote from his job description. For example, what was he doing testifying in favor of normal trade relations with China? I happen to agree with him on the issue—but trade policy is a long way from monetary policy, and he should have stayed out of it.

Even the response to Mr. Lindsey's faux pas was inappropriate. According to Mr. Greenspan's spokesman, his "preference is for high or rising surpluses," but "if growing surpluses become politically infeasible to defend, he would prefer that they be allocated to tax cuts rather than to spending initiatives." I guess the first part of that is O.K.—since monetary policy and fiscal policy are interdependent, it's legitimate for the Fed chief to recommend fiscal restraint. But decisions about whether surpluses should be used to cut taxes or provide benefits— should we eliminate the estate tax or provide the elderly with drug coverage?—are surely matters for the electorate, not for unelected monetary technocrats.

If and when Mr. Greenspan becomes a private citizen, his views on such issues will and should be heard. But as the chairman of the Fed, he has to be careful: he must avoid any hint that he is overstepping the boundaries of his position.

# ELEVEN AND COUNTING

*December 14, 2001*

Embarrassing but true: Just one month ago the James A. Baker III Institute presented Alan Greenspan with its Enron Prize. I'm not suggesting any impropriety; it was just another indication of how deeply the failed energy company was enmeshed with our ruling elite.

And yet Mr. Greenspan also finds himself in Chapter 11. That is, the Fed has now cut interest rates 11 times, and has yet to see any results. What's going on?

One answer is that something has gone wrong with the monetary "transmission mechanism," the drive train that normally links the Fed's actions with the real economy. And one of the people who stripped the Fed's gears is Mr. Greenspan himself.

The Fed's direct power over the economy is actually more limited than is widely appreciated. People often say that the Fed controls interest rates, but what it actually controls is only *an* interest rate, the rate in the overnight federal funds market. And this interest rate is, in itself, of very little economic importance.

Normally, however, a fall in the federal funds rate indirectly affects financial variables that do matter; it leads to higher stock prices, a weaker dollar and—above all—lower long-term interest rates. Goldman Sachs economists have incorporated these variables into a "financial conditions index" that, they show, has historically done a very good job of predicting future economic performance.

Based on past experience, you would have expected the Fed's dramatic rate cuts since January to lower the Goldman Sachs index by about five points—enough to produce a roaring 2002. In fact, however, the index has fallen only about half a point, largely because long-term interest rates have not fallen at all. The Fed, in other words, is getting almost no bang for its bucks. Why?

Part of the explanation is self-defeating optimism. Bond traders continue to believe, despite mounting evidence to the contrary, that Mr. Greenspan is a magician—that he will soon conjure up another dramatic boom, and will then raise interest rates to cool a red-hot economy. Ironically, this very belief helps keep long-term rates high, and thus ensures that no such boom seems imminent.

And then there's the federal budget. Just months ago we were dazzled with projections of huge federal surpluses; there was enough money, the Bush administration insisted, to have a big tax cut, increase spending and still pay off the federal debt. But on Tuesday Paul O'Neill quietly asked Congress to raise the federal government's debt ceiling—something he had previously said would not be necessary until 2008 at the earliest.

Has the sudden return of federal deficits had an impact on long-term interest rates? Of course it has. Just a few months ago everyone expected the federal government to pay off its debt, drastically reducing the supply of bonds; now it turns out that it will actually be borrowing money. Inevitably this depresses bond prices, which is the same as raising long-term interest rates. So the rapid deterioration of federal finances is part of Mr. Greenspan's problem. (Has the negative impact of the tax cut on the economy via its effect on interest rates outweighed the positive effect on consumer spending? Yes, on any reasonable calculation.)

Mr. Greenspan, then, finds himself with much less ability to move the economy than anyone expected. And it's partly his own fault. After all, he did much to cultivate the mystique that now turns out to be a handicap. And let's not forget that he intervened decisively on behalf of large tax cuts back in January, when he urged Congress to prevent what he then saw as a great risk: that surpluses would be too large, and that the federal debt would be paid off too quickly.

It might be helpful if Mr. Greenspan would now say something to dampen self-defeating belief in a sudden economic turnaround. It would be even more helpful if he would concede, however indirectly, that he gave Congress bad advice last January; that might prepare the ground for an eventual return to fiscal responsibility. But the Fed chairman, who was quite willing to intervene in fiscal politics when that was helpful to the Bush administration, has gone oddly silent on the subject now that those surplus projections turn out to have been bad science fiction.

Maybe Mr. Greenspan deserved that Enron Prize after all.

# HERD ON THE STREET

*April 30, 2002*

On Friday the Commerce Department announced that the economy grew 5.8 percent in the first quarter of 2002. The Dow promptly sank below 10,000, making it the stock market's worst week since September 11. And stocks fell again yesterday.

What's going on? Maybe the market is spooked by those orchestrated leaks about attacking Iraq, which everyone agrees are a smoke screen, but nobody is sure for what. Or maybe we should ignore the Dow; an old line says that the stock market has predicted nine of the last five recessions. But the truth is that the numbers, when you look at them closely, are actually quite disappointing. How can 5.8 percent growth be disappointing? Bear with me while I run through a textbook example. This won't hurt (much).

Imagine a company that produces widgets (companies in these examples always produce widgets), normally selling 100 each month. The company tries to keep one month's sales, 100 widgets, in inventory. But for some reason sales drop off, to 90 per month. And it takes a month before the company realizes what has happened.

At the end of that month the company, having produced 100 widgets but sold only 90, finds itself with 110 in inventory, but wants to hold only 90. To eliminate the excess inventory quickly, it might slash production to 70 for the next month, then bump production back up to 90. But unless sales increase again, that's where it ends—production never recovers to its original level.

As go the widget-makers, so goeth the economy. When demand drops, inventories build up, then production drops sharply as businesses work off the overhang. Finally, there's an "inventory bounce" when the overhang is gone. But the bounce doesn't necessarily presage a true recovery—to get that, you need increased sales to final buyers.

And more than half of that 5.8 percent growth was just inventory bounce. Final sales actually grew only 2.6 percent, slower than in the previous quarter. And even that growth rate may not be sustainable: home construction soared, partly because of unusually warm weather, but there are already signs that the housing market is cooling off. Meanwhile, business investment, weighed down by excess capacity and weak profits, actually declined. In short, there is nothing in the data to suggest that a great boom is imminent.

This shouldn't be cause for surprise, but it is—because the great majority of business forecasters have become cheerleaders. As Alan Abelson put it in *Barron's*: "Where we are today . . . is not where we were supposed to be, according to the received wisdom back at the turn of the year. Economically, the perfect storm was to be followed by the perfect recovery."

I've never quite understood where that received wisdom came from. Wall Street economists assured us that business investment was about to surge, yet corporate leaders—who actually make the investment decisions—have consistently been much more pessimistic than the forecasters. Hey, what do they know?

Still, there has been intense pressure on business economists to run with the bullish herd.

Skeptics about the impending economic miracle haven't just

been ridiculed, they have been ostracized. Morgan Stanley's Stephen S. Roach—who was a lonely skeptic in the days of Nasdaq 5,000 and is now one of the few business forecasters with the courage to defy the orthodoxy—signs his e-mails to me "From the wilderness."

Of course, it's still possible that the prophets of boom will be vindicated. But it's also still possible, and I'd say about equally likely, that the recovery will stall. Right now the best bet for the next few quarters is probably a "jobless recovery," in which GDP grows but unemployment stays high. After all, the economy needs to grow at about 3.5 percent just to prevent the unemployment rate from rising—and the odds are at least even that growth will fall short of that mark.

The funny thing is that a slow, jobless (and profitless) recovery is exactly what levelheaded people—like economists at the Federal Reserve—have been predicting for a long time. So how did a far more bullish view become not just prevalent but more or less mandatory on Wall Street? How, with the business landscape still strewn with rubble from the bubble, did manic optimism so quickly become de rigueur again? It seems that hype springs eternal.

# LIVING WITH BEARS

## July 23, 2002

It looks as if the authors of *Dow 36,000*—remember that?—may have had one digit too many in their title. Let's just hope it was an extra "3," not an extra "0."

The bull market is now well and truly over. In fact, if you adjust for inflation the S&P 500—a much better measure than the overused Dow—is now below its level in late 1996, when Alan Greenspan gave his famous "irrational exuberance" speech.

So what should the responsible officials—Mr. Greenspan, George W. Bush and whatshisname, the Treasury secretary—be doing?

A good first step would be to stop trying to talk up the market by extolling the economy's fundamental strength. For one thing, it reeks of desperation. For another, stocks are still richly valued compared with earnings. Most important, the fundamentals aren't actually all that great. Doubts about corporate governance are growing, not fading away. State and local governments are in a desperate fiscal crisis. And even before the sudden plunge in the markets, the data were pointing not to a boom but to a "jobless recovery," in which the economy grows too slowly to make much if any dent in the unemployment rate.

Indeed, the report prepared in support of Mr. Greenspan's recent testimony projected no significant decline in unemployment this year, and not much decline next year. And in the face of plunging markets we have to worry whether even that forecast is overly optimistic.

Given the definitely iffy economic outlook, shouldn't Mr. Greenspan be thinking seriously about another interest rate cut? True, rates are already very low. But if there's one thing we've learned from Japan's experience, it is that when you face the risk of a deflationary trap—still not the most likely scenario, but not as unlikely as it seemed a few months ago—it makes no sense to "save your ammunition," holding interest rate cuts in reserve. The time to fight deflation is before it has time to get built into the nation's psychology.

True, the Fed has been concerned that another cut would panic the markets. But now that the markets have panicked on their own, there's nothing to lose.

What about the rest of the government? Corporate reform is essential; if investors cannot be reassured that they are being treated fairly, they will take their money and go home. But we can't count on reform to provide an immediate boost to the economy; trust, once lost, cannot be restored in a moment. What else can the government do?

Let's ignore the politics and look at the situation objectively. On one side, thanks in part to the end of the bull market, the long-run federal budget outlook has worsened to an extent that has surpassed the expectations of even the biggest pessimists (like yours truly). Realistically, we are looking at a decade of deficits, which will eventually pose serious problems for Social Security and Medicare.

On the other hand, with the recovery still wobbly, this is no time for fiscal austerity—if anything, right now the federal government ought to be pumping more money into the economy than it is.

The obvious answer to this seeming dilemma is to loosen the reins now, but prepare to tighten them once the economy has fully recovered. For example, the Bush administration could move quickly to aid distressed state governments, avoiding harsh (and contractionary) cuts in essential programs. Meanwhile, to assuage worries about the long-run fiscal position, it could put on hold future tax cuts that were written into law back when visions of surplus sugarplums were still dancing in our heads.

And after the administration takes these responsible steps, thousands of pigs will fill the skies over Washington.

Look at it this way: The Bush administration's economic plans have not changed significantly since the fall of 1999, when they were introduced as a way to ward off a challenge from Steve Forbes. Back when the tax cut that eventually became law was announced, *Dow 36,000* was climbing the best-seller lists. The economic environment has changed completely; the administration's plans haven't changed a bit.

Our economic problems are real, but by no means catastrophic. What scares me is the utter inflexibility of the people who should be solving those problems.

# DUBYA'S DOUBLE DIP?

*August 2, 2002*

If the story of the current U.S. economy were made into a movie, it would look something like *55 Days at Peking*. A ragtag group of ordinary people—America's consumers—is besieged by a rampaging horde, the forces of recession. To everyone's surprise, they have held their ground.

But they can't hold out forever. Will the rescue force—resurgent business investment—get there in time?

The screenplay for that kind of movie always ratchets up the tension. The besieged citadel fends off assault after assault, but again and again rescue is delayed. And so it has played out in practice. Consumers kept spending as the Internet bubble collapsed; they kept spending despite terrorist attacks. Taking advantage of low interest rates, they refinanced their houses and took the proceeds to the shopping malls.

But predictions of an imminent recovery in business investment keep turning out to be premature. Most businesses are in no hurry to go on another spending spree. And those that might have started to invest again have been deterred by sliding stock prices, widening bond spreads and revelations about corporate scandal.

Will the rescuers arrive in the nick of time? Not necessarily. This movie may not be *55 Days at Peking* after all. It may be *A Bridge Too Far*.

A few months ago the vast majority of business economists mocked concerns about a "double dip," a second leg to the downturn. But there were a few dogged iconoclasts out there, most notably Stephen Roach at Morgan Stanley. As I've repeatedly said in this column, the arguments of the double-dippers made a lot of sense. And their story now looks more plausible than ever.

The basic point is that the recession of 2001 wasn't a typical postwar slump, brought on when an inflation-fighting Fed raises interest rates and easily ended by a snapback in housing and consumer spending when the Fed brings rates back down again. This was a prewar-style recession, a morning after brought on by irrational exuberance. To fight this recession the Fed needs more than a snapback; it needs soaring household spending to offset moribund business investment. And to do that, as Paul McCulley of Pimco put it, Alan Greenspan needs to create a housing bubble to replace the Nasdaq bubble.

Judging by Mr. Greenspan's remarkably cheerful recent testimony, he still thinks he can pull that off. But the Fed chairman's crystal ball has been cloudy lately; remember how he urged Congress to cut taxes to head off the risk of excessive budget surpluses? And a sober look at recent data is not encouraging.

On the surface, the sharp drop in the economy's growth, from 5 percent in the first quarter to 1 percent in the second, is disheartening. Under the surface, it's quite a lot worse. Even in the first quarter, investment and consumer spending were sluggish; most of the growth came as businesses stopped running down their inventories. In the second quarter, inventories were the whole story: final demand actually fell. And lately straws in the wind that often give advance warning of changes in official statistics, like mall traffic, have been blowing the wrong way.

Despite the bad news, most commentators, like Mr. Greenspan, remain optimistic. Should you be reassured?

Bear in mind that business forecasters are under enormous pressure to be cheerleaders: "I must confess to being amazed at the venom my double dip call still elicits," Mr. Roach wrote yesterday at cbsmarketwatch.com. We should never forget that Wall Street basically represents the sell side.

Bear in mind also that government officials have a stake in accentuating the positive. The administration needs a recovery because, with deficits exploding, the only way it can justify that tax cut is by pretending that it was just what the economy needed. Mr. Greenspan needs one to avoid awkward questions about his own role in creating the stock market bubble.

But wishful thinking aside, I just don't understand the grounds for optimism. Who, exactly, is about to start spending a lot more? At this point it's a lot easier to tell a story about how the recovery will stall than about how it will speed up. And while I like movies with happy endings as much as the next guy, a movie isn't realistic unless the story line makes sense.

# MIND THE GAP

*August 16, 2002*

How much has Japan's economy shrunk since its bubble burst? It's a trick question; Japan's economy hasn't shrunk. It had only two down years over the past decade, and on average it grew 1 percent per year.

Yet Japan's is a genuinely depressed economy. Because growth has been so slow, an ever-increasing gap has opened up between what the economy could produce and what it actually produces. This "output gap" translates into rising unemployment and accelerating deflation. Slow growth can be almost as big a problem as actual output decline.

Now the non-trick question: What would a similar analysis say about the United States?

The U.S. economy's "potential output"—what it could produce at full employment—has lately been growing at about 3.5 percent per year, thanks to the productivity surge that began in the mid-1990's. But according to the revised figures released a couple of weeks ago, actual growth has fallen short of potential for seven of the last eight quarters.

The conventional view is that we had a brief, shallow recession last year, and that recovery has begun. But the output gap tells a different story: Two years ago we went into an economic funk, and it's not over. In a way the whole double-dip controversy is a red herring; the real question is when GDP will start growing fast enough to narrow the output gap. And so far there's no sign of that happening.

There's no mystery about the causes of our funk: the bubble years left us with too much capacity, too much debt and a backlog of business scandal. We shouldn't have expected a quick and easy recovery, and we're not getting one.

Some readers have already guessed where I'm going with this. The U.S. stock bubble in the second half of the 1990's was just as big as Japan's bubble in the second half of the 1980's. Will our two-year funk turn into a five-year or ten-year funk, the way Japan's did?

A loud chorus is already shouting "We're not Japan!" Half the time, depending on what I had for breakfast (rice and pickles?), I'm part of that chorus. But let me share some disquieting thoughts.

Back when I first got professionally obsessed with Japan's problems, around four years ago, I made myself a mental checklist of reasons that Japan's decade of stagnation could not happen to the United States. It went like this:

1. The Fed has plenty of room to cut interest rates, which should be enough to deal with any eventuality.
2. The U.S. long-term budget position is very strong, so there's plenty of room for fiscal stimulus in the unlikely event interest rate cuts aren't enough.
3. We don't have to worry about an Asian-style loss of confidence in our business sector, because we have excellent corporate governance.
4. We may have a stock bubble, but we don't have a real estate bubble.

I've now had to strike the first three items off my list, and I'm getting worried about the fourth.

More and more people are using the B-word about the housing market. A recent analysis by Dean Baker, of the Center for

Economic Policy Research, makes a particularly compelling case for a housing bubble. House prices have run well ahead of rents, suggesting that people are now buying houses for speculation rather than merely for shelter. And the explanations one hears for those high prices sound more and more like the rationalizations one heard for Nasdaq 5,000.

If we do have a housing bubble, and it bursts, we'll be looking a lot too Japanese for comfort.

A recent Federal Reserve analysis of Japan's experience declares that the key mistake Japan made in the early 1990's was "not that policy makers did not predict the oncoming deflationary slump—after all, neither did most forecasters—but that they did not take out sufficient insurance against downside risks through a precautionary further loosening of monetary policy." That's Fedspeak for "if you think deflation is even a possibility, throw money at the economy now and don't worry about overdoing it."

And yet the Fed chose not to cut rates on Tuesday. Why?

Last year some economists began privately referring to the Fed chairman as "Greenspan-san." The joke faded out as optimism about recovery became conventional wisdom. But maybe it's not a bad nickname after all.

# PASSING THE BUCK

*September 3, 2002*

Somewhere I read about a conference on optimal economic planning, some years before the fall of Communism. The Soviet delegate declared that his planning agency always did the best it could under the circumstances. Hence, Soviet planning was always optimal.

The man from Gosplan would have gotten along fine with Alan Greenspan. Mr. Greenspan disclaims any responsibility for the immense market bubble that inflated on his watch: his policy was right, he says, because he did the best he could.

In his keynote speech at last week's Jackson Hole conference, Mr. Greenspan offered two excuses. First, he claimed that it wasn't absolutely clear, even during the manic market run-up of 1999, that something was amiss: "it was very difficult to definitively identify a bubble until after the fact—that is, when its bursting confirmed its existence." Second, he claimed that the Fed couldn't have done anything anyway. "Is there some policy that can at least limit the size of a bubble and, hence, its destructive fallout? . . . the answer appears to be no."

I wasn't alone in finding this speech disturbingly evasive. As *The Financial Times* noted, policy makers always have to act on limited information: "The burden of proof for a central bank should not be absolute certainty." The editorial also reminded readers that while Mr. Greenspan may now portray himself as skeptical but powerless during the bubble years, at the time many saw him as a cheerleader. "The Fed chairman . . . may well have contributed to the explosion of exuberance in the late 1990's with his increasingly bullish observations."

Moreover, there is evidence that Mr. Greenspan actually knew better. In September 1996, at a meeting of the Federal Open Market Committee, he told his colleagues, "I recognize that there is a stock market bubble problem at this point." And he had a solution: "We do have the possibility of . . . increasing margin requirements. I guarantee that if you want to get rid of the bubble, whatever it is, that will do it."

Yet he never did increase margin requirements, that is, require investors to put up more cash when buying stocks. Indeed, aside from giving one speech about irrational exuberance, followed by a small rise in the Fed funds rate, Mr. Greenspan did nothing at all. He now says he could not have done more, but how does he know when he never even tried? What really happened, one suspects, was that in early 1997 Mr. Greenspan discovered that his tentative efforts to deflate the emerging bubble made investors furious, and lost his nerve.

Worse, he then began giving ever more euphoric speeches about the wonders of the new economy. Surely he must have known that these speeches were interpreted by investors as a retraction of his own previous warning, as a signal that soaring stock prices were justified after all.

Still, what's most important about Mr. Greenspan's defensiveness is not what it says about the past, but what it implies about the future.

You see, Mr. Greenspan is the only economic policy maker we have. Fiscal policy is effectively off the table, partly because of long-run deficits worsened by Mr. Greenspan's own bad advice. Funny how he wasn't sure that Nasdaq 5,000 was a bubble, but believed that 10-year surplus projections were reliable enough to justify a huge tax cut. In any case, serious fiscal action is ruled out by the Bush administration's relentless opportunism; every proposal for short-run economic stimulus turns into an attempt to lock in permanent tax cuts for corporations and the wealthy. So if the recovery continues to lose momentum, it's up to the Fed to take matters in hand.

Yet Mr. Greenspan's remarks reinforce a worry I've had for the past few months: that Fed officials will respond to continuing economic weakness not with action but with excuses.

We've seen the process all too clearly in Japan. First officials at the Bank of Japan denied that they had any responsibility to fight economic stagnation; their mandate, they said, was solely to ensure price stability. Then, as inflation gave way to deflation, even price stability was no longer their business. In other words, rather than risk trying to solve Japan's problems and failing, the bank has repeatedly redefined its mission so that it doesn't even have to try.

I never thought the Fed would go down the same path. But after listening to Mr. Greenspan explain why he couldn'ta and shouldn'ta, I'm starting to wonder.

# STOCKS AND BOMBS

*September 13, 2002*

"This stock-market situation—what are the military options?" That was the caption of a *New Yorker* cartoon last month. But these days reality has a way of outrunning satire; way back in June the CNBC pundit Larry Kudlow published a column in *The Washington Times* with the headline "Taking Back the Market—by Force." In it he argued for an invasion of Iraq to boost the Dow.

Pretty amazing stuff, though not as amazing as a July column in *The New York Post* by John Podhoretz, whose headline read, "October Surprise, Please," followed by the injunction, "Go On, Mr. President: Wag the Dog."

In general it's a bad omen when advocates of a policy claim that it will solve problems unrelated to its original purpose. The shifting rationale for the Bush tax cut—it's about giving back the surplus; no, it's a demand stimulus; no, it's a supply-side policy—should have warned us that this was an obsession in search of a justification.

The shifting rationale for war with Iraq—Saddam was behind Sept. 11 and the anthrax attacks; no, but he's on the verge of developing nuclear weapons; no, but he's a really evil man (which he is)—has a similar feel.

The idea that war would actually be good for the economy seems like just one more step in this progression. But one must admit that there are times when war has had positive economic effects. In particular, there's no question that World War II pulled the United States out of the Great Depression. And today's U.S. economy, while not in a depression, certainly could use some help; the latest evidence suggests a recovery so slow and uneven that it feels like a continuing recession. So is war the answer?

No: World War II is a very poor model for the economic effects of a new war in the Persian Gulf. On balance, such a war is much more likely to depress than to stimulate our struggling economy.

There is nothing magical about military spending—it provides no more economic stimulus than the same amount spent on, say, cleaning up toxic waste sites.

The reason World War II accomplished what the New Deal could not was simply that war removed the usual inhibitions. Until Pearl Harbor, Franklin Roosevelt didn't have the determination or the legislative clout to enact really large programs to stimulate the economy. But war made it not just possible but necessary for the government to spend on a previously inconceivable scale, restoring full employment for the first time since 1929.

By contrast, this time around Congress is eager to spend on domestic projects; if the administration wants to pump money into the economy, all it needs to do is drop its objections to things like drought aid for farmers and new communication gear for firefighters. In other words, if the economy needs a burst of federal spending, neither economics nor politics requires that this burst take the form of a war.

And in any case it's not clear how much stimulus war would provide. One assumes that the necessary munitions are already in stock, so there will be no surge in factory orders. There will be spending on peacekeeping—won't there?—but it will be spread over many years.

Meanwhile there is the potential economic downside, which may be summed up in one word: oil.

Iraq itself currently supplies so little oil to the world market that wartime disruption of its production would pose little problem. But neither the Arab-Israeli war of 1973 nor the Iranian revolution of 1979 directly affected oil production.

Instead, the indirect political repercussions of conflict were what caused oil prices to surge. This time around, Arab leaders have warned that an invasion of Iraq would open the "gates of hell." That doesn't sound good for the oil market.

It's worth remembering that each of the oil crises of the 1970's was followed by a severe recession—and that the milder oil price spike before the gulf war was also followed by a recession. Could rising crude prices undermine our weak economic recovery, creating a double-dip recession? Yes.

None of this should deter us from invading Iraq if the administration makes a convincing case that we should do so for security reasons. But it's foolish and dangerous to minimize the potential economic consequences of war, let alone claim that it will be good for the economy.

# THE VISION THING

*September 20, 2002*

This is the way the recovery ends—not with a bang but with a whimper.

O.K., I could be wrong. Industrial production is falling and layoffs are rising. But it's still not a sure thing that the months ahead will be bad enough for the business-cycle referees to declare a renewed recession. And on the other hand, the administration seems determined to have a bang sometime before Nov. 5.

But right now it looks as if the economy is stalling, and also as if the people in charge have no idea what to do. In short, it's feeling a lot like the early 1990's.

It doesn't really matter whether you call what's going on right now a slow recovery or a recession. Most people don't care whether GDP growth is slightly above or below zero; what matters to them is whether they can find jobs and keep them. And the job situation is increasingly dismal. A 5.7 percent unemployment rate doesn't sound that bad, but an unusually large number of workers have given up searching for jobs. The overall unemployment rate also doesn't reflect the rapidly growing number of people who are truly desperate, because they have been out of work for six months or more. And the employment situation has lately taken a significant turn for the worse: the number of people filing new claims for unemployment insurance, a leading indicator of future unemployment, has increased sharply over the past month.

At best, then, this is a recovery that, as far as workers are concerned, might as well be a continuing recession. The Center on Budget and Policy Priorities points out that in terms of job losses and long-term unemployment, the current slowdown is already a match for the nasty recession of the early 1990's.

So this really is like the early 1990's all over again. The economic similarity between our current difficulties and the slump under the first George Bush is stronger than most people realize. In 1990, as in 2001, the economy went into a recession in part because of past excesses—though those quaint old scandals involving junk bonds and real estate speculation seem very tame in the age of Enron and Tyco. In the early 1990's, as today, recession was followed by a "jobless recovery," in which GDP grew but employment didn't. And then as now there was concern that interest rate cuts by the Fed might not be enough to turn the economy around—though back then we didn't yet have the example of Japan to show that the "liquidity trap," in which even a zero interest rate isn't enough to produce an economic recovery, was a real possibility in the modern world.

But the most striking similarity between now and a decade ago, it seems to me, is political. For all the differences between the moderate father and the deeply conservative son, now as then we have an administration whose key figures are fundamentally uninterested in and uncomfortable with economic policy.

That statement may strike you as strange: wasn't the tax cut George W. Bush's central achievement before Osama bin Laden came along? But the tax cut was never intended as an economic policy; it was a political gesture designed to ward off a challenge from Steve Forbes and satisfy the conservative base. Only later did the administration make the providential discovery that it was also just the thing to fight recession, promote family values and cure the common cold.

And it can't seem to come up with anything else, now that the tax cut that wasn't designed to fight a recession has, sure enough, failed to fight a recession. When Treasury Secretary Paul O'Neill was asked for new ideas that came out of the comical Waco summit, his answer was—are you ready?—making the tax cut permanent.

Should we be worried about the administration's lack of the vision thing when it comes to economics? Yes, we should. The excesses of the 1990's dwarfed those of the 1980's, and the economic risks are correspondingly larger. Suppose that, as seems increasingly plausible, the deteriorating job situation finally undermines the dogged optimism of America's consumers. In that case we'll need some decisive action—action determined by what the economy needs, not by what Karl Rove thinks will play in the polls. How much chance is there that we'll get it?

# DEALING WITH W

*October 1, 2002*

TOKYO—I got obsessed with the Japanese economy after it was fashionable.

Americans paid a lot of attention to Japan in the 1980's, when Japanese manufacturers were conquering the world. Remember when airport bookstores were filled with management tomes bearing samurai warriors on their covers? Then Japan's bubble burst, and most Americans concluded that we had nothing to learn from Japan—except how a country can stumble when it lacks adequate business and political leadership. And we, of course, don't have that problem.

Or do we? Jack Welch's gut is starting to look as overrated as those business samurai. And our political leadership doesn't exactly inspire confidence. In fact, lately I've started to have a truly depressing thought: Bad as Japan's policy has been, it's possible that the United States will do even worse.

It's hard to say anything good about how Japan has handled its post-bubble economy. But I've worried for years about how other countries would deal with similar problems. Sure enough, as America tries to cope with its own burst bubble, it's a lot easier to see how bad economic decisions get made.

It's true that Alan Greenspan and his colleagues made a much better start than their counterparts in Japan. They knew that the Bank of Japan cut interest rates too slowly, and that by the time it realized the seriousness of the country's problems it was too late: even a zero interest rate wasn't enough to spark a

94

recovery. So the Fed cut rates early and often; those 11 interest rate cuts in 2001 fueled a boom both in housing purchases and in mortgage refinancing, both of which helped keep the economy from experiencing a much more severe recession.

But it's starting to look as if the interest rate cuts weren't enough. I don't need to tell you about the stock market. Economic indicators strongly suggest that the economy is either sliding into a double-dip, "W-shaped" recession—bet you thought I was talking about the guy in the White House—or close enough as makes no difference. Bond markets are clearly predicting that the Fed will have to cut interest rates again. What if the Fed, like the Bank of Japan, goes all the way to zero and finds that it still hasn't turned the economy around?

Not many people realize that in some ways Japanese economic policy responded quite effectively to a sustained slump. It's easy to make fun of the country's enormous spending on public works—all those bridges to nowhere in particular, highways with no traffic, and so on. Without question enormous sums have been wasted. But it's also clear that all that spending pumped money into the economy, preventing what might otherwise have been a full-fledged depression.

So what will be the U.S. equivalent? Right now we are in effect following the reverse policy: slashing domestic spending in the face of an economic slump. Some of this is taking place at the federal level; the Bush administration is nickel-and-diming public spending wherever it can, shaving a billion here, a billion there off everything from veterans' benefits and homeland security to Medicare payments. More important, the federal government is doing nothing to help as state and local governments, their revenues savaged by recession, make deep cuts in spending on everything that isn't urgently necessary, and many things that are.

It's true that we haven't yet confronted head on the possibility that Uncle Alan may not be able to save us single-handedly. But last fall's debate over economic stimulus suggested that our political leadership cannot make a rational response to economic problems. Where economists saw danger, the White House and its Congressional allies saw opportunity—an opportunity to ram through more tax cuts for corporations and the affluent, measures that suited their political agenda but had almost no relevance to the economy's problems. Remember the proposal to give retroactive tax breaks to ChevronTexaco and Enron?

In the end, the need for stimulus was less urgent than it seemed at the time, but there is no reason to think that we'll do better if, as now seems all too likely, the recovery stumbles.

Of course, the worst thing of all would be if our leadership decides that economics is not its thing, if it simply tries to distract the public from rising unemployment and plunging stocks by going off and invading someone. But we don't have to worry about that, do we?

# MY ECONOMIC PLAN

*October 4, 2002*

Although other news has been drowned out by the barking of
the dogs of war, something ominous is happening on the economic front. It's not dramatic, but month by month the numbers keep coming in worse than expected. Let's put politics
completely aside for once, and review where we are and what
should be done.

The key point is that this isn't your father's recession—it's
your grandfather's recession. That is, it isn't your standard
postwar recession, engineered by the Federal Reserve to fight
inflation, and easily reversed when the Fed loosens the reins.
It's a classic overinvestment slump, of a kind that was normal
before World War II. And such slumps have always been hard
to fight simply by cutting interest rates.

Now there's no question that the Fed's rapid rate reductions
last year helped avert a much bigger slump. But a hard look at
monetary policy suggests that the Fed hasn't done enough—
and possibly can't do enough. Although the Fed funds rate, the
usual measure of monetary policy, is at its lowest level in generations, the real Fed funds rate—the interest rate minus the
inflation rate, which is what matters for investment decisions—
is actually about the same as it was at the bottom of the last
recession, in the early 1990's, because inflation is considerably
lower.

And the drop in the Fed funds rate engineered by Alan
Greenspan & Company, though faster than that in the last

recession, has so far been considerably smaller; last time it fell by 6.75 points, this time it fell by only 4.75. Even if the Fed funds rate falls all the way to zero, that will be a smaller interest rate reduction than the last time around. If you think the excesses of the 1990's were larger than those of the 1980's, that the economy needs more stimulus to pull itself out, then it seems likely that the Fed hasn't done enough, and quite possible that even going all the way to zero still won't be enough.

And this situation may last for a while. The overhang of excess capacity, especially in telecommunications, will be worked off only slowly. It's all too possible that we may be looking at a sluggish economy into 2004, maybe beyond. The Fed should cut rates further—it may not be enough, but it will help. What else should we do?

The answer is that we should have a sensible plan for fiscal stimulus—one that encourages spending now, to bridge the gap until business investment revives. Some of the elements of such a plan are obvious, and were described by Jeff Madrick in yesterday's *Times* [October 3, 2002]. First, extend unemployment benefits, which are considerably less generous now than in the last recession; this will do double duty, helping some of the neediest while putting money into the hands of people who are likely to spend it. Second, provide aid to the states, which are in increasingly desperate fiscal straits. This will also do double duty, preventing harsh cuts in public services, with medical care for the poor the most likely target, at the same time that it boosts demand.

If these elements don't add up to a large enough sum—I agree with Mr. Madrick that $100 billion over the next year is a good target—why not have another rebate, this time going to everyone who pays payroll taxes?

And how will we pay for all of this? You know the answer to

that: Cancel tax cuts scheduled for the future. The economy needs stimulus now; it doesn't need tax cuts for the very affluent five years from now.

This isn't rocket science. It's straightforward textbook economics, applied to our actual situation.

It's also, I'm well aware, politically out of the question. But I think we're entitled to ask why.

# CHAPTER 4

# Crony Capitalism, U.S.A.

## CRONY CAPITALISM, U.S.A.

*January 15, 2002*

Four years ago, as Asia struggled with an economic crisis, many observers blamed "crony capitalism." Wealthy business-men in Asia didn't bother to tell investors the truth about their assets, their liabilities or their profits; the aura of invincibility that came from their political connections was enough. Only when a financial crisis came along did people take a hard look at their businesses, which promptly collapsed.

Does this sound familiar?

On the face of it, the sudden political storm over Enron is puzzling. After all, the Bush administration didn't save the com-pany from bankruptcy. But then why did the administration dis-semble so long about its contacts with Enron? Why did George W. Bush make the absurd claim that Enron's C.E.O., Kenneth Lay, opposed him in his first run for governor, and that the two men got to know each other only after that race? And why does the press act as if there may be a major scandal brewing?

Because the administration fears, and the press suspects,

that the latest revelations in the Enron affair will raise the lid on crony capitalism, American style.

Cronyism is hardly novel in America; the Clinton administration took us to the edge of a trade war on behalf of Chiquita bananas, a major campaign contributor. But the Bush administration, with its sense of entitlement, seems unconcerned by even the most blatant conflicts of interest—like the plan of Marc Racicot, the new chairman of the Republican National Committee, to continue drawing a seven-figure salary as a lobbyist. (He now says he won't lobby—but he will still receive that salary.)

The real questions about Enron's relationship with the administration involve what happened before the energy trader hit the skids. That's when Mr. Lay allegedly told the head of the Federal Energy Regulatory Commission that he should be more cooperative if he wanted to keep his job. (He wasn't, and he didn't.) And it's when Enron helped Dick Cheney devise an energy plan that certainly looks as if it was written by and for the companies that advised his task force. Mr. Cheney, in clear defiance of the law, has refused to release any information about his task force's deliberations; what is he hiding?

And while Enron has imploded, other energy companies retain the administration's ear. Just days before the latest Enron revelations, the administration signaled its intention to weaken pollution rules on power plants; late last week it announced its decision to proceed with a controversial plan to store radioactive waste in Nevada. Each of these decisions was worth billions to companies with very strong connections to Mr. Bush. CBSMarketWatch.com declared, in its story about the nuclear waste decision, that "one group of major energy-business political donors just hit the jackpot."

Notice the source of that quote. In recent months, while

political reporters have been busy waving the flag, business reporters have taken the lead in telling us what's really going on. And they seem disgusted by what they see. It was CBSMarketWatch's executive editor, not some whining political commentator, who warned that "a small group of business leaders exert enormous clout over Bush and his team in getting the rules changed to their benefit."

And the business magazine *Red Herring* has published the biggest exposé to date of the secretive Carlyle Group, an investment company whose story sounds like the plot of a bad TV series.

Carlyle specializes in buying down-and-out defense contractors, then reselling them when their fortunes miraculously improve after they receive new government business. Among the company's employees is former President George H. W. Bush. Among the group's investors, until late October, was the bin Laden family of Saudi Arabia.

Another administration would have regarded the elder Bush's role at Carlyle as unseemly; this administration apparently does not. And Defense Secretary Donald Rumsfeld recently gave his old college wrestling partner Frank Carlucci, head of Carlyle, a very nice gift: Mr. Rumsfeld decided to proceed with the much-criticized Crusader artillery system, which even the Pentagon wanted to cancel. The result was another turnaround for a Carlyle-owned company.

Sad to say, none of this is clearly illegal—it just stinks to high heaven. That's why the Bush administration will try to keep the Enron story narrowly focused on one company during its death throes. Just remember that the real story is much bigger.

# TWO, THREE, MANY?

*February 1, 2002*

Here's a scary question: How many more Enrons are out there?

Even now the conventional wisdom is that Enron was uniquely crooked. O.K., other companies have engaged in "aggressive accounting," the art form formerly known as fraud. But how likely is it that other major companies will turn out, behind their imposing facades, to be little more than pyramid schemes?

Alas, it's all too likely. I can't tell you which corporate icons will turn out to be made of papier-mâché, but I'd be very surprised if we don't have two, three, even many Enrons in our future.

Why do I say this? Like any crime, a pyramid scheme requires means, motive and opportunity.

Lately all three have been there in abundance.

Means: We now know how easily a company that earns a modest profit, or even loses money, can dress itself up to create the appearance of high profitability. Just the simple trick of paying employees not with straight salary, which counts as an expense, but with stock options, which don't, can have a startling effect on a company's reported profits. According to the British economist Andrew Smithers, in 1998 Cisco reported a profit of $1.35 billion; if it had counted the market value of the stock options it issued as an expense, it would have reported a loss of $4.9 billion. And stock options are only one of a panoply of techniques available to make the bottom line look artificially good.

Motive: The purpose of inflating earnings is, of course, to drive up the price of the stock. But why do companies want to do that?

One answer is that a high stock price helps a company grow; it makes it easier to raise money, to acquire other companies, to attract employees and so on. And no doubt most managers have puffed up their stock out of a genuine desire to make their companies grow. But as we watch top executives walk away rich while the companies they ran collapse (there are cases worse than Enron; the founder of Global Crossing has apparently walked away from bankruptcy with $750 million), it's clear that we should also think about the incentives of the managers themselves. Ask not what a high stock price can do for your company; ask what it can do for your personal bottom line.

Not incidentally, a high stock price facilitates the very accounting tricks that companies use to create phantom profits, further driving up the stock price. It's Ponzi time!

But what about opportunity? A confluence of three factors in the late 1990's opened the door for financial scams on a scale unseen for generations.

First was the rise of the "new economy." New technologies have, without question, created new opportunities and shaken up the industrial order. But that creates the kind of confusion in which scams flourish. How do you know whether a company has really found a highly profitable new-economy niche or is just faking it?

Second was the stock market bubble. As Robert Shiller pointed out in his book *Irrational Exuberance*, a rising market is like a natural Ponzi scheme, in which each successive wave of investors generates gains for the last wave, making everything look great until you run out of suckers. What he didn't point out, but now seems obvious, is that in such an environment it's also easy to run deliberate pyramid schemes. When the public believes in magic, it's springtime for charlatans.

And finally, there was (and is) a permissive legal environment. Once upon a time, the threat of lawsuits hung over companies and auditors that engaged in sharp accounting practices. But in 1995 Congress, overriding a veto by Bill Clinton, passed the Private Securities Litigation Reform Act, which made such suits far more difficult. Soon accounting firms, the companies they audited and the investment banks that sold their stock got very cozy indeed.

And here too one must look not only at the motives of corporations, but at the personal motives of executives. We now know that Enron managers gave their investment bankers— not their investment banks but the individual bankers—an opportunity to invest in the shell companies they used to hide debt and siphon off money. Wanna bet that similar deals didn't take place at many other firms?

I hope that Enron turns out to be unique. But I'll be very surprised.

# ENEMIES OF REFORM

*May 21, 2002*

"I would suggest to you that the single most important innova-
tion shaping [America's] capital market was the idea of generally accepted accounting principles." So declared Lawrence
Summers, then deputy secretary of the Treasury, in a 1998
speech. Mr. Summers urged troubled Asian economies, then
in the middle of a disastrous financial crisis, to emulate
American-style "transparency and disclosure."

Now America has its own problems with corporate accounting, exemplified by Enron. So will we follow our own advice?
Will we provide investors with the facts they need to make
informed decisions? Probably not. And that's bad news, because
Enron's case, though extreme, was by no means unique.

For corporate America as a whole, 1997 was a watershed
year. According to government statistics, overall corporate
profits grew rapidly between 1992 and 1997, but then stalled;
after-tax profits in the third quarter of 2000 were barely higher
than they were three years earlier. But the operating earnings
of the S&P 500—that is, the profits companies reported to
investors—grew 46 percent over those three years.

There are technical reasons that these measures of profits
need not grow at exactly the same rate, but they have historically tracked each other fairly well. So why did they suddenly
diverge? Surely the main reason was that after 1997 companies
made increasingly aggressive use of accounting gimmicks to
create the illusion of profit growth.

You see, corporate leaders were desperate to keep their stock prices rising, in an environment where anything short of 20 percent profit growth was considered failure. And why were they desperate? In a word: options. The bull market, combined with ever-more-generous options packages, led to an explosion of executive compensation. In 1980 chief executives at large companies, according to *BusinessWeek*'s estimates, earned 45 times as much as non-supervisory workers. By 1995, however, the ratio had risen to 160; by 1997, it had reached 305. C.E.O.'s wanted to keep the good times rolling, and they did: by 2000, though profits hadn't really increased, they were paid 458 times as much as ordinary workers.

The point here isn't that top executives are overpaid, though they surely are; it's that the way they are paid rewards them for creating the illusion of success, never mind the reality.

Still, that's exactly the kind of thing that accounting standards are supposed to prevent. What allowed our corporate emperors to hide their nakedness was a combination of poorly crafted standards, which I wrote about last week, and compliant auditors. Major accounting firms were all too happy to be deceived by corporate smoke and mirrors, as long as they got lucrative consulting contracts.

Time for reform? Not according to some people. Today the Senate Banking Committee is scheduled to take up a bill drafted by Paul Sarbanes, the committee's chairman, that would take some modest steps toward accounting and auditing reform. The bill has been endorsed by some of the most respected names in finance—people like Paul Volcker, the great former Fed chairman, and John Bogle, the famed investor. But Senator Phil Gramm, throwing his weight behind an all-out lobbying effort by the accounting industry, has made it clear that he will try to kill the bill.

I'd like to be nonpartisan here—really I would. And there are indeed Democrats who have gotten large contributions from accounting firms. But the current effort to prevent any meaningful accounting reform is explicitly a Republican initiative, one directed from the very top: *The New York Times* reports that Mr. Gramm is "working closely with the Bush administration" in his efforts to block the Sarbanes bill.

Let me repeat what I said last time: Honesty in corporate accounting isn't a left-right issue; it's about protecting all investors from exploitation by insiders. By blocking reform of a broken system, the Bush administration is favoring the interests of a tiny corporate oligarchy over those of everyone else.

One final thought: This isn't just a question of treating American investors fairly. Like the Asian nations before their crisis, the United States relies heavily on inflows of foreign capital, inflows that depend on international faith in the integrity of U.S. markets. The Bush administration may believe that investors have nowhere else to go, that the money will keep coming even if we don't reform. That's what Suharto thought, too.

# GREED IS BAD

*June 4, 2002*

"The point is, ladies and gentlemen, greed is good. Greed works, greed is right . . . and greed, mark my words, will save not only Teldar Paper but the other malfunctioning corporation called the U.S.A."

Gordon Gekko, the corporate raider who gave that speech in the 1987 movie *Wall Street*, got his comeuppance; but in real life his philosophy came to dominate corporate practice. And that is the backstory of the wave of scandal now engulfing American business.

Let me be clear: I'm not talking about morality, I'm talking about management theory. As people, corporate leaders are no worse (and no better) than they've always been. What changed were the incentives.

Twenty-five years ago, American corporations bore little resemblance to today's hard-nosed institutions. Indeed, by modern standards they were Socialist republics. C.E.O. salaries were tiny compared with today's lavish packages. Executives didn't focus single-mindedly on maximizing stock prices; they thought of themselves as serving multiple constituencies, including their employees. The quintessential pre-Gekko corporation was known internally as Generous Motors.

These days we are so steeped in greed-is-good ideology that it's hard to imagine that such a system ever worked. In fact, during the generation that followed World War II the nation's standard of living doubled. But then, growth faltered—and the corporate raiders arrived.

The raiders claimed—usually correctly—that they could increase profits, and hence stock prices, by inducing companies to get leaner and meaner. By replacing much of a company's stock with debt, they forced management to shape up or go bankrupt. At the same time, by giving executives a large personal stake in the company's stock price, they induced them to do whatever it took to drive that price higher.

All of this made sense to professors of corporate finance. Gekko's speech was practically a textbook exposition of "principal-agent" theory, which says that managers' pay should depend strongly on stock prices: "Today management has no stake in the company. Together the men sitting here [the top executives] own less than 3 percent of the company."

And in the 1990's corporations put that theory into practice. The predators faded from the scene, because they were no longer needed; corporate America embraced its inner Gekko. Or as Steven Kaplan of the University of Chicago's business school put it—approvingly—in 1998: "We are all Henry Kravis now." The new tough-mindedness was enforced, above all, with executive pay packages that offered princely rewards if stock prices rose.

And until just a few months ago we thought it was working.

Now, as each day seems to bring a new business scandal, we can see the theory's fatal flaw: a system that lavishly rewards executives for success tempts those executives, who control much of the information available to outsiders, to fabricate the appearance of success. Aggressive accounting, fictitious transactions that inflate sales, whatever it takes.

It's true that in the long run reality catches up with you. But a few years of illusory achievement can leave an executive immensely wealthy. Ken Lay, Gary Winnick, Chuck Watson, Dennis Kozlowski—all will be consoled in their early retirement by nine-figure nest eggs. Unless you go to jail—and does anyone think any of our modern malefactors of great wealth will actually do time?—dishonesty is, hands down, the best policy.

And no, we're not talking about a few bad apples. Statistics for the last five years show a dramatic divergence between the profits companies reported to investors and other measures of profit growth; this is clear evidence that many, perhaps most, large companies were fudging their numbers.

Now, distrust of corporations threatens our still-tentative economic recovery; it turns out greed is bad, after all. But what will reform our system? Washington seems determined to validate the judgment of the quite apolitical Web site of Corporate Governance (corpgov.net), which matter-of-factly remarks, "Given the power of corporate lobbyists, government control often equates to de facto corporate control anyway."

Perhaps corporations will reform themselves, but so far they show no signs of changing their ways. And you have to wonder: Who will save that malfunctioning corporation called the U.S.A.?

# FLAVORS OF FRAUD

*June 28, 2002*

So you're the manager of an ice cream parlor. It's not very profitable, so how can you get rich? Each of the big business scandals uncovered so far suggests a different strategy for executive self-dealing.

First there's the Enron strategy. You sign contracts to provide customers with an ice cream cone a day for the next 30 years. You deliberately underestimate the cost of providing each cone; then you book all the projected profits on those future ice cream sales as part of this year's bottom line. Suddenly you appear to have a highly profitable business, and you can sell shares in your store at inflated prices.

Then there's the Dynegy strategy. Ice cream sales aren't profitable, but you convince investors that they will be profitable in the future. Then you enter into a quiet agreement with another ice cream parlor down the street: each of you will buy hundreds of cones from the other every day. Or rather, pretend to buy—no need to go to the trouble of actually moving all those cones back and forth. The result is that you appear to be a big player in a coming business, and can sell shares at inflated prices.

Or there's the Adelphia strategy. You sign contracts with customers, and get investors to focus on the volume of contracts rather than their profitability. This time you don't engage in imaginary trades, you simply invent lots of imaginary customers. With your subscriber base growing so rapidly, analysts give you high marks, and you can sell shares at inflated prices.

Finally, there's the WorldCom strategy. Here you don't create imaginary sales; you make real costs disappear, by pretending that operating expenses—cream, sugar, chocolate syrup—are part of the purchase price of a new refrigerator. So your unprofitable business seems, on paper, to be a highly profitable business that borrows money only to finance its purchases of new equipment. And you can sell shares at inflated prices.

Oh, I almost forgot: How do you enrich yourself personally? The easiest way is to give yourself lots of stock options, so that you benefit from those inflated prices. But you can also use Enron-style special-purpose entities, Adelphia-style personal loans and so on to add to the windfall. It's good to be C.E.O.

There are a couple of ominous things about this menu of mischief. First is that each of the major business scandals to emerge so far involved a different scam. So there's no comfort in saying that few other companies could have employed the same tricks used by Enron or WorldCom—surely other companies found other tricks. Second, the scams shouldn't have been all that hard to spot. For example, WorldCom now says that 40 percent of its investment last year was bogus, that it was really operating expenses. How could the people who should have been alert to the possibility of corporate fraud—auditors, banks and government regulators—miss something that big? The answer, of course, is that they either didn't want to see it or were prevented from doing something about it.

I'm not saying that all U.S. corporations are corrupt. But it's clear that executives who want to be corrupt have faced few obstacles. Auditors weren't interested in giving a hard time to companies that gave them lots of consulting income; bank executives weren't interested in giving a hard time to companies that, as we've learned in the Enron case, let them in on some of those lucrative side deals. And elected officials, kept compliant by campaign contributions and other inducements, kept the regulators from doing their job—starving their agencies for funds, creating regulatory "black holes" in which shady practices could flourish.

(Even while loudly denouncing WorldCom, George W. Bush is trying to appoint the man who drafted the infamous "Enron exemption"—a law custom-designed to protect the company from scrutiny—to a top position with a key regulatory agency. And some congressmen seem more interested in clamping down on New York's attorney general, Eliot Spitzer, than in doing something about the corruption he has been investigating.)

Meanwhile the revelations keep coming. Six months ago, in a widely denounced column, I suggested that in the end the Enron scandal would mark a bigger turning point for America's perception of itself than Sept. 11 did. Does that sound so implausible today?

## EVERYONE IS OUTRAGED

*July 2, 2002*

Arthur Levitt, Bill Clinton's choice to head the Securities and Exchange Commission, crusaded for better policing of corporate accounting—though he was often stymied by the power of lobbyists. George W. Bush replaced him with Harvey Pitt, who promised a "kinder and gentler" S.E.C. Even after Enron, the Bush administration steadfastly opposed any significant accounting reforms. For example, it rejected calls from the likes of Warren Buffett to require deduction of the cost of executive stock options from reported profits.

But Mr. Bush and Mr. Pitt say they are outraged about World-Com.

Representative Michael Oxley, the Republican chairman of the House Financial Services Committee, played a key role in passing a 1995 law (over Mr. Clinton's veto) that, by blocking investor lawsuits, may have opened the door for a wave of corporate crime. More recently, when Merrill Lynch admitted having pushed stocks that its analysts privately considered worthless, Mr. Oxley was furious—not because the company had misled investors, but because it had agreed to pay a fine, possibly setting a precedent. But he also says he is outraged about World-Com.

Might this sudden outbreak of moral clarity have something to do with polls showing mounting public dismay over crooked corporations?

Still, even a poll-induced epiphany is welcome. But it probably isn't genuine. As the Web site dailyenron.com put it, last week "the foxes assured Americans that they are hot on the trail of those missing chickens."

The president's supposed anger was particularly hard to take seriously. As Chuck Lewis of the nonpartisan Center for Public Integrity delicately put it, Mr. Bush "has more familiarity with troubled energy companies and accounting irregularities than probably any previous chief executive." Mr. Lewis was referring to the saga of Harken Energy, which now truly deserves a public airing.

My last column, describing techniques of corporate fraud, omitted one method also favored by Enron: the fictitious asset sale. Returning to the ice cream store, what you do is sell your old delivery van to XYZ Corporation for an outlandish price, and claim the capital gain as a profit. But the transaction is a sham: XYZ Corporation is actually you under another name. Before investors figure this out, however, you can sell a lot of stock at artificially high prices.

Now to the story of Harken Energy, as reported in *The Wall Street Journal* on March 4. In 1989 Mr. Bush was on the board of directors and audit committee of Harken. He acquired that position, along with a lot of company stock, when Harken paid $2 million for Spectrum 7, a tiny, money-losing energy company with large debts of which Mr. Bush was C.E.O. Explaining what it was buying, Harken's founder said, "His name was George Bush."

Unfortunately, Harken was also losing money hand over fist. But in 1989 the company managed to hide most of those losses with the profits it reported from selling a subsidiary, Aloha Petroleum, at a high price. Who bought Aloha? A group of Harken insiders, who got most of the money for the purchase by borrowing from Harken itself. Eventually the Securities and

Exchange Commission ruled that this was a phony transaction, and forced the company to restate its 1989 earnings.

But long before that ruling—though only a few weeks before bad news that could not be concealed caused Harken's shares to tumble—Mr. Bush sold off two-thirds of his stake, for $848,000. Just for the record, that's about four times bigger than the sale that has Martha Stewart in hot water. Oddly, though the law requires prompt disclosure of insider sales, he neglected to inform the S.E.C. about this transaction until 34 weeks had passed. An internal S.E.C. memorandum concluded that he had broken the law, but no charges were filed. This, everyone insists, had nothing to do with the fact that his father was president.

Given this history—and an equally interesting history involving Dick Cheney's tenure as C.E.O. of Halliburton—you could say that this administration is uniquely well qualified to chase after corporate evildoers. After all, Mr. Bush and Mr. Cheney have firsthand experience of the subject.

And if some cynic should suggest that Mr. Bush's new anger over corporate fraud is less than sincere, I know how his spokesmen will react. They'll be outraged.

# SUCCEEDING IN BUSINESS

*July 7, 2002*

On Tuesday, George W. Bush is scheduled to give a speech intended to put him in front of the growing national outrage over corporate malfeasance. He will sternly lecture Wall Street executives about ethics and will doubtless portray himself as a believer in old-fashioned business probity.

Yet this pose is surreal, given the way top officials like Secretary of the Army Thomas White, Dick Cheney and Mr. Bush himself acquired their wealth. As Joshua Green says in *The Washington Monthly*, in a must-read article written just before the administration suddenly became such an exponent of corporate ethics: "The 'new tone' that George W. Bush brought to Washington isn't one of integrity, but of permissiveness. . . . In this administration, enriching oneself while one's business goes bust isn't necessarily frowned upon."

Unfortunately, the administration has so far gotten the press to focus on the least important question about Mr. Bush's business dealings: his failure to obey the law by promptly reporting his insider stock sales. It's true that Mr. Bush's story about that failure has suddenly changed, from "the dog ate my homework" to "my lawyer ate my homework—four times." But the administration hopes that a narrow focus on the reporting lapses will divert attention from the larger point: Mr. Bush profited personally from aggressive accounting identical to the recent scams that have shocked the nation.

In 1986, one would have had to consider Mr. Bush a failed

businessman. He had run through millions of dollars of other people's money, with nothing to show for it but a company losing money and heavily burdened with debt. But he was rescued from failure when Harken Energy bought his company at an astonishingly high price. There is no question that Harken was basically paying for Mr. Bush's connections.

Despite these connections, Harken did badly. But for a time it concealed its failure—sustaining its stock price, as it turned out, just long enough for Mr. Bush to sell most of his stake at a large profit—with an accounting trick identical to one of the main ploys used by Enron a decade later. (Yes, Arthur Andersen was the accountant.) As I explained in my previous column, the ploy works as follows: corporate insiders create a front organization that seems independent but is really under their control. This front buys some of the firm's assets at unrealistically high prices, creating a phantom profit that inflates the stock price, allowing the executives to cash in their stock.

That's exactly what happened at Harken. A group of insiders, using money borrowed from Harken itself, paid an exorbitant price for a Harken subsidiary, Aloha Petroleum. That created a $10 million phantom profit, which hid three-quarters of the company's losses in 1989. White House aides have played down the significance of this maneuver, saying $10 million isn't much, compared with recent scandals. Indeed, it's a small fraction of the apparent profits Halliburton created through a sudden change in accounting procedures during Dick Cheney's tenure as chief executive. But for Harken's stock price—and hence for Mr. Bush's personal wealth—this accounting trickery made all the difference.

Oh, and Harken's fake profits were several dozen times as large as the Whitewater land deal—though only about one-seventh the cost of the Whitewater investigation.

Mr. Bush was on the company's audit committee, as well as on a special restructuring committee; back in 1994, another member of both committees, E. Stuart Watson, assured reporters that he and Mr. Bush were constantly made aware of the company's finances. If Mr. Bush didn't know about the Aloha maneuver, he was a very negligent director.

In any case, Mr. Bush certainly found out what his company had been up to when the Securities and Exchange Commission ordered it to restate its earnings. So he can't really be shocked over recent corporate scams. His own company pulled exactly the same tricks, to his considerable benefit. Of course, what really made Mr. Bush a rich man was the investment of his proceeds from Harken in the Texas Rangers—a step that is another, equally strange story.

The point is the contrast between image and reality. Mr. Bush portrays himself as a regular guy, someone ordinary Americans can identify with. But his personal fortune was built on privilege and insider dealings—and after his Harken sale, on large-scale corporate welfare. Some people have it easy.

# THE INSIDER GAME

*July 12, 2002*

The current crisis in American capitalism isn't just about the specific details—about tricky accounting, stock options, loans to executives, and so on. It's about the way the game has been rigged on behalf of insiders.

And the Bush administration is full of such insiders. That's why President Bush cannot get away with merely rhetorical opposition to executive wrongdoers. To give the most extreme example (so far), how can we take his moralizing seriously when Thomas White—whose division of Enron generated $500 million in phony profits, and who sold $12 million in stock just before the company collapsed—is still secretary of the Army?

Yet everything Mr. Bush has said and done lately shows that he doesn't get it. Asked about the Aloha Petroleum deal at his former company Harken Energy—in which big profits were recorded on a sale that was paid for by the company itself, a transaction that obviously had no meaning except as a way to inflate reported earnings—he responded, "There was an honest difference of opinion . . . sometimes things aren't exactly black-and-white when it comes to accounting procedures."

And he still opposes both reforms that would reduce the incentives for corporate scams, such as requiring companies to count executive stock options against profits, and reforms that would make it harder to carry out such scams, such as not allowing accountants to take consulting fees from the same firms they audit.

The closest thing to a substantive proposal in Mr. Bush's tough-talking, nearly content-free speech on Tuesday was his call for extra punishment for executives convicted of fraud. But that's an empty threat. In reality, top executives rarely get charged with crimes; not a single indictment has yet been brought in the Enron affair, and even "Chainsaw Al" Dunlap, a serial book-cooker, faces only a civil suit. And they almost never get convicted. Accounting issues are technical enough to confuse many juries; expensive lawyers make the most of that confusion; and if all else fails, big-name executives have friends in high places who protect them.

In this as in so much of the corporate governance issue, the current wave of scandal is prefigured by President Bush's own history.

An aside: Some pundits have tried to dismiss questions about Mr. Bush's business career as unfair—it was long ago, and hence irrelevant. Yet many of these same pundits thought it was perfectly appropriate to spend seven years and $70 million investigating a failed land deal that was even further in Bill Clinton's past. And if they want something more recent, how about reporting on the story of Mr. Bush's extraordinarily lucrative investment in the Texas Rangers, which became so profitable because of a highly incestuous web of public policy and private deals? As in the case of Harken, no hard work is necessary; Joe Conason laid it all out in Harper's almost two years ago.

But the Harken story still has more to teach us, because the S.E.C. investigation into Mr. Bush's stock sale is a perfect illustration of why his tough talk won't scare well-connected malefactors.

Mr. Bush claims that he was "vetted" by the S.E.C. In fact, the agency's investigation was peculiarly perfunctory. It somehow decided that Mr. Bush's perfectly timed stock sale did not reflect inside information without interviewing him, or any other members of Harken's board. Maybe top officials at the S.E.C. felt they already knew enough about Mr. Bush: his father, the president, had appointed a good friend as S.E.C. chairman. And the general counsel, who would normally make decisions about legal action, had previously been George W. Bush's personal lawyer—he negotiated the purchase of the Texas Rangers. I am not making this up.

Most corporate wrongdoers won't be quite as well connected as the young Mr. Bush; but like him, they will expect, and probably receive, kid-glove treatment. In an interesting parallel, today's S.E.C., which claims to be investigating the highly questionable accounting at Halliburton that turned a loss into a reported profit, has yet to interview the C.E.O. at the time—Dick Cheney.

The bottom line is that in the last week any hopes you might have had that Mr. Bush would make a break from his past and champion desperately needed corporate reform have been dashed. Mr. Bush is not a real reformer; he just plays one on TV.

# THE OUTRAGE CONSTRAINT

*August 23, 2002*

The high pay of America's C.E.O.'s reflects intense competition among companies for the best managerial talent. Stock options and other typical forms of executive compensation are designed to provide incentives for performance. These incentives align the personal interests of managers with those of shareholders.

Nothing in the preceding paragraph is true. That's the message of an extraordinary research paper circulated by the National Bureau of Economic Research, an economics think tank. The paper is must reading for anyone trying to understand what's really going on in our economy.

I first read this paper, "Executive compensation in America: Optimal contracting or extraction of rents?" by Lucian Bebchuk, Jesse Fried and David Walker (of Harvard, Berkeley and Boston University respectively), last December. It was largely due to their analysis that I concluded, early in the game, that Enron would be only the first of many scandals.

What they show is that the official theory of the corporation, in which the C.E.O. serves at the pleasure of a board that represents shareholder interests, is thoroughly misleading. In practice, modern C.E.O.'s set their own compensation, limited only by the "outrage constraint"—outrage not on the part of the board, whose members depend on the C.E.O.'s good will for many of their perks, but on the part of outside groups that can make trouble. And the true purpose of many features of executive pay packages is not to provide incentives but to provide "camouflage"—to let C.E.O.'s reward themselves lavishly while minimizing the associated outrage.

The most obvious case in point is stock options. There is a good argument for linking an executive's pay to his company's stock price, but a true incentive scheme would have features that one almost never sees in practice. For example, an executive's pay should depend on his company's stock price compared with a benchmark index composed of other, similar companies, so that what he gets reflects the job he is doing, not general market conditions.

In fact, however, a C.E.O. almost always receives stock options at the current market price—end of story. If the stock price goes up, he cashes in. If it goes down, he receives new options at the lower price. There are, to be fair, quirks in the tax law that encourage this practice. But the main reason executives are paid this way is that it gives them an almost sure thing—unless the stock falls steadily, sooner or later an executive who keeps getting options at the current price makes a lot of money—yet does so in a way that camouflages the sweetness of the deal. The options grant often isn't even counted as a corporate expense, and the payoff, when it comes, can always be represented as a reward for achievement.

Thanks to the growing skill of companies at camouflage, and also to a steady erosion of old inhibitions against apparent excess, the average pay of C.E.O.'s at major companies has skyrocketed. It was "only" 40 times that of an average worker a generation ago; it's 500 times as much today. That's a lot of money, but the direct expense is not the main problem. Instead, it's the fact that the tricks used to camouflage exorbitant pay give executives an enormous incentive to get the stock price up in time to cash in their options.

We're only beginning to see the extent to which that incentive distorts corporate behavior. We now know that some companies engaged in grandiose programs of acquisition and expansion that ended in grief—but only after top executives had profited immensely. We also know that companies eager to meet or surpass analysts' expectations engaged in creative accounting on a grand scale: in each of the last few years of the bubble most big companies reported double-digit profit growth, yet national statistics show that true corporate profits were hardly growing at all.

I'm not claiming that C.E.O.'s are conscious villains, twirling their mustaches and chortling over their evil doings. People are very good at rationalizing their actions—even Jeff Skilling reportedly regards himself as a victim—and the great majority of C.E.O.'s surely stayed within the letter of the law.

But the fact is that we have a corporate system that gives huge incentives for bad behavior. And I would be very surprised if Wednesday's plea by Enron's Michael Kopper is the beginning of the end; at best, it's the end of the beginning.

# BUSINESS AS USUAL

*October 22, 2002*

The mood among business lobbyists, according to a jubilant official at the Heritage Foundation, is one of "optimism, bordering on giddiness." They expect the elections on Nov. 5 to put Republicans in control of all three branches of government, and have their wish lists ready. "It's the domestic equivalent of planning for postwar Iraq," says the official.

The White House also apparently expects Christmas in November. In fact, it is so confident that it has already given business lobbyists the gift they want most: an end to all this nonsense about corporate reform. Back in July George W. Bush declared, "Corporate misdeeds will be found and will be punished," touting a new law that "authorizes new funding for investigators and technology at the Securities and Exchange Commission to uncover wrongdoing." But that was then; don't you know there's a war on?

The first big step in undermining reform came when Harvey Pitt, chairman of the S.E.C., backtracked on plans to appoint a strong and independent figure to head a new accounting oversight board.

But that was only a prelude. The S.E.C. has been underfunded for years, and most observers—including Richard Breeden, who headed the agency when Mr. Bush's father was president—thought that even the budget Mr. Bush signed back in July was seriously inadequate. But now the administration wants to cancel most of the "new funding" Mr. Bush boasted about.

Administration officials claim that the S.E.C. can still do its job with a much smaller budget. But the S.E.C. is ludicrously underfinanced: staff lawyers and accountants are paid half what they could get in the private sector, usually find themselves heavily outnumbered by the legal departments of the companies they investigate, and often must do their own typing and copying. Officials say there are investigations that they should pursue but can't for lack of resources. And the new law expands the S.E.C.'s responsibilities.

So what's going on? Here's a parallel. Since 1995 Congress has systematically forced the Internal Revenue Service to shrink its operations; the number of auditors has fallen by 28 percent. Yet it's clear that giving the I.R.S. more money would actually reduce the federal budget deficit; the agency estimates that it loses at least $30 billion a year in uncollected taxes, mainly because high-income taxpayers believe they can get away with tax evasion. So starving the I.R.S. isn't about saving money, it's about protecting affluent tax cheats.

Similarly, top officials don't really believe that the S.E.C. can do its job with less money; the whole point is to prevent the agency from doing its job.

In retrospect, it's hard to see why anyone believed that our current leadership was serious about corporate reform. To an extent unprecedented in recent history, this is a government of, by and for corporate insiders. I'm not just talking about influence, I'm talking about personal career experience. The Bush administration contains more former C.E.O.'s than any previous administration, but as James Surowiecki put it in *The New Yorker*, "Almost none of the C.E.O.'s on the Bush team headed competitive, entrepreneurial businesses." Instead they come out of a world of "crony capitalism, in which whom you know is more important than what you do and how you do it." Why would they turn their backs on that world?

And don't forget the personal incentives. Almost all of those ex-C.E.O.'s in the administration became wealthy thanks to the connections they had acquired in Washington; the exception is Mr. Bush himself, who became wealthy thanks to the connections his father had acquired in Washington. This process continues. Senator Phil Gramm, who pushed through legislation that exempted Enron's trading practices from regulation while his wife sat on the company's board, is retiring and taking a new job: he's going to UBS Warburg, the company that bought Enron's trading operation. Somehow, crusaders against business abuse don't get similar offers.

The bottom line is that you shouldn't worry about those TV images of men in suits doing the perp walk. That was for public consumption; now that the public is focused on other things, it's back to business—insider business—as usual.

*Part Two*

# FUZZY
# MATH

I ONCE read a story about a Latin American country whose politicians were in the habit of promising something for nothing. One party even promised to improve gas mileage by designing all roads to run downhill.

Now the joke's on us.

There's an obvious similarity between the Bush tax cut of 2001 and the Reagan tax cut 20 years earlier. But the politics were quite different this time around, and much scarier. I'm not an admirer of Reagan, but at least he presented his plan honestly: he didn't deny that he was proposing big tax cuts for the rich, and didn't hide the fact that his tax cuts looked afford-able only if you accepted his supply-side economic theories. When Bush proposed a similar plan, however, he misrepre-sented everything about it: He pretended that it was a tax cut mainly for the middle class, and he claimed that it would fit easily within a responsible budget. It took only a bit of home-work to show that both claims were just plain untrue—but for some reason almost nobody in the media was willing to do that homework.

In the early months of the 2000 campaign I had trouble

believing what was happening. Was the presidential candidate of a major political party really lying, blatantly, about the content of his own program? Were the media really letting him get away with it? He was, and they were.

The result? Bush has pulled the largest bait-and-switch operation in history. First he described a budget-busting tax cut, which delivered the bulk of its benefits to the very affluent, as a modest plan to return unneeded revenue to ordinary families. Then, when the red ink began flowing in torrents, he wrapped himself and his policies in the flag, blaming deficits on evil terrorists and forces beyond his control. As an economist I understood what was going on, and tried to explain it in my column. Critics called me a Cassandra, and they were right—for though nobody believed Cassandra's prophecies, they did come true.

Chapter 5 describes the selling of the Bush tax cut—the tricks, evasions, and outright lies that he used first to sell his campaign on the election trail, then to pass it through Congress. A subtext of that story is the failure of the institutions and individuals who should have protected the public interest. The press failed, disastrously, to explain the issues; Bush was allowed to get away with incredibly blatant lies about the budget. And men who had cast themselves as guardians of fiscal probity threw away their supposed principles; most notably, Alan Greenspan, high priest of fiscal discipline during the Clinton years, tied himself into intellectual knots to lend support to the thoroughly irresponsible Bush tax cut.

It was clear to me that the Bush plan would squander the hard-won budget surplus. What I didn't foresee was just how quickly things would fall apart, with record surpluses transformed in the blink of an eye into record deficits. And of course I didn't know that September 11 would offer the administration an opportunity to cover its tracks, to blame the torrent of red ink on foreign evildoers. Chapter 6 chronicles the post–September 11 budget debate, as the scale of the budget disaster became apparent—and nobody seemed to care.

Well, why should we care? Apologists for the Bush administration tell us that by historical standards the federal government's debt isn't that big relative to the economy, and the current budget deficit, while unprecedented in dollar terms, also isn't that exceptional compared with the size of the economy. But such historical comparisons are deeply misleading: the administration's policies arc ruinously irresponsible, setting us up for a huge crisis in the not too distant future. Why? Because we are only a few years from B-Day: the day on which the baby boomers start retiring.

The U.S. government is best viewed as a big insurance company that also happens to have an army. The giant retirement programs—Social Security and Medicare—already dominate the federal budget; they'll become much more expensive a decade from now. If we have to pay those bills, and also pay interest on a big national debt, something will have to give. So now would be a good time to run surpluses and pay off the federal debt. It's hard to imagine a worse time to be running huge deficits.

But why not reform Social Security and Medicare instead? Sounds good—and Bush's plan for Social Security "reform" played well during the campaign. As chapter 7 explains, however, that plan was a fraud from the start. When you came down to it, Bush was insisting that $2 - 1 = 4$—that diverting part of the Social Security system's revenue into private accounts would strengthen the system's finances, when simple arithmetic showed that it would do exactly the reverse. The mendacity in the administration's Medicare plans was subtler, but equally stark. In both cases, the supposed cures for the programs' woes would actually make things much, much worse—and compound the problems created by irresponsible fiscal policy.

Where will it all lead? While putting this part of the book together, I took a good hard look at the nation's fiscal future—and switched to a fixed-rate home mortgage. One of these years, and probably sooner than you think, the financial markets will look at the situation, and realize that the U.S. government has made inconsistent promises—promises of benefits to future retirees, repayment to those who buy its debt, and tax rates far below what is necessary to pay for all of it. Something will have to give, and it won't be pretty. In fact, I think the United States is setting itself up for a Latin American–style financial crisis, in which fears that the government will try to resolve its dilemma by inflating away its debt cause interest rates to soar.

You read it here first.

# CHAPTER 5

# The Bait . . .

## OOPS! HE DID IT AGAIN

*October 1, 2000*

It's confession season on the financial news. With many companies admitting that profits won't measure up to market expectations, programs like CNN's *Moneyline* have become painful to watch: night after night executives squirm as interviewers grill them about why earnings fell short of estimates. Needless to say, honest accounting is a given. After all, the interviewers do their homework—they would pounce on any obviously wrong numbers.

But I guess some people get special treatment.

I really, truly wasn't planning to write any more columns about George W. Bush's arithmetic. But his performance on *Moneyline* last Wednesday was just mind-blowing. I had to download a transcript to convince myself that I had really heard him correctly. It was as if Mr. Bush's aides had prepared him with a memo saying: "You've said some things on the stump that weren't true. Your mission, in the few minutes you have, is to repeat all of those things. Don't speak in generalities—give specific false numbers. That'll show them!"

First, Mr. Bush talked about the budget—"There's about $4.6 trillion of surplus projected," he declared, which is true, even if the projections are dubious. He then went on to say: "I want some of the money, nearly a trillion, to go to projects like prescription drugs for seniors. Money to strengthen the military to keep the peace. I've got some views about education around the world. I want to—you know, I've got some money in there for the environment."

Nearly a trillion? The budget statement released by the candidate's campaign three weeks ago shows total spending on new projects of $474.6 billion—less than half a trillion. Mr. Bush presumably wants to convey the sense that he's a compassionate guy who really cares about education, the environment and all that. But that doesn't excuse claiming to spend twice as much on these good things as the number given in his own budget.

He continued: "But there's still a quarter unspent, about $1.3 trillion [the size of Mr. Bush's tax cut]. I think we ought to send it back to the people who pay the bills." Alas, 4 times 1.3 is 5.2, not 4.6—and anyway, the full budget cost of that tax cut, including interest, is $1.6 trillion, more than a third of the projected surplus.

Next came Social Security. Here a bit of explanation is needed. The reason Social Security is in trouble is that the system has a large "hole"—basically a hidden debt—because previous generations of retirees were paid benefits out of the contributions of younger workers. That hole also means that you can't justify privatizing Social Security—which Mr. Bush advocates—by comparing the rate of return that an individual could get by investing in government bonds and the implied rate of return on his Social Security contributions. That comparison ignores a multitrillion-dollar debt that somebody has to pay.

Mr. Bush, wasting no time, went straight to that bogus comparison. "But the safest of all safe—of about 4 percent [a reference to government bonds]—is twice what they get in the Social Security trust today."

Is there any way to explain away Mr. Bush's remarks—three major self-serving misstatements in the course of only a couple of minutes? Not that I can see. We're not talking questionable economic analysis here, just facts: what Mr. Bush said to that national television audience simply wasn't true.

What is really striking here is the silence of the media—those "liberal media" conservatives complain about. *Moneyline* would never let a C.E.O. get away with claiming to spend twice as much on research as the sum announced in the company's own press release. But when Mr. Bush declared that he would spend twice as much on new programs as the sum announced by his own campaign, the interviewer said nothing—and nobody else picked up on it.

As I said, I don't want to keep writing about this. But reporters seem to be too busy chasing rats and dogs to look at what the candidates say about their actual policy proposals. So someone has to point out that in an interview intended to showcase his economic program, Mr. Bush did it again: he vastly exaggerated his spending plans, greatly understated the cost of his tax cut and misrepresented the issues on Social Security.

## WE'RE NOT RESPONSIBLE

*October 18, 2000*

However this election turns out, future historians are likely to see this as the year that America failed a big political test.

After decades of bipartisan irresponsibility, by the 1990's the United States had, miraculously, started to look like a grown-up nation—a nation able to plan ahead, to take advantage of good times to prepare for the rainier days to come. But it was an illusion: We were, it turns out, just playing at being grown-up.

The basic rule of fiscal responsibility for a national government is pretty much the same as the rule for a family: Pay off your debts and build up financial reserves when things are good, so that you can draw on those reserves later. And these are the best of times for America's government, in at least three ways.

First, we are at peace, with no significant military rivals. You don't have to believe in a new cold war to think that things are unlikely to stay this easy, that one way or another defense spending will eventually have to rise from its current low.

Second, our demography is as good as it's going to be for the foreseeable future. The modern U.S. government is in large part in the business of insuring the income and medical expenses of older citizens. Starting just 10 years from now, the population eligible for Medicare and Social Security will start rising, and rising, and rising, with no end in sight. And so will the bills. If taxes on the diminishing fraction of our population that isn't retired are to stay tolerable, we'd better start saving now.

Finally, right now the U.S. economy—and indirectly the federal budget—benefits from the perception in the rest of the world that America is the place to invest your money. Huge inflows of foreign capital have been keeping U.S. interest rates down and stock prices up, both of which also keep the money flowing into federal coffers. Some economists think that these capital inflows, like the similar inflows into Asian nations before 1997, are only setting us up for a future crisis—and I won't say that I'm not worried. But even without a crisis we know that foreigners (and American investors too) will eventually discover more opportunities outside the United States, that the inflows will someday become outflows, and that we will be sorry if we haven't prepared for that day.

So the responsible, sensible thing for the U.S. government to do is to run very big surpluses right now. Indeed, budget analysts who take the long view argue that even without the tax cuts and spending initiatives proposed by the presidential candidates we would not be running as large a surplus over the next decade as we should—that if anything we should be raising taxes and cutting spending.

But how do you explain that long view to the public? The truth is that our leaders never really tried. Instead, even politicians who were trying to be responsible resorted to half-truths. All that business about putting Social Security and Medicare in "lockboxes" is an attempt to sell fiscal responsibility to the voters without really trying to explain why it is necessary. So maybe we should not be surprised that we have ended up with the worst of all worlds. On one side the public feels, correctly, that politicians like Al Gore, who use those half-truths to push for half-responsible policies, are talking down to them. On the other side the public feels, quite wrongly, that politicians like George W. Bush, who tell them that they can have their cake and eat it too, are men of the people.

Mr. Bush's willingness to trust in the public's innumeracy continues to boggle the mind. In the second debate he offered possibly the biggest misrepresentation yet, this time declaring about his tax plan that "most of tax reductions go to the people at the bottom end of the economic ladder." (That sound you hear is the giggling of millionaires and the guffawing of multi-millionaires.)

But the gleefulness of the crowds who picked up that Orwellian chant of "no fuzzy numbers" (Orwellian because what it really meant was "no clear numbers—we don't want to know") suggests that this country just wasn't ready for the hard thinking that would have let us act responsibly. Maybe better politicians could have made a better case for the right policies. Or maybe the fault is not in our politicians but in ourselves.

# FUZZIER AND FUZZIER

*October 25, 2000*

Did you know that if Al Gore is elected president, and his economic plan is put into effect, 2.3 million Americans will die next year? Supercilious Washington insiders may try to confuse you by pointing out that even if Mr. Gore isn't elected, 2.3 million Americans will die—that next year's mortality rate has nothing to do with who wins the election. But you can deal with that by chanting, "No fuzzy math!" until the election is over.

No, George W. Bush hasn't blamed Mr. Gore for American mortality. But he's done something comparable. Mr. Gore has been pointing out, correctly, that Mr. Bush has promised $1 trillion in Social Security taxes to two different groups of people—telling young workers that he will allow them to invest the money in personal accounts, while assuring older workers that it will be available to pay for their retirement. So Mr. Bush has responded by charging that Mr. Gore's Social Security plan will add no less than $40 trillion to the national debt.

That seems like an awfully big number. It turns out to be an estimate of the total value of payments from the general government budget to Social Security, including interest, that will take place over the next 50 years. And I could bore you by explaining why that number is meaningless.

The really amazing thing, however, is that the number has nothing to do with Mr. Gore. It's true that Social Security will need transfers from general revenue if Mr. Gore's plan is put into effect. But it will need just as much money if Mr. Gore's plan isn't put into effect. The only way to reduce the required aid would be to reduce the benefits promised to retirees.

Meanwhile, Mr. Bush has said nothing about reducing benefits. So his plan for Social Security would cost just as much as his opponent's—or rather considerably more, because to honor those contradictory promises he has to find another pot of money somewhere.

Maybe blaming Mr. Gore for future mortality wouldn't have worked; but Mr. Bush's advisers seem to think that blaming him for the entire future liabilities of the Social Security system will, or at least can serve temporarily to confuse voters who might otherwise have started to think too clearly about the subject. Only two weeks to go until the election, and we can clean up the mess later, right?

But what a mess it's going to be. Those Social Security payments aren't the only sums being promised to two different groups of people.

Mr. Bush's plans—and, to a lesser extent, Mr. Gore's plans—are based on projections that assume there will be no increase in federal discretionary spending over the next 10 years. But over the last few months, while you weren't looking, Congress went on a bipartisan spending spree—with a cost estimated by both Democratic and Republican analysts at more than $800 billion over the next decade.

How will the next president deal with this bad news? Mr. Gore has a bit of slack in his budget, and has proclaimed that protecting the surplus is his highest priority; maybe he would decide to jettison his unloved and unlovely targeted tax cuts. But Mr. Bush's budget even now adds up thanks only to creative accounting, and he has made it clear that he cannot conceive of anything that would make him renege on his tax-cutting promises. (Did someone say, "Read my lips"?)

The odds, then, are that soon—perhaps as soon as next year—those projections of future budget surpluses will have been revised dramatically downward, and longer-term projections will show deficits as far as the statistical eye can see. This will pose real economic risks; it will also be a severe blow to our self-confidence. We will shake our heads at our earlier optimism and wonder what we were thinking.

But the answer, of course, is that we weren't thinking, and in general disapproved of those who did. However the election turns out, the reaction to the debates made it clear that voters have a visceral dislike for candidates who seem intellectual, let alone try to make the electorate do arithmetic.

Indeed, the motto for this election year—and the epitaph for the soon-to-be-departed budget surplus—should be: Real men don't think. Unfortunately, what you refuse to think about can still hurt you.

# ET TU, ALAN?

*January 28, 2001*

Despite his legendary obscurity, what Alan Greenspan has to say is usually quite clear and intellectually coherent once translated into English. But his testimony last Thursday before the Senate Budget Committee was evasive and often inconsistent. It was hard to avoid the impression that Mr. Greenspan's intent was to give aid and comfort to the new administration, while retaining plausible deniability.

True, Mr. Greenspan explicitly rejected the administration's argument that we must immediately cut taxes to prevent a recession. While conceding that the economy may grow little if at all this quarter, he suggested that a recovery would probably be under way before tax cuts could have any impact. By the way, new evidence suggests that manufacturing, which suffered a nasty downturn in the last few months, has already started to rebound.

Nonetheless, the headlines were all about Mr. Greenspan's endorsement of tax cuts—something the Fed chairman must have known would happen. And when you look at the tortured logic by which Mr. Greenspan arrived at that endorsement, you have to wonder whether those headlines weren't exactly what he wanted.

His argument went as follows: given its projected surpluses over the next decade, the federal government may not only pay off its debt, but actually find itself using surplus cash to buy private assets. This could cause problems, he suggested, because it would be "difficult to insulate the government's investment decisions from political pressures." So we should engage in "pre-emptive smoothing of the glide path," which turns out to mean cutting taxes enough so that the federal government never does pay off its debt, after all.

Now I would quarrel with those surplus projections. I would also point out that in declaring "it is far better . . . that the surpluses be lowered by tax reductions than by spending increases," Mr. Greenspan was out of bounds. Since when is it the Fed's business to say that we should have a tax cut rather than, say, a new prescription drug benefit—or for that matter a missile defense system? (Neither program is factored into those surplus projections.) Mr. Greenspan himself seemed aware that he was on shaky ground, offering the very inadequate excuse that "I speak for myself and not necessarily for the Federal Reserve."

But the really strange thing about his argument was that he seemed to ignore the fact that the main reason the federal government will one day become an investor is the buildup of assets in the hands of the Social Security and Medicare systems—and those funds must accumulate assets to prepare for the future demands of the baby-boom generation. Indeed, by all estimates even the huge projected surpluses of those trust funds will be inadequate to the task. "Certainly," Mr. Greenspan declared, "we should make sure that Social Security surpluses are large enough to meet our long-term needs." Well, I'm sorry, but you can't do that without allowing the federal government to become an investor.

So if that prospect was what was really worrying Mr. Greenspan, he should have focused on the problem of how to prevent the government's position as an investor from being abused. And there are many ways to do that—including, by the way, realistic plans for partial privatization of Social Security, which (unlike the fantasy promises of the Bush campaign) would require the federal government to ante up trillions of dollars to pay off existing obligations, solving the "problem" of excessive surpluses quite easily.

But Mr. Greenspan seemed determined to arrive at tax cuts as an answer. After dismissing the argument that we need a tax cut to fend off a recession now, and conceding that tax cuts have historically "proved difficult to implement in the time frame in which recessions have developed and ended," he waffled: "Should current economic weakness spread beyond what now seems likely, having a tax cut in place may, in fact, do noticeable good." But by the same token, if the economy is strong again by the time a tax cut goes into effect, won't that tax cut do noticeable harm? Mr. Greenspan declined to answer questions along those lines.

When a man who is usually a clear thinker ties himself in intellectual knots in order to find a way to say exactly what the new president wants to hear, it's not hard to guess what's going on. But it's not a pretty sight.

# SLICING THE SALAMI

*February 11, 2001*

The selling of George W. Bush's tax cut relies heavily on salami tactics—slicing away opposition a bit at a time. To understand how fundamentally misleading that sales pitch is, we must look at the whole salami.

Basically, there are three federal taxes on individuals. The payroll tax, which is levied at a flat rate of 15.3 percent of income up to a maximum of almost $70,000, is the main tax paid by about four out of five families. The income tax is less than 10 percent of income for most families, but it rises to around 30 percent of the income of million-dollar earners. And the inheritance tax, which applies only to estates of more than $675,000 (twice that for couples), is a tax on only the very well off: a mere 2 percent of estates pay any tax, and most of the tax is paid by a few thousand multimillion-dollar estates each year.

Now for the salami tactics.

Conservatives who decry the burden of taxes always include the payroll tax in their calculations. And when arguing for tax cuts, the administration starts with numbers that include the whole salami. Again and again we hear about that projected surplus of $5.6 trillion. You shouldn't believe that projection, but for what it's worth more than half of it (the more credible half) comes from Social Security and Medicare—programs financed by payroll taxes.

When it comes to tax cuts, however, Mr. Bush's people ignore the payroll tax—that is, they propose no cut in the tax that is most of what most families pay, while demanding a large cut in the income tax, which falls mainly on the affluent. And they want to eliminate the inheritance tax, which is overwhelmingly a tax on the downright wealthy.

By proposing to eliminate a tax that falls entirely on the rich, to cut a tax that falls mainly on the well off, but to ignore the main tax paid by most people, the administration has made a deliberate decision to tilt tax relief strongly toward the top of the scale. Families earning $50,000 per year would on average get a tax break of about $800 annually; families earning $1 million would get about $50,000. Yes, well-off families currently pay a higher share of their income in taxes—but not that much higher. And no, it's not "class warfare" to point out that the tax cut disproportionately benefits the very, very affluent.

Now you could try to justify tax cuts tilted toward the top by claiming that a rising tide lifts all boats, and that cutting taxes on the rich will make the economy grow faster. But that is not the case that the administration is making—perhaps because given the extraordinary boom of the Clinton years, it's hard to claim that excessive taxes have been a drag on economic growth.

Instead, the administration pretends that it is offering broad tax relief for working families. Last week Treasury Secretary Paul O'Neill declared that the plan "would focus on helping those people who are close to the low-income and middle-income brackets," adding that "it would affect every American that currently pays taxes." This statement isn't technically a lie: "close to" need not actually mean "in," and "affect" need not mean that a family's taxes are actually reduced. But one has to say that Mr. O'Neill, whom the press has portrayed as a straight talker, is learning his new trade very quickly.

The pretense that this is a populist tax cut is aided by careful slicing of that salami. The Bush people love to point out that families in the lower brackets will see a greater proportional reduction in their income taxes than those in the top bracket; they hope you won't notice that the main burden on such families is not the income tax but the payroll tax, which will not be cut, and that the children of the wealthy will receive large additional tax relief from the elimination of the inheritance tax.

Those staged events with "tax families" slice the salami even thinner, carefully avoiding any reference to the major beneficiaries. The only high-income taxpayer, and the only likely inheritor of a taxable estate, ever mentioned at these events is Mr. Bush himself.

Otto von Bismarck is supposed to have declared that "people will sleep better not knowing how their sausage and politics are made." Mr. Bush no doubt agrees; he hopes that the American people won't look too closely either at the composition of the tax salami or at how he proposes to slice it.

# THE MONEY PIT

*March 18, 2001*

So this contractor is renovating your house. Funny how he got the job: you checked the wrong box on a confusing form, and the judge—a close friend of the contractor—ruled that you were stuck. Anyway, though you told him that your priority was replacing your leaky roof, he insists that first he wants to put in a luxurious powder room.

Back when he was trying to get your business, the contractor said that he could put in the powder room for only $10,000, though others insisted that estimate was way too low. Now it turns out, sure enough, that it will cost at least $25,000. But he claims that he can save enough money on other parts of the job to make up the difference. And one of his employees has offered his personal assurance that the roof won't be neglected—though he admits that in the end it's not his decision, and his boss refuses to put anything in writing.

Last May, when George W. Bush was claiming that he planned only a trillion-dollar tax cut—remember the routine with the dollar bills?—independent experts estimated the actual 10-year budget cost of his tax plan at close to $2 trillion. They also warned that under Mr. Bush's plan a hitherto obscure aspect of the tax code, the alternative minimum tax, would become a major issue—and resolving that issue would sharply increase the cost of the plan.

Sure enough, earlier this month the bipartisan Congressional Joint Tax Committee estimated that Mr. Bush's proposal would reduce revenues over the next decade by $2.2 trillion. And the J.T.C. also produced some shocking estimates about the alternative minimum tax.

Most people have never heard of this tax, which was supposed to prevent the wealthy from avoiding taxes but ends up mainly affecting upper-middle-income families with lots of deductions. When the tax kicks in, it's infuriating; you've carefully calculated everything, then you discover that you have to do another calculation, and you end up owing a lot more. But right now this happens to only 1.5 percent of taxpayers. The J.T.C. concluded, however, that under the Bush plan this number would rise to one-third of taxpayers. Without question the law will be changed so that this doesn't happen—but the fix will add at least $300 billion to the cost of the plan.

So the "trillion-dollar tax cut" has become $2.5 trillion and counting—which means that Mr. Bush can pay for initiatives like missile defense and prescription drug coverage only by raiding Social Security and Medicare.

Last week Tommy Thompson, secretary of health and human services, tried to allay suspicions about such a raid by offering his personal assurance that the money Medicare has been accumulating to care for the baby boomers will not be diverted into other uses—even though Mr. Bush includes that money in his "contingency fund." But Mr. Thompson admitted that it isn't really up to him—and the administration's allies in the Senate blocked a measure that would have made Mr. Thompson's promise binding. Somehow I'm not reassured.

The latest news is that Mr. Bush wants additional tax cuts this year to stimulate the economy; he has apparently just realized that cuts that will take 10 years to phase in won't do anything to increase spending today. This will add hundreds of billions to the budget cost of his plan. You might think that he would admit that this increases the cost of his tax cut, and perhaps that he would offer to scale back those future tax cuts. Not a chance: administration officials claim that tax cuts this year don't affect their arithmetic because their budget is for 2002 through 2011, so what happens this year doesn't count. I am not making this up.

The important point is that the estimated cost of the tax cut hasn't exploded because of new information; it has exploded because the original estimates were simply dishonest. Mr. Bush knew from the start that he was misleading the public about the budget impact of his proposals, just as he knows that he is misleading people now about whose taxes will be cut and by how much. This contractor didn't make an honest error; he deliberately deceived the homeowner. And as long as he keeps getting away with it, he sees no reason to change the way he does business.

# THE UNIVERSAL ELIXIR

*May 16, 2001*

Scenes from the selling of the tax cut:

January 2001: The White House economic adviser Lawrence Lindsey argues that George W. Bush's tax cut—not interest rate cuts—is the right solution to the economic slowdown, because the tax cut has a "much bigger heft." Economists are puzzled by the attempt to sell a long-term tax cut as the answer to a short-run economic slowdown, especially given the fact that most of the cuts proposed by Mr. Bush wouldn't take place until the second half of the decade. Later, when Congress passes a budget resolution authorizing $1.35 trillion in tax cuts, administration allies try to eliminate language requiring that $100 billion of that total be reserved for immediate tax breaks to stimulate the economy. They would prefer to use the money for tax breaks for high-income families, even though those breaks will not phase in fully until 2006.

March 2001: President Bush declares that "nationwide there are more than 17.4 million small-business owners and entrepreneurs who stand to benefit from dropping the top rate from 39.6 to 33 percent." A press release from the Treasury Department seems to back him up, declaring that "it is evident that at least 17.4 million small-business owners and entrepreneurs, many of whom currently pay at the 39.6 percent rate, stand to benefit from the president's tax relief plan." Economists are puzzled, since only about a million taxpayers have any income taxed at the 39.6 percent rate, and most of those are not small-business owners. Independent estimates suggest that only about 1 percent of small businesses would receive any benefit from a cut in the top rate, giving a new meaning to the term "many."

May 2001: Mr. Bush is asked what his administration plans to do in the face of high gasoline prices. "Let me say it again, see if I can be more clear," he replies. "To the Congress, who is interested in helping consumers pay high gas prices: 'Pass the tax relief as quickly as possible.' We've set aside $100 billion to help consumers with high energy prices. That's the quickest way to help consumers. I am deeply concerned about consumers. I'm deeply concerned about high gas prices. To anybody who wants to figure out how to help the consumers, pass the tax relief package as quickly as possible." Economists are puzzled, since the poorest families, who are most affected by the gasoline price spike, will receive no tax cut under the Bush plan. Also, that $100 billion that Mr. Bush says he has set aside "to help consumers with high energy prices" is the short-term tax cut that his Congressional allies tried to eliminate from the budget resolution.

June 2001: Soaring electricity prices cause hardship for many families and small businesses in several parts of the United States. Mr. Bush continues to insist that there are no short-term solutions to energy problems, that the answer is to drill for oil in the Arctic National Wildlife Refuge. However, he adds that his tax relief package will help families afford electricity, or buy candles and propane lamps.

July 2001: Foot-and-mouth disease breaks out in the United States, and spreads rapidly. Mr. Bush denies that the outbreak calls into question planned cuts in the Agriculture Department budget. The best answer, he argues, is broad tax relief, which will help farmers buy new animals, help consumers pay higher food prices and allow housewives to take courses in vegetarian cooking.

August 2001: Adverse weather conditions and lax pollution regulations lead to severe air-quality problems in Houston, which during Mr. Bush's governorship took the lead from Los Angeles in ozone pollution. Mr. Bush denies that the pollution is a warning sign for his production-oriented energy policy, and argues that his tax cut will help alleviate the problem, by giving families the money with which to pay for air filters, respirators and medical care.

September 2001: Critics pan the new fall television lineup, describing it as "must-avoid TV" and calling it the worst set of new programs in decades. Mr. Bush declares that he is "very concerned" about the deteriorating quality of broadcast entertainment. He urges TV viewers to support his plan for tax relief, which will provide families with money they can use to subscribe to HBO, allowing them to watch *The Sopranos*.

# BAD HEIR DAY

*May 30, 2001*

There's a scene in the 1966 British comedy *The Wrong Box* in which the son of an irascible plutocrat pushes his father's wheelchair along the top of a cliff, responding with a dutiful "Yes, Father" to each outpouring of verbal abuse. Then the old man waves his hand at the industrial landscape below, and declares, "When I'm gone, all this will be yours." "Yes, Father," replies the son—and pushes him off the cliff.

That scene came back to me as I delved further into the absurd piece of tax legislation that a House-Senate conference devised and that George W. Bush triumphantly signed last weekend.

The Bush tax plan was always peculiar: in order to hide the true budget impact, its authors delayed many of the biggest tax cuts until late into the 10-year planning period; repeal of the estate tax, in particular, was put off to 2010. But even that left the books insufficiently cooked, so last week the conferees added a "sunset" clause, officially causing the whole bill to expire, and tax rates to bounce back to 2000 levels, at the beginning of 2011.

So in the law as now written, heirs to great wealth face the following situation: If your ailing mother passes away on Dec. 30, 2010, you inherit her estate tax-free. But if she makes it to Jan. 1, 2011, half the estate will be taxed away. That creates some interesting incentives. Maybe they should have called it the Throw Momma from the Train Act of 2001.

That's by no means the only weird element in the tax bill. Almost as bizarre is the sudden tax increase for upper-middle-income families scheduled for the end of 2004. Anyone who has been following the tax debate—in particular via the extremely informative Web site of the Center on Budget and Policy Priorities—knows that the alternative minimum tax [A.M.T.] is a major land mine lurking in the road ahead. Under the tax bill just passed, the number of taxpayers subject to this tax will balloon from 1.5 million to more than 36 million, with the result that many people—typically well-off but not rich families who already pay high state and local taxes—will find the tax cut they thought they were getting snatched away.

So why not fix the law? Because that would raise the budget impact of the tax cut by hundreds of billions of dollars. Still, the conferees felt they had to do something; so they included a partial fix for the A.M.T. problem. But even that partial fix, if maintained over the whole decade, would have made the tax cut too big to fit the budget resolution. So guess what? The A.M.T. fix is scheduled to expire in 2004, which means that according to the law millions of families will face a sudden large tax increase.

In short, the tax bill is a joke. But if the administration has its way, the joke is on us. For the bill is absurd by design. The administration, knowing that its tax cut wouldn't fit into any responsible budget, pushed through a bill that contains the things it wanted most—big tax cuts for the very, very rich—and used whatever accounting gimmicks it could find to make the overall budget impact seem smaller than it is. The idea is that when the absurdities become apparent—when mobs of angry junior vice presidents from New Jersey start demonstrating against the A.M.T., or when elderly multimillionaires develop a suspiciously high rate of fatal accidents—Congress will always respond with further tax cuts. And if the result of all those tax cuts is to prevent the government from ever providing the things Mr. Bush promised during the campaign, like prescription drug coverage under Medicare or increased aid to education—well, that was also part of the plan.

Someday, responsible politicians—or is that an oxymoron?—will have to untangle this mess. And yes, that means that some of the tax cuts Congress just approved will have to be rescinded. (How about a deal that fixes the A.M.T. and pays for the fix by returning tax rates on the top bracket to their 2000 level? Just a thought.)

But for now, it's a defensive game. The administration, having successfully rammed through a ridiculous tax bill, will try to bamboozle us on other matters. So the next question is whether men of honor will insist on honest accounting when it comes to Social Security reform. Yes, Senator Moynihan, this means you.

# PANTS ON FIRE

*August 24, 2001*

To: Mitch Daniels, Office of Management and Budget

Dear Mitch: I have a suggestion. It's dishonest and irresponsible—but I suspect that doesn't bother you. And it would help you squirm out of a problem that we both know isn't going away.

True, your bobbing and weaving have been impressive. Some people have actually bought your line that the surplus has vanished because of Congressional big spending, even though the spending numbers have hardly changed since your previous, bullish projection. And most reporters, bless their tiny little heads, have written about the budget shortfall as if it were a temporary problem; they haven't looked at Table 3 of your own report, which despite all your cooking of the books projects only a razor-thin non–Social Security surplus for the next five years.

But there's more trouble ahead. You bullied the Congressional Budget Office into delaying its own budget projection until next week, so that you could get your numbers out first. Still, when the C.B.O. numbers come out everyone knows that they will look considerably worse than yours.

And of course we both know that the truth is actually even worse than that, because the C.B.O. must pretend to believe what politicians tell it. For example, when you claim that you can provide prescription drug insurance for a third of what anyone else thinks it will cost, or that you won't adjust the alternative minimum tax even when millions of irate voters ask why their tax cut has been snatched away, the C.B.O. duly puts those claims into its numbers.

It's a good thing that reporters were too lazy to read last week's report by the International Monetary Fund. I admit, "2001 Article IV Consultation" isn't a very catchy title, but the contents are hot stuff. Basically what the I.M.F. said was, "Liar, liar, pants on fire." When the I.M.F. staff points out the truth, such as the fact that the "$1.35 trillion" tax cut will actually cost at least $2.5 trillion, it becomes all too obvious that you'll be raiding the Social Security surplus year after year, with no end in sight.

So here's my suggestion: Declare that the defense budget is actually part of Social Security. The military provides security to society, doesn't it? Then you can say with a straight face that there isn't any Social Security surplus; including defense spending, the program is actually in deficit! And that will get you off the hook, because you won't have to worry about protecting a surplus that you have declared doesn't exist.

My idea is, of course, just an expanded version of your administration's Medicare scam.

Medicare's hospital insurance program is run the same way as Social Security: it collects revenue from payroll taxes, and it is accumulating a trust fund to help pay benefits when the baby boomers retire. If you treated the hospital insurance surplus the same way you treat the Social Security surplus—which you should, since the two programs work the same way—it would already be obvious that you are paying for the tax cut with money that was supposed to be reserved for future retirees.

However, Medicare also runs a supplemental insurance program. This program has always been paid for out of general revenue—just like defense—but your administration insists that it must be lumped in with hospital insurance. That lets you declare that there is no Medicare surplus, and use the hospital insurance surplus to pay for tax cuts.

Some people have pointed out that this is a very strange way to make policy. Even aside from the blatantly dishonest accounting, surely a country with an aging population should be putting money aside to pay for future retiree health care. But you've done a good job of shouting those people down. So I don't see why you can't do the same thing when you start billing the costs of missile defense to the Social Security Administration.

In the end, we both know, the truth will become apparent. Eventually there will be no disguising the fact that thanks to the tax cut the nation has failed to make adequate preparations for the demographic deluge, that money that was supposed to be accumulated to pay retirement benefits has been used instead to provide big tax cuts to the very, very affluent.

But then that's been the plan all along, hasn't it?

## CHAPTER 6

# . . . And the Switch

## HITTING THE TRIFECTA

*December 7, 2001*

Shortly after Sept. 11, George W. Bush interrupted his inveighing against evildoers to crack a joke. Mr. Bush had repeatedly promised to run an overall budget surplus at least as large as the Social Security surplus, except in the event of recession, war or national emergency. "Lucky me," he remarked to Mitch Daniels, his budget director. "I hit the trifecta."

Lucky him, indeed. The Enron analogy will soon become a tired cliché, but in this case the parallel is irresistible. Enron management and the administration Enron did so much to put in power applied the same strategy: First, use cooked numbers to justify big giveaways at the top. Then, if things don't work out, let ordinary workers who trusted you pay the price. But Enron executives got caught; Mr. Bush believes that the events of Sept. 11 will let him off the hook.

Earlier this year Mr. Bush used projections of vast budget surpluses to push through a huge, 10-year tax cut. Most of that tax cut went to people with incomes of more than $200,000 per year. Now Mr. Daniels tells us that the budget—not just the budget outside Social Security, but the whole enchilada—will be in deficit through 2004. Since the administration's phony budget math ("fuzzy" just doesn't cut it at this point) gets phonier the further you go into the future, this means that we have effectively returned to a state of permanent deficit.

However, with television busy reporting from the caves of Tora Bora, this revelation—which shows that the tax cut was sold on utterly false premises—wasn't even considered headline news.

Administration officials insist that the economic slowdown and the war on terror, not the tax cut, are responsible for the red ink. But this is flatly untrue: antiterror spending is a minor factor, and the persistence of projected deficits into the indefinite future tells us that it's not caused by the recession either.

Anyway, they're missing the point. Opponents of the administration's plan always warned that it was foolish to lock in a giant tax cut on the basis of hypothetical surplus projections. They urged, to no avail, that we wait to see the actual budget results. Now their warnings have proved prophetic—and ordinary Americans will suffer because they were ignored.

The administration now says that the tax cut was necessary to fight the current recession. But nobody is questioning the $40 billion in rebates actually paid out so far, and few would complain about another round of temporary tax cuts for the year ahead. It's the huge further tax cuts that will take place after 2002—tax cuts that are now the law of the land—that are the problem. But we're supposed to accept those future cuts as a fait accompli. Hey, Mr. Bush hit the trifecta.

Meanwhile, the return of budget deficits has real, nasty consequences. Prescription drug insurance is, of course, dead. Bolstering Social Security? Don't be silly: payroll tax receipts are being used neither to acquire assets nor to pay down federal debt; instead, they are subsidizing deficits in the rest of the government.

And austerity rules, even in areas you might have thought were of the highest priority. Money to rebuild New York? Sorry, no. The government's own experts say we need $3 billion to guard against bioterrorism? Cut the number in half. Tax cuts are more important.

Meanwhile, state and local governments, savaged both by recession and by new security expenses, are firing teachers and slashing services. How about some revenue-sharing from the Feds? Never mind.

Whenever they were asked, voters said that the "compassionate" parts of Mr. Bush's campaign promises—securing Social Security, providing more money for prescription drugs and education—were more important to them than tax cuts. But they were assured that there was enough money for everything. Those assurances were false—but the tax cut is sacrosanct, while the rest is expendable.

Mr. Bush could try to undo some of the damage, by canceling future tax cuts for the top income bracket. Instead, he wants to accelerate those cuts. That's the moral equivalent of the big bonuses Enron gave to executives just days before it went bankrupt.

Horse racing is a zero-sum game; so, it seems, is budget politics. Mr. Bush hit the trifecta; the great majority of Americans lost, big time.

# THE QUIET MAN

*January 8, 2002*

On Sunday newspapers headlined George W. Bush's declaration that future tax cuts would be canceled "over my dead body." But the only news there was Mr. Bush's choice of words—words he hasn't repeated, probably because his aides realized that they didn't sound very presidential, and were in poor taste in light of recent events.

The interesting news story on economic policy, it seems to me, involves someone else—and it involves his silence, not his words. Whatever happened to Alan Greenspan, the high priest of fiscal responsibility?

About Mr. Bush: surely nobody expected him to give an inch, even though the surplus projections that were used to sell the tax cut have turned out to be nonsense. The Bush administration operates on the principle of "no enemies on the right"; it also operates on the principle that Mr. Bush is infallible. Whatever policies he may have proposed in the past, his aides always insist that they are perfectly suited to the present—indeed, were devised with the present situation in mind. It's actually quite funny, though nobody dares say so.

Last month, for example, Karl Rove explained that the tax cut, although originally proposed amid an economic boom, was designed to cope with the current recession. "All the signs were there in the second, if not the second, the third quarter of 2000," Mr. Rove said. When a questioner gently pointed out that

Mr. Bush had laid out his tax plan way back in 1999, Mr. Rove brushed him aside.

And since Mr. Bush is infallible, why should he ever reconsider his decisions?

But back to Alan Greenspan. A year ago Mr. Greenspan gave the new Bush administration decisive aid in its push for a large tax cut. Worrying that the national debt would be paid off too quickly, he urged Congress to cut taxes in order to put the budget on a "glide path" of gradually declining surpluses.

Some glide path; more like a nosedive. In 2000 America ran a record surplus; now, analysts from both parties agree that the federal budget will be in deficit for at least the next several years. They still project surpluses for late in the decade—but if you believe those projections, I've got some Enron stock you might want to buy.

Mr. Greenspan ought to be upset. It's not just that during the Clinton years he became an icon of fiscal probity; the sudden plunge back into deficit undoes his own handiwork.

You see, back in the early 1980's, before he became Fed chairman, Mr. Greenspan headed a commission that was supposed to secure the future of Social Security. The main result of that commission was an increase in payroll taxes, even as Ronald Reagan was cutting income taxes. The purpose of this regressive tax increase—payroll taxes fall most heavily on low- and middle-income families—was to generate a surplus that would, in turn, make it easier for the federal government to pay benefits to an aging population.

But now, thanks to the disappearance of the budget surplus, the excess revenue collected by the payroll tax isn't being used to acquire assets, or even to pay down the federal debt; it's being used to cover deficits elsewhere in the budget. We're not talking small numbers here; only about 70 cents of each dollar in Social Security revenue is used to pay current benefits. In effect, the other 30 cents has now been expropriated for other uses—mainly tax cuts for the richest few percent of the population.

Was this what Mr. Greenspan intended—to raise taxes on the poor and the middle class, so that they could be cut for the rich? If not, why doesn't he say something? After all, a word from him could alter the landscape of economic debate, just as it did a year ago.

It's true that to give that word Mr. Greenspan would have to admit, at least tacitly, that he was wrong last year. But he's not a politician up for re-election—and if he's worried about his reputation, he should realize that if he continues to be silent history will not judge him kindly. Right now the provisional verdict is that he was a hypocrite: he sternly demanded fiscal responsibility while Democrats were in office, but had no complaints—indeed, acted as an enabler—as a Republican administration quickly squandered the fruits of all that austerity.

That verdict doesn't have to stand. All it would take would be a few carefully chosen remarks. I'm all ears.

# OUR WRETCHED STATES

*January 11, 2002*

Many Americans are surprised at the speed with which assurances that immense federal surpluses were here to stay gave way to the reality of deficits. Some of us, however, aren't surprised; we're simply following a trail blazed in places like Richmond and Austin. In the 1990's most states had Republican governors; and they applied the same strategy—using what-me-worry forecasts and bogus accounting to justify tax cuts for the affluent—that the Bush administration applied at a national level in 2001. In both cases the consequences were predictable.

The difference is that state governments are generally prohibited by their constitutions from borrowing to cover deficits. Eventually the federal government, too, must live within its means—but spin and denial can delay the reckoning. State chickens come home to roost a lot faster. In other words, the state of the states is the shape of national things to come.

How bad is the state fiscal crisis? The National Governors Association recently reported that its members faced a combined shortfall—that is, a gap between projected revenue and projected spending—of at least $40 billion, and quite possibly $50 billion. The latter number would be almost 10 percent of states' budgets, a very large number indeed.

If 10 percent doesn't sound that big to you, remember that much state spending, like much federal spending, cannot be cut—especially on short notice. A budget shortfall of 6.5 percent in the early 1990's led to severe cuts in services and forced 44 states to raise taxes; this one looks considerably worse.

How did states get themselves in this fix? The biggest proximate cause of the budget crunch is the end of the great 1990's boom; second place goes to surging medical costs. Expenses for homeland security add a final insult.

But stuff happens; why didn't states prepare for a rainy day? Although they can't borrow in bad times, state governments can accumulate reserves in good times. Instead, however, many governors acted as if the boom would never end.

They increased spending—though not all that much; spending by state and local governments was about the same share of GDP at the end of the 1990's as it was at the beginning.

More important, they cut taxes. Now it's true that state governments raised taxes in the early 1990's—but as new work by the Center on Budget and Policy Priorities shows, they didn't cut the same taxes they had previously raised. Increases in regressive taxes—that is, taxes like the sales tax, which bear most heavily on lower- and moderate-income families—by and large were never reversed. Instead, states cut taxes that bear most heavily on upper-income families. The end result was a redistribution of the tax burden away from the haves toward the have-nots. A family earning, say, $30,000 per year pays considerably more in state taxes than a family with the same constant-dollar income did in 1990, while a family earning $600,000 per year pays considerably less.

The way for these selective tax cuts was cleared not just with forecasts that made no allowance for contingencies, but with creative accounting worthy of Enron. For example, in 1999 the governor of Texas—yes, him—justified new corporate tax breaks with a budget that not only understated Medicaid costs by $550 million but hid regular payments for nursing care and other services by moving them from the last month of fiscal 2001 to the first month of 2002. Just last year, with the fiscal picture already darkening, Governor James Gilmore of Virginia (who resigned as head of the Republican National Committee after his party lost the Virginia and New Jersey state houses) evaded a "trigger" rule that was supposed to postpone tax cuts in the event of a revenue shortfall; he booked an estimate of the entire value of future payments from tobacco companies as current revenue.

Now the states must deal with the effects of past chicanery even as they face recession, soaring health care costs and the fiscal impact of terrorism. The result will be layoffs of teachers and policemen, medical care denied to the poor, delayed repairs to roads and bridges, and—eventually, when it can no longer be avoided—tax increases. And why do I think I know whose taxes will go up?

It's not a pretty picture, but you should get accustomed to it. As the states go, so goes America.

# BUSH'S AGGRESSIVE ACCOUNTING

*February 5, 2002*

Senator Kent Conrad [D-ND] actually got it wrong yesterday when he criticized the Bush administration's new budget for its Enron-like accounting. Last year's budget, the one that included that big tax cut, was the one with a strong touch of Enron about it. This year's budget involves a different, though equally pernicious, kind of aggressive accounting.

Enron's illusion of profitability rested largely on "mark to market" accounting. The company entered into contracts that would yield profits, if at all, only over a number of years. But Enron jumped the gun: it treated the capitalized value of those hypothetical future gains as a current profit, which could then be used to justify high stock prices, big bonuses for executives, and so on.

And that's more or less what happened in last year's budget. The Bush administration took a bullish 10-year surplus projection—a projection that had a built-in upward bias, and in any case should have been regarded as no more than a guess—and treated it as if it were hard fact. On the basis of those surplus fantasies the administration—aided by an audit committee, otherwise known as the U.S. Congress, that failed to exercise due diligence—gave itself a big bonus in the form of a huge tax cut.

A year later the wrongness of the assumptions behind last year's budget is there for all to see, and in a rational world the administration would be called to account for misleading the American public. But instead the Bush administration has turned to the political equivalent of another increasingly common accounting trick: the "one-time charge."

According to Investopedia.com, one-time charges are "used to bury unfavorable expenses or investments that went wrong." That is, instead of admitting that it has been doing a bad job, management claims that bad results are caused by extraordinary, unpredictable events: "We're making lots of money, but we had $1 billion in special expenses associated with our takeover of XYZ Corporation." And of course extraordinary events do happen; the trick is to make the most of them, as a way of evading responsibility. (Some companies, such as Cisco, have a habit of incurring "one-time charges" over and over again.)

The events of Sept. 11 shocked and horrified the nation; they also presented the Bush administration with a golden opportunity to bury its previous misdeeds. Has more than $4 trillion of projected surplus suddenly evaporated into thin air? Pay no attention to the tax cut: it's all because of the war on terrorism.

In short, the administration's strategy is to prevent criticism of what amounts to a fiscal debacle by wrapping its budget in the flag. And I mean that literally: the budget report released yesterday came wrapped in a red, white and blue cover depicting the American flag.

But why am I so cynical? Isn't the war on terrorism a big deal?

The answer is that emotionally, morally, it is indeed a big deal; but fiscally it's very nearly a rounding error.

It's true that the administration is using the terrorist threat to justify a huge military buildup. But there are a couple of funny things about that buildup. First, if we really have to give up butter in order to pay for all those guns, shouldn't we reconsider future tax cuts that were conceived in a time of abundance?

"Not over my dead body" isn't really an answer. And it's particularly hard to take all the grim war talk seriously when the administration is, at the very same time, proposing an additional $600 billion in tax cuts.

Second, the military buildup seems to have little to do with the actual threat, unless you think that Al Qaeda's next move will be a frontal assault by several heavy armored divisions. We nondefense experts are a bit puzzled about why an attack by maniacs armed with box cutters justifies spending $15 billion on 70-ton artillery pieces, or developing three different advanced fighters (before Sept. 11 even administration officials suggested that this was too many). No politician hoping for reelection will dare to say it, but the administration's new motto seems to be "Leave no defense contractor behind."

I could go on, but you get the point. The administration insists, and may even believe, that the war on terror has become a mission. But as far as the budget goes, it's not a mission; it's an excuse.

# TRUE BLUE AMERICANS

*May 7, 2002*

Remember how hard New York's elected representatives had to fight to get $20 billion in aid for the stricken city—aid that had already been promised? Well, recently Congress agreed to give farmers $180 billion in subsidies over the next decade. By the way, the population of New York City is about twice as large as America's total farm population.

I've been a stern critic of the Bush administration, but this is one case where Democrats in the Senate were the lead villains. To its credit, the administration initially opposed an increase in farm subsidies, though as in the case of steel protection, it didn't take long before political calculation trumped the administration's alleged principles. But politics aside, maybe the farm bill debacle will help us, finally, to free ourselves from a damaging national myth: that the "heartland," consisting of the central, relatively rural states, is morally superior to the rest of the country.

You've heard the story many times: the denizens of the heartland, we're told, are rugged, self-reliant, committed to family; the inhabitants of the coast are whining yuppies. Indeed, George W. Bush has declared that he visits his stage set—er, ranch—in Crawford to "stay in touch with real Americans." (And what are those of us who live in New Jersey—chopped liver?)

But neither the praise heaped on the heartland nor the denigration of the coasts has any basis in reality.

I've done some statistical comparisons using one popular definition of the heartland: the "red states" that—in an election that pitted both coasts against the middle—voted for Mr. Bush.

How do they compare with the "blue states" that voted for Al Gore?

Certainly the heartland has no claim to superiority when it comes to family values. If anything, the red states do a bit worse than the blue states when you look at indicators of individual responsibility and commitment to family. Children in red states are more likely to be born to teenagers or unmarried mothers—in 1999, 33.7 percent of babies in red states were born out of wedlock, versus 32.5 percent in blue states. National divorce statistics are spotty, but per capita there were 60 percent more divorces in Montana than in New Jersey.

And the red states have special trouble with the Sixth Commandment: the murder rate was 7.4 per 100,000 inhabitants in the red states, compared with 6.1 in the blue states, and 4.1 in New Jersey.

But what's really outrageous is the claim that the heartland is self-reliant. That grotesque farm bill, by itself, should put an end to all such assertions; but it only adds to the immense subsidies the heartland already receives from the rest of the country. As a group, red states pay considerably less in taxes than the federal government spends within their borders; blue states pay considerably more. Over all, blue America subsidizes red America to the tune of $90 billion or so each year.

And within the red states, it's the metropolitan areas that pay the taxes, while the rural regions get the subsidies. When you do the numbers for red states without major cities, you find that they look like Montana, which in 1999 received $1.75 in federal spending for every dollar it paid in federal taxes. The numbers for my home state of New Jersey were almost the opposite. Add in the hidden subsidies, like below-cost provision of water for irrigation, nearly free use of federal land for grazing and so on, and it becomes clear that in economic terms America's rural heartland is our version of southern Italy: a region whose inhabitants are largely supported by aid from their more productive compatriots.

There's no mystery about why the heartland gets such special treatment: it's a result of our electoral system, which gives states with small populations—mainly, though not entirely, red states—disproportionate representation in the Senate, and to a lesser extent in the Electoral College. In fact, half the Senate is elected by just 16 percent of the population.

But while this raw political clout is a fact of life, at least we can demand an end to the hypocrisy. The heartland has no special claim to represent the "real America." And the blue states have a right to ask why, at a time when the federal government has plunged back into deficit, when essential domestic programs are under assault, a small minority of heavily subsidized Americans should feel that they are entitled to even more aid.

# THE GREAT EVASION

*May 14, 2002*

Last week Stanley Works, a Connecticut tool company, postponed its plan to evade taxes by incorporating itself in Bermuda. The decision reflected pressure from the White House, which denounced the move as unpatriotic in a time of national emergency.

I am, of course, making that last part up. The shareholders' vote approving Stanley's move was challenged by Connecticut officials; also, the company has been put in the spotlight by David Cay Johnston, *The New York Times*'s invaluable tax reporter. But the Bush administration, always quick to question the patriotism of anyone who gets in its way, has said nothing at all about Stanley Works, and little about the growing number of U.S. corporations declaring themselves foreign for tax purposes.

To be fair, the administration didn't create the loophole Stanley wants to exploit. And it's not enough just to denounce corporations that exploit tax loopholes; the real answer is to deny them the opportunity. Still, the administration's silence is peculiar. What's going on?

The closest we have to an official statement on the issue of companies moving offshore comes from the Treasury Department's chief of tax enforcement: "We may need to rethink some of our international tax rules that were written 30 years ago when our economy was very different and that now may be

impeding the ability of U.S. companies to compete internation-
ally."

Unfortunately, that statement misrepresents the issue. For
one thing, U.S. companies don't necessarily pay higher taxes
than their foreign counterparts; Germany's corporate tax rate is
significantly higher than ours, France's rate is about the same,
and Britain's is only marginally lower. Anyway, the Treasury
statement makes it sound as if we're losing revenue because
U.S.-based companies are moving their headquarters to lower-
cost locations, or because they are losing market share to foreign rivals. Neither proposition is true. In fact, we're losing
revenue because profitable U.S. companies are using fancy
footwork to avoid paying taxes.

By incorporating itself in Bermuda, a U.S.-based corporation
can—without moving its headquarters or anything else—shelter its overseas profits from taxation. Better yet, the company
can then establish "legal residence" in a low-tax jurisdiction
like Barbados, and arrange things so that its U.S. operations are
mysteriously unprofitable, while the mail drop in Barbados
earns money hand over fist. In other words, this isn't about
competition; it's about tax evasion.

The natural answer would seem to be to crack down on the
evaders—to find a way to tax companies on the profits they
really earn in the U.S., and prevent them from using creative
accounting to make the profits appear somewhere else. It's
hard, but not impossible.

But here's the key point: Administration officials don't want
to help collect the corporate profits tax. Unable to push major
corporate tax breaks through Congress, the administration has
used whatever leeway it has to offer such breaks without legislation. The Hill, a nonpartisan publication covering Congres-

sional affairs, recently reported on "a series of little-noticed executive orders . . . that will provide corporations with billions of dollars in tax relief without the consent of Congress."

And now the silence on Stanley becomes comprehensible. The administration doesn't want to say outright that it's in favor of tax evasion; but it also doesn't really want to collect the taxes. Better to say nothing at all.

The trouble is that hinting, even by silence, that it's O.K. not to pay taxes is a dangerous game, because it can quickly grow into a major revenue loss. Accountants and tax planners have taken the hint; they now believe that it's safe to push the envelope. Tax receipts this year are falling far short of expectations, even taking the recession into account; my bet is that it will turn out that newly aggressive tax avoidance by corporations (and wealthy individuals) is an important part of the story. And it will get worse next year.

Furthermore, what does it say to the nation when companies that are proud to stay American are punished, while companies that are willing to fly a flag of convenience are rewarded?

If the administration wants to eliminate the corporate profits tax, let's have a real, open debate—starting with an explanation of how the lost revenue will be replaced in a time of severe budget deficits. Meanwhile, let's crack down on tax evasion.

# SPRINGTIME FOR HITLER

*October 18, 2002*

You may recall that George W. Bush promised, among other things, to change the tone in Washington. He made good on that promise: the tone has certainly changed.

As far as I know, in the past it wasn't considered appropriate for the occupant of the White House to declare that members of the opposition party weren't interested in the nation's security. And it certainly wasn't usual to compare anyone who wants to tax the rich—or even anyone who estimates the share of last year's tax cut that went to the wealthy—to Adolf Hitler.

O.K., maybe we should discount remarks by Senator Phil Gramm. When Mr. Gramm declared that a proposal to impose a one-time capital gains levy on people who renounce U.S. citizenship in order to avoid paying taxes was "right out of Nazi Germany," even the ranking Republican on the Senate Finance Committee, Charles Grassley, objected to the comparison.

But Mr. Grassley must have thought better of his objection, since just a few weeks later he decided to use the Hitler analogy himself: "I am sure voters will get their fill of statistics claiming that the Bush tax cut hands out 40 percent of its benefits to the top 1 percent of taxpayers. This is not merely misleading, it is outright false. Some folks must be under the impression that as long as something is repeated often enough, it will become true. That was how Adolf Hitler got to the top."

For the record, Robert McIntyre of Citizens for Tax Justice— the original source of that 40 percent estimate—is no Adolf

Hitler. The amazing thing is that Mr. Grassley is sometimes described as a moderate. His remarks are just one more indicator that we have entered an era of extreme partisanship—one that leaves no room for the acknowledgment of politically inconvenient facts. For the claim that Mr. Grassley describes as "outright false" is, in fact, almost certainly true; in a rational world it wouldn't even be a matter for argument.

You might imagine that Mr. Grassley has in hand an alternative answer to the question, "How much of the tax cut will go to the top 1 percent?"—that the administration has, at some point, produced a number showing that the wealthy aren't getting a big share of the benefits. In fact, however, administration officials have never answered that question. When pressed, they have always insisted on answering some other question.

But last year the Treasury Department did release a table showing, somewhat inadvertently, that more than 25 percent of the income tax cut will go to people making more than $200,000 per year. This number doesn't include the effects of estate tax repeal; in 1999 only 2 percent of estates paid any tax, and half of that tax was paid by only 0.16 percent of estates. The number also probably doesn't take account of the alternative minimum tax, which will snatch away most of the income tax cut for upper-middle-class families, but won't affect the rich.

Put all this together and it becomes clear that, sure enough, something like 40 percent of the tax cut—it could be a bit less, but probably it's considerably more—will go to 1 percent of the population. And the administration's systematic evasiveness on the question of who benefits from the tax cut amounts to a plea of nolo contendere.

Which brings us back to the new tone in Washington.

When Ronald Reagan cut taxes on rich people, he didn't deny that that was what he was doing. You could agree or disagree with the supply-side economic theory he used to justify his actions, but he didn't pretend that he was increasing the progressivity of the tax system.

The strategy used to sell the Bush tax cut was simply to deny the facts—and to lash out at anyone who tried to point them out. And it's a strategy that, having worked there, is now being applied across the board.

Michael Kinsley recently wrote that "The Bush campaign for war against Iraq has been insulting to American citizens, not just because it has been dishonest, but because it has been unserious. A lie is insulting; an obvious lie is doubly insulting." All I can say is, now he notices? It's been like that all along on economic policy.

You see, some folks must be under the impression that as long as something is repeated often enough, it will become true. That was how George W. Bush got to the top.

# IS THE MAESTRO A HACK?

*February 7, 2003*

It's probably wishful thinking, but some people hope that the old Alan Greenspan—the man we used to respect—will make a return appearance next week.

During the Clinton years Mr. Greenspan became an icon of fiscal probity, constantly lecturing politicians on the importance of eliminating deficits and paying off debt. Then George W. Bush took office, and Mr. Greenspan became—or was revealed as—a different man.

First the Fed chairman lent decisive support to the Bush tax cut, urging Congress to reduce taxes lest the country run too large a budget surplus and pay off its debt too quickly. No, really.

Then when the budget plunged into deficit, Mr. Greenspan not only refused to reconsider, he supported plans to make the tax cut permanent. The stern headmaster had become an indulgent uncle.

But now the fiscal deterioration has reached catastrophic proportions. In its first budget, the Bush administration projected a 2004 surplus of $262 billion. In its second budget, released a year ago, it projected a $14 billion deficit for the same year. Now it projects a deficit of $307 billion. That's a deterioration of $570 billion, just for next year—matched by comparable deterioration in each following year. You know, $570 billion here and $570 billion there, and pretty soon you're talking real money.

Not my fault, says Mr. Bush. "A recession and a war we did

not choose have led to a return of deficits," he declared. Really? Will the recession and war cost $570 billion per year, every year? Besides, Mr. Bush knew all about the recession and Osama bin Laden (remember him?) a year ago, when his projections showed a return to surpluses by 2005. Now they show deficits forever—even though they don't include the costs of an Iraq war.

Anyway, isn't a leader supposed to solve problems, not look for excuses? But Mr. Bush proposes to make the problem worse. Contrary to all previous practice, he wants to cut taxes even further in the face of "wartime" deficits.

Although financial reporters have started to realize that Mr. Bush is out of control—he has "lost his marbles," says *CBS Market Watch*—the sheer banana-republic irresponsibility of his plans hasn't been widely appreciated. That $674 billion tax cut you've heard about literally isn't the half of it. Even according to its own lowball estimates, the administration wants $1.5 trillion in tax cuts over the next decade—more than it pushed through in 2001. Another $575 billion or so will be needed to fix the alternative minimum tax—something officials have said they'll do, but haven't put in the budget.

The administration has used gimmicks to postpone most of the cost of these tax cuts until after 2008—and whaddya know, the Office of Management and Budget has suddenly stopped talking about 10-year projections and now officially looks only five years ahead. But there are long-term projections tucked away in the back of the budget; they're overoptimistic, but even so they suggest a fiscal disaster once the baby boomers start collecting benefits from Social Security and Medicare. ("We will not pass along our problems to other Congresses, other presidents, other generations," declared Mr. Bush in the State of the Union. And with a straight face, too.)

So where does Mr. Greenspan come in? Next week he will testify before the Senate Banking Committee. Will he, at long last, acknowledge the administration's fecklessness?

Mr. Greenspan must know that many people, whatever they say in public, now regard him as a partisan hack. That very much includes Republicans, who assume that he will support anything Mr. Bush proposes. What he does next week will determine whether that perception sticks.

He has certainly run out of excuses. As a famous fiscal scold, he can't adopt the administration's "deficits, schmeficits" approach. And he can't make the supply-side claim that tax cuts actually increase revenues, when just two years ago he argued for a tax cut to reduce the surplus.

If Mr. Greenspan nonetheless finds ways to rationalize Mr. Bush's irresponsibility, or if he takes refuge in Delphic utterances that could mean anything or nothing, history will remember him as a man who urged hard choices on others, but refused to make hard choices himself.

This may be Alan Greenspan's last chance to save his reputation—and the country's solvency.

# CHAPTER 7

## $2 - 1 = 4$

### THE PIG IN THE PYTHON

*June 21, 2000*

Demographers describe the baby-boom generation as "the pig in the python": a huge bulge in an otherwise skinny age distribution, gradually moving down the distribution as the boomers age. As the pig's snout approaches the python's nether regions, it poses two distinct policy problems: a narrow "financial" problem and a broader "real" problem. But the debate in the presidential campaign doesn't seem to be about either.

The "financial" problem is how to pay for Social Security. This problem is a legacy of Social Security's pay-as-you-go past: because the baby boomers' contributions were used to provide generous benefits to earlier generations, there isn't enough money in the system to pay the benefits promised to the boomers themselves. The good news is that solving this financial problem isn't all that difficult. Despite the apocalyptic rhetoric you sometimes hear, affordable injections of money would allow the system to run untroubled for at least 50 more years. It's just a matter of facing up to facts.

The "real" problem is that in a few decades the age distribution of the U.S. as a whole will look like that of Florida today. How will a relatively small number of workers be able to produce enough both to live well themselves and to provide the huge population of retirees with the standard of living it expects?

This problem is much harder to solve. The only answer—other than allowing large-scale immigration—is to make tomorrow's workers as productive as possible. We can hope for a technological fix; with smart enough machines, who needs workers? But a responsible government would meanwhile try to ensure that national savings—public plus private—are high, so that future workers are well equipped with capital and not burdened with large foreign debts.

Alas, the campaign seems to be revolving around a quite different issue: the perception that Americans get too low a return on their contributions to Social Security. As I've explained in earlier columns, the implicit return on Social Security contributions is low only because today's workers are in effect being taxed to pay the system's debts from the past. You may not like that, just as you may not like the fact that 15 percent of your federal tax dollar goes to pay interest on a debt mainly run up in the 80's and early 90's. But in both cases the debts are a fact of life.

Yet the salesmanship surrounding George W. Bush's Social Security plan is all about the meaningless contrast between the returns that an unburdened individual can get on investments and the implicit return that a very-much-burdened Social Security system can offer. And Al Gore's new plan for subsidized retirement accounts also isn't about the real problems; it's a response to that salesmanship.

That said, Mr. Gore's plan could have been worse. It won't

break the budget; it probably will encourage somewhat more private saving. And, like Social Security itself, it will be progressive—that is, it will tend to narrow disparities in wealth.

You also have to give Mr. Gore some points for honesty. The details of his plan are fully spelled out; he has also come clean about how he will extend the life of the Social Security system— namely, by transferring money over from the general budget. By contrast, Mr. Bush has said nothing about how much he plans to reduce benefits in return for allowing workers to invest their contributions elsewhere, let alone how he will deal with the overhang of obligations from the past. All he offers are magic asterisks: "*details to be provided later." My guess is that if and when Mr. Bush finally does provide the details, the size of the proposed benefit cuts will start a political firestorm, forcing him to use general revenue to rescue Social Security after all. But that won't happen until after the election.

And where will the money come from? Remember that Mr. Bush is also proposing huge tax cuts. Aside from eliminating a surplus that might have been used to help Social Security, those cuts will encourage the nation as a whole to consume more and save less, exactly the opposite of what an aging society should be doing.

Meanwhile the pig is still in the python, inching inexorably toward its destiny. Is anyone paying attention?

# PRESCRIPTION FOR FAILURE

*July 26, 2000*

In denouncing President Clinton's plan to extend Medicare coverage to prescription drugs, and in touting their own counter-proposal, Republicans have rolled out the usual rhetoric. They excoriate the administration plan as a bureaucratic, "one size fits all" solution. They claim that their plan offers more choice.

And for once their claims are absolutely right. The Republican plan does offer more choice.

Unfortunately, this is one of those cases in which more choice is actually bad for everyone. In fact, by trying to give people more choices the Republican plan would end up denying them any choice at all.

Where Democrats want to offer drug coverage directly to Medicare recipients, the Republicans propose to offer money to private insurance companies instead, to entice them into serving the senior market. But all indications are that this plan is a non-starter. Insurance companies themselves are very skeptical; there haven't been many cases in which an industry's own lobbyists tell Congress that they don't want a subsidy, but this is one of them. And an attempt by Nevada to put a similar plan into effect has been a complete dud—not a single insurer licensed to operate in the state has shown any interest in offering coverage.

The reason is "adverse selection"—a problem that afflicts many markets, but insurance markets in particular. Basically, adverse selection is the reason you shouldn't buy insurance from companies that say "no medical exam necessary": when insurance is sold to good and bad prospects at the same price, the bad risks drive out the good.

Why can't the elderly buy prescription drug insurance? Suppose an insurance company were to offer a prescription drug plan, with premiums high enough to cover the cost of insuring an average Medicare recipient. It turns out that annual spending on prescription drugs varies hugely among retirees—depending on whether they have chronic conditions, and which ones. Healthy retirees, who know that their bills won't be that high, would be unwilling to buy insurance that costs enough to cover the bills of the average senior—which means that the insurance plan would attract only those with above-average bills, meaning higher premiums, driving still more healthy people away, and so on until nobody is left. Insurance companies understand this logic very well—and are therefore simply not interested in getting into the market in the first place.

The root of the problem is that private drug insurance could be offered at a reasonable price only if people had to commit to paying the necessary premiums before they knew whether they would need expensive drugs. Such policies cannot be offered if those who find out later that they don't require such drugs can choose to stop paying what turn out to be unnecessarily high premiums.

And while in principle one could write a contract that denies the insured the choice of opting out, just try to imagine the legal complications if a private company tried to force a healthy retiree to keep paying high premiums for decades on end, even though he turns out not to need the company's benefits. As a practical matter the only way to avoid this opt-out problem, to enforce the kind of till-death-do-us-part commitment needed to make drug insurance work, is to make the coverage part of a government program.

All of this is more or less textbook economics. So why are Republican leaders insisting on a plan that almost nobody familiar with the issue thinks will work?

Cynical politics no doubt plays an important role.

So does money; the insurance industry is by and large against the Republican plan, but the pharmaceutical industry is very anxious to avoid anything that might push down drug prices, and fears that the administration plan will do just that. But sincere fanaticism also enters the picture. Republican leaders in the House, in particular, are true believers in the miraculous powers of the free market—they are in effect members of a sect that believes that markets will work even when the businessmen actually involved say they won't, and that government involvement is evil even where conventional analysis says it is necessary.

The Republican plan is, in short, an assertion of a faith that transcends mundane economic logic.

But what's in it for us heathens?

# A RETIREMENT FABLE

*October 11, 2000*

There once was a land where people lived only two years. In the first year they worked; in the second year they lived off their personal savings.

There came a time when the government decided to help out the elderly. So it instituted a system called Social Security. Every young, working individual would pay a tax, which would be used to pay benefits that same year to each older, retired individual.

For the first generation of beneficiaries, Social Security was a great deal. They had not been obliged to pay in when young, yet got the benefits anyway. But subsequent generations misunderstood the system. They thought of their required contributions as investments, though they really were tax payments, needed to pay benefits to their parents' generation. And they imagined that they could get higher returns investing that money in the market.

So eventually an ambitious politician came along, declaring: "It's your money! I trust the people, not the government!" He said he would let workers invest half their contributions themselves. When critics tried to point out that this money had already been promised to older citizens (whose own contributions had been used to pay benefits to the previous generation of retirees), they were drowned out by chants of "No fuzzy numbers!" And so the scheme was put into effect.

And the next year Social Security went broke. Without

enough money coming in, retirees could not be paid their promised benefits.

I wish I could say that this fable oversimplifies this year's Social Security debate in some important way. But it really is that simple, and George W. Bush's proposal—which calls for putting part of Social Security contributions into individual accounts, without any replacement for the diverted funds— really is that irresponsible. Because Americans live more than two years, the drama will take longer to play out. Social Security won't go broke for about 30 years, so the victims will be those who are currently middle-aged, not those who are already retired. But the crisis will come much sooner, as the impending disaster becomes obvious.

Mr. Bush has made an important political discovery. Really big misstatements, it turns out, cannot be effectively challenged, because voters can't believe that a man who seems so likable would do that sort of thing. In last week's debate Mr. Bush again declared that he plans to spend a quarter of the surplus on popular new programs, even though his own budget shows that he plans to spend less than half that much. ("No fuzzy numbers!" roared the crowd—but these are his own numbers.) And he insists that he has a plan to save Social Security, when his actual proposal, as it stands, would bankrupt the system.

But aren't there good economists, even experts on Social Security, who support Mr. Bush's proposal? Think of it as a Faustian bargain—selling their souls not for power or wealth (maybe that too, but that's not my department) but for reform.

For there is a good case for Social Security reform—if we are prepared to pay the price. The current system in effect promises today's workers that future generations will take care of them, just as they are taking care of today's retirees. As a Bush adviser, Martin Feldstein, has pointed out, this makes people feel richer than they really are, leading them to consume too much and save too little.

But to fix this problem would take a lot of money—money to pay off the system's existing obligations. Or to put it differently (making the same point from a different angle): Since the problem with Social Security is that it makes people feel artificially rich, any real reform has to make them feel poorer. But that, of course, is not what Mr. Bush is selling.

What economists who support his proposal presumably believe is that after the election this can all be fixed. When the real plan is announced, it will actually make sense.

But it's hard to see how. Try to imagine a victorious Mr. Bush explaining that he has to slash benefits after all, or abandoning his tax cut so that he has enough money to pay for Social Security reform.

What is certain is that Mr. Bush's actual Social Security proposal would bankrupt the system.

That's not a fuzzy number—it's a cold, hard fact.

# NO GOOD DEED

*November 5, 2000*

It started with a good deed. Back in the 1980's Congress decided
to act responsibly, making early provision for a crisis that,
though predictable, was still 30 years away.

Until the 1980's Social Security had been run on a pure pay-
as-you-go basis: just about all of each year's tax receipts were
used to pay current benefits. But by 1980 it was already clear
that, beginning some 30 years later, this system would run into
big trouble. The baby boomers are the villains: once the
boomers start to retire, the number of workers paying into
Social Security will plateau, while the number of retirees the
system must support will soar. Right now there are about 3.4
workers for every retiree; by 2030 there will be only two. So a
pay-as-you-go system would be forced into drastic tax
increases, drastic benefit cuts, or both.

What Congress did in the 1980's was to raise Social Security
taxes—a moderate increase, two percentage points—in order to
ward off much more severe consequences later. In the runup to
the demographic crisis the system would build up a large
reserve, postponing the day of reckoning, perhaps even putting
it off entirely. It may not be a permanent solution, but it has
given us a lot of breathing room. The system can run as is until
at least 2037; modest additional measures could easily extend
its life to 2050 and beyond.

But any political action that takes such a long view risks

being undermined by later politicians, who will be tempted to raid the cookie jar. Which brings us to the current dispute.

George W. Bush wants to rescind that two-point tax increase. True, he doesn't propose to give it back in cash, but he wants to put it into personal accounts, which would belong mainly to young workers and therefore be unavailable to support the currently middle-aged workers that reserve was supposed to protect. And?

For surely there must be an "and." If the money that was supposed to provide benefits to the baby boomers is being used for another purpose, we have to do something else—cut benefits, transfer in additional money from other sources, something. Right?

But Mr. Bush has never finished his sentence. His ads continue to proclaim that he will put Social Security on a sound financial footing—but his proposal does nothing, literally nothing, to shore up the system's finances. It doesn't even try. This isn't even a debatable issue—there are no measures to debate.

I'm not sure why the press corps has done such a bad job of making this clear. Maybe reporters just don't dare say that the governor has no clothes, that a key proposal by the man who may well be president contains no measures that even try to do what he claims that proposal will do.

Even now most coverage makes excuses for Mr. Bush's nonplan, saying that it doesn't threaten the benefits of today's retirees because there is still enough money to maintain benefits at current levels for 20 years or so. But that's moving the goal posts. The whole demand for reform of Social Security has been driven by charges that the system is unsustainable in the long run—now, suddenly, we're supposed to accept a "reform" that actually cuts the system's remaining life by 14 years?

Anyway, what do you think would really happen? Would the Social Security Administration really continue to pay full benefits for the next two decades—then suddenly, one day, make an announcement: "Sorry, folks, the money's all gone. We're cutting benefits 40 percent, effective immediately"? The reality is that the pressure to cut benefits would begin as soon as the diversion of taxes into individual accounts was put into effect; many of today's retirees would feel the pinch.

Maybe, if Mr. Bush wins, he will reveal a secret plan—one that pretty much has to involve benefit cuts, because where else can he find the money? (The budget surplus will have been eliminated by tax cuts.) Or maybe he will tell a bipartisan commission to devise a plan, and then blame the Democrats for the commission's inability to find a way to create something from nothing.

It's ironic. The responsible actions of Congress in the 1980's set the stage, it turns out, for a blatantly irresponsible political ploy. But you know the saying: No good deed goes unpunished.

## 2016 AND ALL THAT

### July 22, 2001

I knew that the commission on Social Security reform appointed by George W. Bush would produce a slanted report, one designed to bully Congress into privatizing the system. But the draft report released last week is sheer, mean-spirited nonsense.

The commission, in an attempt to sow panic, claims that Social Security is in imminent peril—that the system will be in crisis as soon as 2016. That's wildly at odds with the standard projection, which says that Social Security reserves will last until 2038. And even that projection is based on quite pessimistic assumptions about future economic growth and hence future payroll tax receipts. If you use more optimistic assumptions—say, the assumptions in the budget forecasts that were used to justify Mr. Bush's tax cut—the system will still be financially sound in 2075.

So how did the commission reach its pessimistic conclusion? Through a truly Orwellian exercise in doublethink—the art of believing two mutually contradictory things at the same time.

It's true that in 2016, according to (pessimistic) projections, benefit payments will start to exceed payroll tax receipts. By then, however, the Social Security system will have accumulated a multitrillion-dollar "trust fund." Just as a private pension fund uses earnings on its assets to pay benefits, the Social Security system can use earnings from this trust fund to pay benefits. And that trust fund will extend the life of the system for decades, perhaps indefinitely.

But the commission declares that these accumulated assets aren't "real," and don't count as resources available to pay future benefits. Why? Because they are invested in government bonds—perfectly good assets when they are accumulated by private pension funds but worthless, says the commission, when accumulated by a government agency.

Does this make any sense? There is a school of thought that says that Social Security shouldn't have a separate budget, that Social Security receipts should be regarded simply as part of general revenue, and outlays as part of general expenditure. But in that case it's hard to see why we should get worked up about 2016: who cares if the payroll tax, which is only one of many taxes, collects less money than the government spends on retirement benefits, which are only one of many government expenses? Social Security benefits can be paid out of the general budget—a transfer of revenue that is clearly justified if payroll tax receipts have meanwhile been used to pay off the national debt, releasing large sums that would otherwise have been consumed by interest payments.

Alternatively, you could say that for political reasons it's important that Social Security have its own separate account. But in that case, we should count government bonds in the trust fund as real assets, just as we would if Social Security were a private pension fund. (Here's a proposal: let's launder the trust fund by putting it in private banks, which then buy government bonds. Will that make the assets "real"?)

So the commission is trying to have it both ways. When Social Security runs surpluses, it doesn't get any credit because it's just part of the government. But when it runs deficits, Social Security is on its own. This twisted logic in effect expropriates all of the extra money workers have paid into the system since 1983, when Senator Daniel Patrick Moynihan, among others, pushed through an increase in payroll taxes—an increase whose purpose was to build up the trust fund that the commission, co-chaired by Mr. Moynihan, now says isn't real.

And how big will the Social Security deficit be once the trust fund has been expropriated? The commission says 37 percent of payroll tax receipts, which sounds immense; but that's only about 2 percent of GDP. That's an interesting number: it's about what the federal government now pays in interest on its debt—the debt that Social Security surpluses are being used to pay off.

Oh, and there's another budget item that's about the same size as the putative Social Security shortfall: the Bush tax cut, which will eventually reduce revenue by about 1.7 percent of GDP.

There is a case for reforming Social Security; there is even a case for privatization. But we can't have a meaningful debate about reform unless the parties to the debate are willing to discuss the issues honestly. And the members of the commission, including Mr. Moynihan, have just disqualified themselves.

# SINS OF COMMISSION

*July 25, 2001*

You began saving for your retirement 18 years ago. You could have bought stocks and corporate bonds, but your nephew persuaded you to keep it in the family. So ever since you have been lending him money. Your contributions helped him through some bad financial patches, and recently he used money he borrowed from you to pay off his mortgage.

But now he tells you that you had better start investing for your retirement. After all, he says, you don't have any real assets. "What about the money you owe me?" you ask. "That's not a real asset," he replies. "It's just a promise. The only way I could honor that promise is by earning more or spending less money on myself. And you can't expect me to do that." Meanwhile, you happen to know that he has ordered himself a yacht—and that the payments on that yacht would be enough to cover the debt he owes you.

Most people would regard your nephew's attitude as inexcusable. But George W. Bush's handpicked commission on the reform of Social Security thinks your nephew has the right idea. The Social Security system has been running surpluses since 1983, when the payroll tax was increased in order to build up a trust fund out of which future benefits could be paid. These surpluses could have been invested in stocks or corporate bonds, but it seemed safer and less problematic to buy U.S. government debt instead. The system now has $1.2 trillion in its rapidly growing trust fund. But the commission says that the government bonds in that trust fund aren't real assets.

That's like saying that when you paid off your nephew's mortgage, you did nothing to improve his cash flow.

Every dollar that the Social Security system puts in government bonds—as opposed to investing in other assets, such as corporate bonds—is a dollar that the federal government doesn't have to borrow from other sources. If the Social Security trust fund hadn't used its accumulated surpluses to buy $1.2 trillion in government bonds, the government would have had to borrow those funds elsewhere. And instead of crediting the trust fund with $65 billion in interest this year, the government would have had to cough up at least that much extra in actual, cash interest payments to private bondholders. So the trust fund makes a real contribution to the federal budget. Doesn't that make it a real asset?

Because the trust fund has been used to pay off debt, it reduces the amount the government spends on debt service, and makes it easier to pay benefits to retirees. Still, it's true that when the Social Security system starts cashing in its i.o.u.'s the federal government will have to have higher taxes and/or lower spending than it would if it could simply renege on its promises. But are we actually, as the commission claims, talking about a crushing burden?

Here's some arithmetic: If we had 2040 demographics today (48 retirees per 100 workers, instead of the current 30), Social Security benefit payments this year would exceed payroll tax receipts by about $180 billion. That sounds like a lot. But it so happens that if the Bush tax cut passed two months ago (your nephew's new yacht) were fully phased in today, it would reduce revenue this year by about $170 billion.

Yesterday the ever more partisan Alan Greenspan—who, 18 years ago, led the commission that increased payroll taxes and thus created the Social Security surplus—told a Senate hearing that the Bush tax cut was "quite modest." Well, if it's a modest tax cut, then the sums Social Security will need to cover its cash shortfall are also modest. You can't have it both ways.

But having it both ways—what George Orwell called double-think—is what this commission report is all about. We're supposed to believe that Social Security surpluses are meaningless, because it's all one budget, but that Social Security deficits are a terrible thing, because the program must stand on its own. We're supposed to believe that $170 billion a year is a modest sum if it's a tax cut for the affluent, but that it's an insupportable burden on the budget if it's an obligation to retirees.

And we're supposed to listen seriously to the recommendations of a commission that has just issued a biased, internally inconsistent and intellectually dishonest report.

# BAD MEDICINE

*March 19, 2002*

Sunday's front-page story in *The Times* on doctors who shun patients with Medicare may have been alarming enough; it seems that recent cuts in Medicare payments are inducing many doctors to avoid treating Medicare recipients at all. But this is just the beginning of a struggle that will soon dominate American politics.

Think of it as the collision between an irresistible force (the growing cost of health care) and an immovable object (the determination of America's conservative movement to down-size government). For the moment the Bush administration and its allies still won't admit that there is any conflict between their promises to retirees and their small-government ideology. But we're already past the stage where this conflict can be hidden with fudged numbers. The effort to live within unrealistically low targets for Medicare expenses has already translated into unrealistically low payments to health-care providers. And it gets worse from here.

Why do health-care costs keep on rising? It's not because doctors and hospitals are greedy; it's because of medical progress. More and more conditions that once lay beyond doctors' reach can now be treated, adding years to the lives of patients and greatly increasing the quality of those years—but at ever greater expense. A triple coronary bypass does a lot more for you than a nice bedside manner, but it costs a lot more, too.

During the 1990's the upward trend in health-care costs seemed to level off. But it's now clear that this was a one-time cost squeeze due to the shift to H.M.O.'s. Now medical costs have resumed their upward march.

If medicine were purely a private matter, medical progress would pose no more of a dilemma than, say, progress in home entertainment systems. But in fact the United States, like every advanced country, treats essential health care as a right, not a privilege. Our Medicare/Medicaid combination provides this right somewhat haphazardly; still, the intent of our system is that nobody should be denied life-saving treatment for lack of funds.

Why don't we just leave medical care up to individuals? Basically, even in the United States there are limits to how much inequality the public is prepared to tolerate. It's one thing if the rich can afford bigger houses or fancier vacations than ordinary families; Americans accept such differences cheerfully. But a society in which rich people get their medical problems solved, while ordinary people die from them, is too harsh even for us.

And so we have Medicare and Medicaid. And the public overwhelmingly supports the extension of Medicare to include prescription drugs, for the same reason: it seems wrong to most Americans that drugs that make a big difference to people's lives should be available only to those wealthy enough to pay for those drugs out of pocket. Including drug coverage in Medicare is not so much a matter of extending the program as of remaining true to its original intent.

But meeting the public's expectations for medical care—that is, ensuring that every American, and in particular every retired American, gets essential care—will require a lot of government spending. And the conservative movement in general, and the Bush administration in particular, are not prepared to make the money available; after all, government spending must ultimately be paid for with taxes.

Yet they dare not say openly that they are prepared to deny essential health care to those who cannot afford it. So what can they do?

The Bush administration is still trying to fake it; the budget proposal it released last month had health-care economists rubbing their eyes. It assumed a far lower rate of growth in Medicare expenses than anyone else thinks plausible—over all, it budgeted $300 billion less over the next decade than the nonpartisan Congressional Budget Office projects will be needed. And it also repeated the implausible claim that we can have prescription drug insurance on the cheap—setting aside half or less what others think such a program will cost.

But we have already reached the point at which we must either come up with more money or deny health care to retirees. The moral of Sunday's story is that Medicare payments have already been squeezed beyond their limits, to the point where recipients can't find doctors willing to take them. Something will have to give, and soon.

# FEAR OF ALL SUMS

*June 21, 2002*

"It is difficult to get a man to understand something," wrote Upton Sinclair, "when his salary depends upon his not understanding it." To make sense of what passes for debate over Social Security reform, one must realize that advocates of privatization—of replacing the current system, at least in part, with a system of personal accounts—are determined not to understand basic arithmetic. Otherwise they would have to admit that such accounts would weaken, not strengthen, the system's finances.

Social Security as we know it is a system in which each generation's payroll taxes are mainly used to support the previous generation's retirement. If contributions from younger workers go into personal accounts instead, the problem should be obvious: who will pay benefits to today's retirees and older workers? It's just arithmetic: $2 - 1 = 1$. So privatization creates a financial hole that must be filled by slashing benefits, providing large financial transfers from the rest of the government or both.

During the 2000 election campaign, George W. Bush was able to get away with the nonsensical claim that private accounts would not only yield high, low-risk returns, but save Social Security at the same time. For whatever reason, few reporters pointed out that he was claiming that $2 - 1 = 4$. But when it came time to produce concrete plans, the arithmetic could no longer be avoided.

# 2 − 1 = 4

Sure enough, the plans laid out by Mr. Bush's Commission to Strengthen Social Security, though presented as confusingly as possible, involve both severe benefit cuts and huge "magic asterisks," infusions of trillions of dollars from an undisclosed location. The extent of the damage is documented in a new Center on Budget and Policy Priorities report by Peter Diamond of the Massachusetts Institute of Technology and Peter Orszag of the Brookings Institution. (Mr. Diamond, who is one of the world's most eminent economists, and is arguably the world's leading expert on retirement systems, was my colleague when I taught at M.I.T.)

The Diamond-Orszag report is informative; even I was surprised by a couple of revelations. For example, the mystery money infusions that the commission assumes will somehow be forthcoming are almost enough to preserve Social Security exactly as it is, with no benefit cuts, forever. Also, the commission's plans include severe cuts in disability benefits, a crucial part of Social Security that privatizers have a habit of overlooking.

But in a way, the most interesting thing about the new report is the administration's reaction.

Charles Blahous, who was executive director of the commission and is now on the White House staff, quickly responded with a memo best described as hysterical. The number of non sequiturs and misrepresentations Mr. Blahous manages to squeeze into just a few pages may set a record. Among other things, he angrily accuses Mr. Diamond and Mr. Orszag of failing to address issues they cover quite clearly. Of one such accusation, Mr. Orszag remarks drily that "in his haste to issue a response to our paper, the Executive Director appears to have overlooked the final box . . . which addresses precisely that issue and provides the comparisons he requested (though he may not be pleased with the results). We direct his attention to that box."

A sample of Mr. Blahous's tactics is his insistence that private accounts don't weaken Social Security, because diverting money from the trust fund into those accounts doesn't reduce the total sum of money available—if you still count private accounts as part of the total. As they say in the technical literature, "Well, duh." Of course the money doesn't disappear—but it is no longer available to pay benefits to older Americans, whose own Social Security contributions were used to pay benefits to previous generations.

As the facts about Social Security privatization gradually emerge, the general strategy of the privatizers seems to be to keep the public confused as long as possible. Indeed, Republicans are now being told to deny that personal accounts—which expose their owners to all the risks of any private investment—constitute "privatization." "Do not be complicit in Democratic demagoguery," urges one party memo. So it looks like a duck and walks like a duck, but it isn't a duck—not until after the next election.

But whatever they say, it is a duck. And the administration economists who claim that privatization will strengthen Social Security are, more than ever, revealed as quacks.

*Part Three*

# VICTORS AND SPOILS

H ow did we get here? How did the American political system, which produced such reasonable economic leadership during the 1990s, lead us into our current morass of dishonesty and irresponsibility? This is not a question I ever expected to be answering: I still don't regard myself primarily as a political columnist. In fact, as I explained in the Introduction to this book, I originally expected my *New York Times* column to be mainly focused on business and international economics, not domestic politics. But as the wreckage accumulates, I've found it necessary to try to explain just why our policies are so bad.

A partial answer, I believe, is that American politics has become highly polarized: the center did not hold. Underlying that political polarization is the growing inequality of income. The result is a form of class warfare—driven not by attempts of the poor to soak the rich, but by the efforts of an economic elite to expand its privileges. Chapter 8 looks at the polarization of American politics along economic lines, paralleling the polarization of the income distribution. It also described how ideas that would have been beyond the pale not long ago—inherited privilege is good, poor people don't pay enough taxes—have been edging their way into political discourse.

The crusade against the welfare state rests on an ideology that denigrates almost everything, other than national defense, that the government does. Today's conservatives want to dislodge the government even from traditional roles like environmental protection, securities regulation, and air traffic control. Some—including the *Times* editorial page—thought that the terrorist attack on September 11, which bore no resemblance to conventional military conflict, might change that attitude. But no—as chapter 9 documents, the Bush administration and its Congressional allies were unmoved. For example, only days after September 11, they still tried to prevent a public takeover of airline security. And after a few days of effusive sympathy for New York and photo-ops with firemen, promises of aid began to be broken. In February 2003, the logic of privatization reached the point of absurdity: Having done almost nothing to strengthen homeland security, the administration urged the public to protect itself with duct tape and plastic sheeting.

It's understandable why many people expected the Bush administration to scale back its domestic agenda after September 11. After all, the administration said it was war—and tradition says that war is not a time to pursue policies that divide the nation. Most famously, after Pearl Harbor FDR declared that "Dr. New Deal" had to be replaced with "Dr. Win the War": he put his political agenda on hold in the interest of national unity.

After September 11, however, the Bush administration did the opposite: It treated terrorism as a partisan political opportunity. Few things I have written have generated as much hate mail as the columns in which I accused the administration of exploiting September 11 for political gain, of wrapping itself in the flag while it sought weakened environmental regulation, tax cuts for corporations and the rich, and above all an upper hand in the midterm election. But as chapter 10 explains, exploitation began within hours after the attack—and gradually it became apparent, not just to me but to a growing number of other observers, that we had some very unscrupulous people running the country. Every administration contains its share of cynical political operators—without them, even the best man has no chance of achieving high office. But this administration seems to have nothing but cynical political operators, who use national tragedy for political gain, don't even try to come to grips with real problems, and figure that someone else will clean up the mess they leave behind.

So how did we end up being ruled by these people? Chapter 11 is a look at the dirty not-so-secret secret of recent American politics: the increasing manipulation of the media and the political process by lavishly funded right-wing groups. Yes, Virginia, there is a vast right-wing conspiracy. It's not even especially hidden: anyone with a modem and some spare time can inform himself about the network of institutions that systematically harass prominent liberals and bully news sources that don't toe the line. (I have, of course, been a target myself.) But it isn't often discussed in major newspapers; here you can read about it.

# CHAPTER 8

# Things Pull Apart

## AMERICA THE POLARIZED

*January 4, 2002*

When Congress returns to Washington, the battles will resume—and each party will accuse the other of partisanship. Why can't they just get along?

Because fundamental issues are at stake, and the parties are as far apart on those issues as they have ever been.

A recent article in *Slate* led me to Keith Poole and Howard Rosenthal, political scientists who use data on Congressional voting to create "maps" of politicians' ideological positions. They find that a representative's votes can be predicted quite accurately by his position in two dimensions, one corresponding to race issues, the other a left vs. right economic scale reflecting issues such as marginal tax rates and the generosity of benefits to the poor.

And they also find—not too surprisingly—that the center did not hold. Ralph Nader may sneer at "Republicrats," but Democrats and Republicans have diverged sharply since the 1980's, and are now further apart on economic issues than they have been since the early 20th century.

Whose position changed? Tom Daschle doesn't seem markedly more liberal than, say, the late Tip O'Neill. On the other hand, Tom DeLay, who will soon be House majority leader, is clearly to the right of previous Republican leaders. In short, casual observation suggests that American politics has become polarized because Republicans have shifted to the right, and Democrats haven't followed them. And sure enough, the Poole-Rosenthal numbers that show a divergence between the parties also show that this divergence reflects a Republican move toward more conservative economic policies, while Democrats have more or less stayed put. As people like James Jeffords and Lincoln Chafee have found, it has become very hard to be what we used to call a moderate Republican.

But why did the Republicans move to the right?

It could be a matter of sheer intellectual conviction. Republicans have realized that low taxes and small government are good for everyone, and Democrats just don't get it. But ideas tend to take root when the soil has been fertilized by social and economic trends. Dr. Poole suggests that the most likely source of political polarization is economic polarization: the sharply widening inequality of income and wealth.

I know from experience that even mentioning income distribution leads to angry accusations of "class warfare," but anyway here's what the (truly) nonpartisan Congressional Budget Office recently found: Adjusting for inflation, the income of families in the middle of the U.S. income distribution rose from $41,400 in 1979 to $45,100 in 1997, a 9 percent increase. Meanwhile the income of families in the top 1 percent rose from $420,200 to $1.016 million, a 140 percent increase. Or to put it another way, the income of families in the top 1 percent was 10 times that of typical families in 1979, and 23 times and rising in 1997.

It would be surprising indeed if this tectonic shift in the economic landscape weren't reflected in politics.

You might have expected the concentration of income at the top to provoke populist demands to soak the rich. But as I've said, both casual observation and the Poole-Rosenthal numbers tell us that the Democrats haven't moved left, the Republicans have moved right. Indeed, the Republicans have moved so far to the right that ordinary voters have trouble taking it in; as I pointed out in an earlier column, focus groups literally refused to believe accurate descriptions of the stimulus bill that House Republican leaders passed on a party-line vote back in October.

Why has the response to rising inequality been a drive to reduce taxes on the rich? Good question. It's not a simple matter of rich people voting themselves a better deal: there just aren't enough of them. To understand political trends in the United States we probably need to think about campaign finance, lobbying and the general power of money to shape political debate.

In any case, the moral of this story is that the political struggles in Washington right now are not petty squabbles. The right is on the offensive; the left—occupying the position formerly known as the center—wants to hold the line. Many commentators still delude themselves with the comforting notion that all this partisanship is a temporary aberration. Sorry, guys: this is the way it's going to be, for the foreseeable future. Get used to it.

# THE SONS ALSO RISE

*November 22, 2002*

America, we all know, is the land of opportunity. Your success in life depends on your ability and drive, not on who your father was.

Just ask the Bush brothers. Talk to Elizabeth Cheney, who holds a specially created State Department job, or her husband, chief counsel of the Office of Management and Budget.

Interview Eugene Scalia, the top lawyer at the Labor Department, and Janet Rehnquist, inspector general at the Department of Health and Human Services. And don't forget to check in with William Kristol, editor of *The Weekly Standard*, and the conservative commentator John Podhoretz.

What's interesting is how little comment, let alone criticism, this roll call has occasioned. It might be just another case of kid-gloves treatment by the media, but I think it's a symptom of a broader phenomenon: inherited status is making a comeback.

It has always been good to have a rich or powerful father. Last week my Princeton colleague Alan Krueger wrote a column for *The Times* surveying statistical studies that debunk the mythology of American social mobility. "If the United States stands out in comparison with other countries," he wrote, "it is in having a more static distribution of income across generations with fewer opportunities for advancement." And Kevin Phillips, in his book *Wealth and Democracy*, shows that robber-baron fortunes have been far more persistent than legend would have it.

But the past is only prologue. According to one study cited by Mr. Krueger, the heritability of status has been increasing in recent decades. And that's just the beginning. Underlying economic, social and political trends will give the children of today's wealthy a huge advantage over those who chose the wrong parents.

For one thing, there's more privilege to pass on. Thirty years ago the C.E.O. of a major company was a bureaucrat—well paid, but not truly wealthy. He couldn't give either his position or a large fortune to his heirs. Today's imperial C.E.O.'s, by contrast, will leave vast estates behind—and they are often able to give their children lucrative jobs, too. More broadly, the spectacular increase in American inequality has made the gap between the rich and the middle class wider, and hence more difficult to cross, than it was in the past.

Meanwhile, one key doorway to upward mobility—a good education system, available to all—has been closing. More and more, ambitious parents feel that a public school education is a dead end. It's telling that Jack Grubman, the former Salomon Smith Barney analyst, apparently sold his soul not for personal wealth but for two places in the right nursery school. Alas, most American souls aren't worth enough to get the kids into the 92nd Street Y.

Also, the heritability of status will be mightily reinforced by the repeal of the estate tax—a prime example of the odd way in which public policy and public opinion have shifted in favor of measures that benefit the wealthy, even as our society becomes increasingly class-ridden.

It wasn't always thus. The influential dynasties of the 20th century, like the Kennedys, the Rockefellers and, yes, the Sulzbergers, faced a public suspicious of inherited position; they overcame that suspicion by demonstrating a strong sense of noblesse oblige, justifying their existence by standing for high principles. Indeed, the Kennedy legend has a whiff of Bonnie Prince Charlie about it; the rightful heirs were also perceived as defenders of the downtrodden against the powerful.

But today's heirs feel no need to demonstrate concern for those less fortunate. On the contrary, they are often avid defenders of the powerful against the downtrodden. Mr. Scalia's principal personal claim to fame is his crusade against regulations that protect workers from ergonomic hazards, while Ms. Rehnquist has attracted controversy because of her efforts to weaken the punishment of health-care companies found to have committed fraud.

The official ideology of America's elite remains one of meritocracy, just as our political leadership pretends to be populist. But that won't last. Soon enough, our society will rediscover the importance of good breeding, and the vulgarity of talented upstarts.

For years, opinion leaders have told us that it's all about family values. And it is—but it will take a while before most people realize that they meant the value of coming from the right family.

# HEY, LUCKY DUCKIES!

*December 3, 2002*

Carping critics of the conservative movement have been known to say that its economic program consists of little more than tax cuts, tax cuts and more tax cuts. I may even have said that myself.

If so, I apologize. Emboldened by the midterm election, key conservative ideologues have now declared their support for tax increases—but only for people with low incomes.

The public debut of this idea came, as such things often do, on the editorial page of *The Wall Street Journal.* The page's editors, it seems, are upset that some low-income people pay little or nothing in income taxes. Not, mind you, because of the lost revenue, but because these "lucky duckies"—the *Journal*'s term, not mine—might not be feeling a proper hatred for the government.

The *Journal* considers a hypothetical ducky who earns only $12,000 a year—some guys have all the luck!—and therefore, according to the editorial, "pays a little less than 4% of income in taxes." Not surprisingly, that statement is a deliberate misrepresentation; the calculation refers only to income taxes. If you include payroll and sales taxes, a worker earning $12,000 probably pays well over 20 percent of income in taxes. But who's counting?

What's interesting, however, is what the *Journal* finds wrong with this picture: The worker's taxes aren't "enough to get his or her blood boiling with rage."

In case you're wondering what this is about, it's an internal squabble of the right. The *Journal* is terrified that future tax cuts might include token concessions to ordinary families; it wants to ensure that everything goes to corporations and the wealthy. But the political theory revealed by the editorial—policy should be nasty to people with low incomes, lest they have any good feelings about government—may explain a lot of what has been happening lately.

For example, House Republicans recently refused to extend unemployment insurance. Their inaction means that later this month more than 800,000 workers will receive Merry Christmas letters from the government, telling them that their benefits have been cut off. This would have been a harsh decision under any circumstances. At a time when the administration says we need further tax cuts to stimulate demand, slashing the incomes of the very households most likely to cut their spending sounds like a lose-lose proposition. But once you realize that pain is good because it makes citizens hate their government, it all makes sense.

An even better example is the failure of Congress to provide adequate funds for the State Children's Health Insurance Program. The details of the legislative maneuvering are complex, but what it comes down to is that conservatives showed no interest in maintaining adequate funding for this highly successful program. The sums involved are not large, by Washington standards. But the results will be dramatic: according to Office of Management and Budget estimates, 900,000 children will lose health insurance over the next three years.

We are, of course, now living in what George W. Bush has called the "era of personal responsibility": if a child chooses to have parents who can't afford health care, that child will have to accept the consequences. But there may also be political calculation involved. Again, the government mustn't do anything good, because then people might not realize that government is bad. Understand?

What do we learn from this catalog of cruelties? We learn that "compassionate conservatism" and "leave no child behind" were empty slogans—but while this may have come as a surprise to the faith-based John J. DiIulio, some of us thought it was obvious all along. More important, we learn how relentless and extremist today's conservative movement really is.

Some people—moderate Republicans who aren't ready to admit what has happened to their party, and Democrats who think their party can appease the right by making its own promises of smaller government—still don't get it. They imagine that at some point the right will decide that it has gotten what it wants.

But the right's ambitions have no limits, and nothing moderates can offer will appease it. Eventually the public, which actually benefits from most of the programs the right is determined to abolish, will figure that out. But how fast voters figure it out depends a lot on whether moderate politicians clearly articulate the issues, or try to escape detection by sounding like conservatives.

# CHAPTER 9

# *The Private Interest*

## PAYING THE PRICE

*September 16, 2001*

Right now most Americans are focused on punishing the perpetrators. But Tuesday's tragedy was partly self-inflicted. Why did we leave ourselves so vulnerable?

For this is a tale not just of villainy, but also of penny-pinching that added up to disaster—and a system that encouraged, even forced, that penny-pinching. It's a problem that goes beyond terrorism. Something is amiss with our political philosophy: we are a nation that is unwilling to pay the price of public safety.

In retrospect, our national neglect of airport security boggles the mind. We've known for many years that America was a target of terrorists. And every expert warned that the most likely terrorist plots would involve commercial airlines.

Yet airports throughout the United States rely on security personnel who are paid about $6 an hour, less than they could earn serving fast food. These guardians of our lives receive only a few hours of training, and more than 90 percent of the people screening bags have been on the job for less than six months.

It didn't have to be that way. Last year a report by the General Accounting Office castigated the state of U.S. airport security, comparing it unfavorably with the systems of other advanced nations. In Europe, the people screening your bags are paid about $15 an hour plus benefits, and they get extensive training. Why didn't the United States take equal care?

The answer is that in Europe, airport security is treated as a law-enforcement issue and paid for by either the airport or the national government. In the United States, however, airport security is paid for by the airlines; not surprisingly, they spend as little as possible. Don't blame them—the fault lies in ourselves, for depending on private companies to do a job that properly belongs in the public domain.

There have been many proposals over the years to put the job in the right hands. For example, in 1997 Robert Crandall, chairman of American Airlines, proposed a national nonprofit corporation to handle airport security. But such proposals went nowhere. They were too much at odds with the spirit of the times, which was all about shrinking the role of government, not expanding it.

And the spirit of the times was definitely against anything that looked like an increase in government spending, unless it was explicitly military. If you look at the sad history of precautions not taken, again and again sums of money that now look trivial were the sticking point. Back in 1996 a government advisory committee on airline security recommended spending $1 billion per year—about $2 per passenger—on improvements. The panel rejected the idea of a special airport tax to pay for these improvements, arguing that since this was a national security issue, the money should come out of general tax revenues. But officials at the Office of Management and Budget warned that the committee had "unrealistic expectations regarding the outlook of discretionary funds"—that is, don't expect politicians to come up with the money. And they didn't.

This is an issue that goes well beyond terrorism. Last year Laurie Garrett, the author of *The Coming Plague*, followed up with a chilling book titled *Betrayal of Trust: The Collapse of Global Public Health*. The story she tells is ominously similar to that of airport security: a crucial but unglamorous piece of our public infrastructure has been allowed to fray to the point of collapse—partly because we have relied on the private sector to do the public sector's job, partly because public agencies have been starved of resources by politicians busily posturing against "big government." Don't be surprised if it turns out that we have left ourselves as vulnerable to an attack by microbes as we were to an attack by terrorists, and for exactly the same reasons.

I hope we bring the perpetrators of last week's attack to justice. But I also hope that once the rage has died down, Americans will be willing to learn one of the key lessons of last week's horror: there are some things on which the government must spend money, and not all of them involve soldiers. If we refuse to learn that lesson, if we continue to nickel-and-dime crucial public services, we may find—as we did last week—that we have nickel-and-dimed ourselves to death.

# THE PUBLIC INTEREST

*October 10, 2001*

I've identified a government agency that, by the usual criteria, should be a prime target for downsizing—maybe even abolition.

Some would argue for leaving much of this agency's function to private initiative. And there is no question that the agency's costs would be reduced if its work were outsourced to private companies, which wouldn't have to obey strict rules on hiring and firing workers. In fact, many of the agency's employees are paid considerably more than people with equivalent qualifications in the private sector.

What agency am I describing? The New York City Fire Department.

Why does New York need a fire department? It is, or should be, obvious why we can't leave fire protection up to individual building owners: a fire that starts in my building can spread to yours.

It may be less obvious why New York shouldn't hire private companies to do its firefighting. The basic answer is that the city can't write a contract to cover all eventualities, and so a private firm would always have an incentive to pinch pennies at the expense of public safety. And that's just not acceptable when the stakes are so high, and in particular when what we need are proud public servants, prepared to do whatever it takes to protect us—people like New York's heroic firefighters—rather than employees who feel that they are paid as little as possible by a company focused on the bottom line.

In short, there are some things that governments must do. Which brings us to the issue of the moment: airport security.

Study after study has urged the federalization of airport security, for pretty much the same reasons city governments take responsibility for firefighting. Maybe we don't expect airport security personnel to put their lives on the line, but we do place our lives in their hands. To that list of reasons has been added another: the need to share sensitive information about potential terrorists. Did recent events finally persuade the doubters?

Not a chance. Representative Bob Barr, Republican of Georgia, put it this way: "To me as a conservative, I look at a problem and ask, Is this a federal function?"

Think about that for a minute. Terrorists board planes in Boston, and use those planes to kill thousands of innocent people in New York—and Mr. Barr still can't see why airport security is a federal function? What would convince him that a federal role is warranted? One suspects that if the U.S. Army didn't already exist, he would oppose its creation—maybe he would argue that state militias, assisted by a few independent contractors (that is, companies of mercenaries) could do the job.

And Mr. Barr is by no means exceptional in his views. Congressional Republican leaders have declared themselves dead set against any proposal to federalize airport security, on the grounds that it would create a new federal bureaucracy—they have even denounced federalization as "socialism." And they have reportedly told the Bush administration that they would prefer no airport security bill to one that creates any new federal functions.

The story here is bigger than airport security. What's now clear, in case you had any doubts, is that America's hard right is simply fanatical—there is literally nothing that will persuade these people to accept the need for increased federal spending. And we're not talking about some isolated fringe; we're talking about the men who control the Congressional Republican Party—and seem, once again, to be in control of the White House.

For the Bush administration, after flirting with moderation in the weeks following the terrorist attack, seems in the last few days to have returned to its conviction that the hard right—which is relentless, and bears grudges—must always be deferred to, even in times of national crisis.

At some level, I have to admit, I don't get it. I can understand why people might oppose anything that smacks of income redistribution, even though I disagree. But how can you be opposed in principle to a program whose sole purpose is to protect the public and restore confidence?

Whatever the explanation, the dispute over airport security leaves no doubt about one thing: The right's fanatical distrust of government is the central fact of American politics, even in a time of terror.

# THE 55-CENT SOLUTION

*November 21, 2001*

When Gerald Ford turned down New York City's appeal for financial aid, the front page of *The Daily News* screamed: "Ford to City: Drop Dead." Those were the days.

These days, only diligent newspaper readers know that George W. Bush has backed off his personal pledge to provide aid to the battered city. And only serious policy wonks know that this is part of a broader picture—that the economic measures now being discussed in Washington will impoverish state and local governments across the country.

Gerald Ford didn't really deserve that headline. He had never promised anything to a city whose fiscal woes were, without question, largely self-inflicted. Why should he have felt compelled to help?

This time, the story is different. Mr. Bush, you may recall, had a rocky couple of days after the terrorist attack. Some questioned his movements on Sept. 11; in New York there was some anger that he did not quickly visit the city. The White House responded to the first criticism with its story about a "credible threat" to Air Force One. More important, Mr. Bush quickly mended his fences in New York by promising members of the state's Congressional delegation that he would provide ample aid—he told Senator Charles Schumer that the city had a "blank check."

Mr. Bush may not have been specific about the details, but all involved thought they knew what he had promised. Every news story I've been able to find from those early days declared that Mr. Bush would allocate half the $40 billion proposed antiterrorism package to New York. And this was widely regarded as only a first installment.

But last week the House Appropriations Committee finally filled in the details. And the antiterrorism package, which closely followed the administration's guidelines, contained only $9 billion for New York, less than half the promised $20 billion. In last-minute negotiations with irate Republican congressmen this was raised to $11 billion; but that's still only 55 cents on the dollar.

Administration officials say they will eventually provide the full $20 billion. But since they haven't kept Mr. Bush's promise to include that sum in the antiterrorism package, why should we believe them? As the memory of the attack recedes, as the administration returns to its pre–Sept. 11 embrace of hard-line conservatives—which has pretty much happened already—it becomes less and less likely that New York will see the rest of the money.

There may never be a specific day when the Bush administration tells the city to drop dead. Instead there will be vague promises, and then a lot of creative accounting—for example, the costs of deploying the National Guard will be counted as part of the $20 billion. But more and more it seems that the aid New Yorkers thought they had been promised, the aid that was supposed to help rebuild the city, was a mirage.

As I said, this is part of a broader picture. The combination of an economic slump and the effects of Sept. 11 has placed state and local governments across the country in a severe financial squeeze. Since almost all state governments are required by law to balance their budgets, this will force draconian cuts in spending.

You might have expected the "stimulus" packages being floated in Washington to provide some help to state governments in this difficult time. On the contrary, they will compound the damage. Proposals that would exempt large chunks of corporate profits from federal taxes will also reduce the profits subject to state taxes. Next year, in all likelihood, will present quite a spectacle: big tax cuts for corporations and people who make more than $300,000 per year, even as desperate state governments slash spending—with the biggest cuts falling on education and medical care for the poor.

Coming back to New York, what puzzles me is how little attention the story of the promise that wasn't is getting. In the weeks after Sept. 11, everyone took it for granted that there would be a great national effort to help rebuild the city. Now it is clear that this won't happen; the administration may claim to be providing what it promised, but New York will have to beg for every dollar of that $20 billion.

Where's the outrage? Have New Yorkers, of all people, forgotten how to complain?

## MONEY-GRUBBING GAMES

*February 8, 2002*

First there is a promise. Then there is no promise. Then there is a promise—until your attention is diverted again.

In the immediate aftermath of Sept. 11, before George W. Bush began his stratospheric ascent in the polls—and just before his first post-terror visit to New York—he made a personal promise: The city would receive at least $20 billion in reconstruction aid. At the time everyone thought that was a floor, not a ceiling.

Then a funny thing happened: Only $11 billion in aid to the city was actually budgeted. I wrote about this in a column last November titled "The 55-percent solution"—but was lambasted by critics, who insisted that of course Mr. Bush would honor his promise.

Now we have the Bush administration's $2.1 trillion budget proposal. Strange to say, it contains no additional aid to New York. It seems that the bucks stop here, at 55 percent of the original commitment.

New York legislators were quick to react, and demanded that Mitch Daniels, the White House budget director, explain the absence. Mr. Daniels first responded that he intended to count $5 billion in relief to victims of Sept. 11 as part of the aid package—a clear violation of everyone's understanding of what the promise meant. Then he lashed out at New York's representatives, saying, "It's strange to me to treat this as a little money-grubbing game."

The White House quickly tried to undo the damage. Mr. Daniels retracted his remarks, and Mr. Bush reiterated his promise to provide $20 billion—just in time to have another photo-op with New York police officers and firefighters. But the money is still not in the budget. And that fact—together with the fact that Mr. Daniels's initial remarks surely represented his true feelings—says volumes about the administration's priorities.

To place the stiffing of New York in context, you need to realize that when it comes to tax cuts and military spending, the Bush administration's budget is an exercise in unrestrained self-indulgence. There is a lot of stirring rhetoric, warning the nation that this is a time of war, in which everyone must make sacrifices—but this austerity does not extend to the wealthiest few percent of the population, who will not only get the lion's share of the future tax cuts already written into law, but would get most of the additional $600 billion in tax cuts the administration now proposes. (Actually it's about $1 trillion without the accounting tricks, but who's counting?)

And while there is much talk of hard choices, the administration seems loath to make any choices at all when it comes to defense spending. Does a subsidiary of the Carlyle Group have a 70-ton artillery piece that made sense, if it ever did, only in the Cold-War era? We'll buy it. Do two competing contractors offer advanced fighters designed to fight a nonexistent next generation of MiG's? We'll take both.

But there are big cuts elsewhere, and big diversions of resources that will force future cuts. You know about the diversion of the Social Security surplus to cover deficits in the rest of the government—deficits that would be much smaller if the administration would forgo some of those tax cuts, and would vanish if it also exercised some restraint in its weapons purchases. But did you know that the administration has budgeted $300 billion less for Medicare than the Congressional Budget Office says is needed to maintain current benefits—never mind add-ons like prescription drug insurance? It's unclear whether the administration actually intends to deny medical care to retirees, or is simply trying to hide the sheer scale of the looming fiscal disaster.

The broken promise to New York is actually small change compared with all of this. And that, in a way, makes it puzzling. Since the budget is already deeply in deficit for the foreseeable future, why not put it another $9 billion in deficit for one year, and avoid offering critics such an easy target?

One answer is that terror or no terror, key Republican lawmakers retain an abiding dislike for the Big Apple—and this administration never offends its supporters on the right.

But my guess is that it comes down to sheer arrogance. Buoyed by those approval ratings, this administration simply believes that its former promises don't matter. After all, don't people know that there's a war on?

# THE LONG HAUL

*September 10, 2002*

Americans should be proud of their reaction to Sept. 11. They didn't respond to calls for sacrifice, because no such calls were made. But they did respond to horror with calm and tolerance. There was no panic; while there were a handful of hate crimes, there were no angry mobs attacking people who look different. The American people remained true to what America is all about.

Yet a year later there is great uneasiness in this nation. Corporate scandals, dropping stocks and rising unemployment account for much of the malaise. But part of what makes us uneasy is that we still don't know how to think about what happened to us. Our leaders and much of the media tell us that we're a nation at war. But that was a bad metaphor from the start, and looks worse as time goes by.

In both human and economic terms the effects of Sept. 11 itself resembled those not of a military attack but of a natural disaster. Indeed, there were almost eerie parallels between Sept. 11 and the effects of the earthquake that struck Japan in 1995. Like the terrorist attack, the Kobe earthquake killed thousands of innocent people without warning. Like the terrorist attack, the quake left a nation afflicted by nightmares and deep feelings of insecurity. And like the terrorist attack, the quake struck a nation already struggling with the aftermath of a financial bubble.

Yet the Kobe earthquake had only fleeting effects on the

Japanese economy—suggesting that the effects of Sept. 11 on the U.S. economy would be equally fleeting. And so it has proved. Kobe had longer-term effects on Japan's psyche, just as Sept. 11 has had on ours. But Japan has mostly moved on, and so will we.

Of course there is a difference between an act of God and a deliberate atrocity. We were angry as well as shocked, determined to pursue and punish the perpetrators. It was natural to think of Sept. 11 as the moral equivalent of Pearl Harbor, and of the struggle that began that day as this generation's equivalent of World War II.

But if this is war, it bears little resemblance to the wars America has won in the past. Where is the call for sacrifice, for a great national effort? How will we know when or if we've won? One doesn't have to be a military expert to realize that the struggle ahead won't involve any D-Days, nor will there ever be a V-J Day. There will never be a day when we can declare terrorism stamped out for good. It will be more like fighting crime, where success is always relative and victory is never final, than like fighting a war.

And the metaphor we use to describe our struggle matters: some things that are justifiable in a temporary time of war are not justifiable during a permanent fight against crime, even if the criminals are murderous fanatics.

This is true even of how we deal with pedestrian matters like the federal budget. Wars are traditionally a valid reason to run budget deficits, because it makes sense for the government to borrow to cover the expense of a severe but temporary emergency. But this emergency is neither severe nor temporary. Is there any reason to expect spending on homeland security and national defense to fall back to pre–Sept. 11 levels, let alone far enough to restore budget balance, anytime in the foreseeable future? No, there isn't. So we had better figure out how to pay the government's bills on a permanent basis.

Far more important, of course, is the question of law and civil liberties. Great democratic leaders have broken the rules in times of war: had Abraham Lincoln not suspended the writ of habeas corpus in 1861, there would be no United States today. But the situation was extreme, and the lapse was temporary: victory in the Civil War brought a return to normal legal procedure. Can anyone think of an event that would persuade our current leaders that they no longer need extraordinary powers?

The point is that our new, threatened condition isn't temporary. We're in this for the long haul, so any measures we take to fight terrorism had better be measures that we are prepared to live with indefinitely.

The real challenge now is not to stamp out terrorism; that's an unattainable goal. The challenge is to find a way to cope with the threat of terrorism without losing the freedom and prosperity that make America the great nation it is.

# CHAPTER 10

# *Exploiting September 11*

## THE ONE-EYED MAN

*October 31, 2001*

Somewhere I read that to really understand legislation you have to look for the clause giving special consideration to one-eyed bearded men with a limp—that is, you have to look for the provision that turns a bill ostensibly serving a public purpose into a giveaway for some special interest.

Most of the commentary about the "stimulus" bill passed by the House last week focuses on the huge benefits it lavishes on giant corporations. But that doesn't tell us much about the specific interests being served. What's good for corporate America is good for General Motors; it would be hard to devise a bill that consists mainly of corporate giveaways without giving a lot of money to the biggest companies. To understand what the bill is really about, you have to look at the big payoffs to not-so-big companies.

One piece of the bill is custom-designed to benefit a small group of multinational financial firms. Another is clearly there for the sake of certain health insurors. But the most remarkable thing is how much of the benefit from repeal of the alternative minimum tax—a measure that is also included in the Bush administration's supposed stimulus plan, and which seems to be one of the administration's key priorities—goes to companies that are not all that big.

For example, it's not too surprising that calculations by Citizens for Tax Justice show General Motors, with its 380,000 workers, getting a check for $800 million. But it's quite amazing that TXU (formerly Dallas Power and Light), a company with only 16,000 employees, would get a check for $600 million. And there are a number of medium-sized companies that, like TXU, are in line for surprisingly big benefits. These companies include ChevronTexaco, Enron, Phillips Petroleum, IMC Global and CMS Energy. What do they have in common?

Well, they tend to be in the energy or mining businesses; and they tend to be based in or near Texas. In other words, the one-eyed bearded man with a limp looks a lot like Dick Cheney.

There is almost certainly a lot of overlap between the companies that would derive large benefits from alternative minimum tax repeal and those that would have received large subsidies under the energy plan devised by Mr. Cheney's task force. You may remember that the administration, in apparent defiance of the law, refused to make the records of that task force's meetings available to Congress; that's one of those issues that seems to have been dropped after Sept. 11.

And I guess it's superfluous to point out that the big winners in all this seem to be companies that gave large, one-sided donations to the Republican Party in the last election. (This is not to suggest that Democrats are any less susceptible to the influence of money.)

To me, the story of the Bush administration is starting to look like the plot of *Victor/Victoria*. First we had a candidate who was supposed to be a moderate. Then we learned, or thought we learned, that this was a mask; he was really a hard-line conservative who pretended to be a moderate in order to gain office.

But the latest economic proposals from the administration, like the Cheney energy plan, don't look as if they came from serious free-marketeers. They don't make sense in terms of either demand-side or supply-side economics, but they do give a lot of money to certain companies. So maybe ideology was just another mask for someone who was really the candidate of corporations—not corporations in general, but a small group of companies with a quite specific set of business interests—and who is only pretending to be a hard-line conservative who pretended to be a moderate in order to gain office.

It's an interesting and all too plausible picture. But it's a picture that most people will never see on their TV, and that many people would refuse to accept no matter how strong the evidence. That, of course, is what makes the whole thing possible. In the land of the blind, the one-eyed bearded man with a limp is king.

# AN ALTERNATE REALITY

*November 25, 2001*

Most Americans get their news from TV. And what they see is heartwarming—a picture of a nation behaving well in a time of crisis. Indeed, the vast majority of Americans have been both resolute and generous.

But that's not the whole story, and the images TV doesn't show are anything but heartwarming. A full picture would show politicians and businessmen behaving badly, with this bad behavior made possible—and made worse—by the fact that these days selfishness comes tightly wrapped in the flag. If you pay attention to the whole picture, you start to feel that you are living in a different reality from the one on TV.

The alternate reality isn't deeply hidden. It's available to anyone with a modem, and some of it makes it into quality newspapers. Often you can find the best reporting on what's really going on in the business section, because business reporters and commentators are not expected to view the world through rose-colored glasses.

From an economist's point of view, the most revealing indicator of what's really happening is the post–Sept. 11 fondness of politicians for "lump-sum transfers." That's economese for payments that aren't contingent on the recipient's actions, and which therefore give no incentive for changed behavior. That's good if the transfer is meant to help someone in need, without reducing his motivation to work. It's bad if the alleged purpose of the transfer is to get the recipient to do something useful, like invest or hire more workers.

So it tells you something when Congress votes $15 billion in aid and loan guarantees for airline companies but not a penny for laid-off airline workers. It tells you even more when the House passes a "stimulus" bill that contains almost nothing for the unemployed but includes $25 billion in retroactive corporate tax cuts—that is, pure lump-sum transfers to corporations, most of them highly profitable.

Most political reporting about the stimulus debate describes it as a conflict of ideologies. But ideology has nothing to do with it. No economic doctrine I'm aware of, right or left, says that an $800 million lump-sum transfer to General Motors will lead to more investment when the company is already sitting on $8 billion in cash.

As Jonathan Chait points out, there used to be some question about the true motives of people like Dick Armey and Tom DeLay. Did they really believe in free markets, or did they just want to take from the poor and give to the rich? Now we know.

Of course, it's not all about lump-sum transfers. Since Sept. 11 there has also been a sustained effort, under cover of the national emergency, to open public lands to oil companies and logging interests. Administration officials claim that it's all for the sake of national security, but when you discover that they also intend to reverse rules excluding snowmobiles from Yellowstone, the truth becomes clear.

So what's the real state of the nation? On TV this looks like World War II. But though our cause is just, for 99.9 percent of Americans this war, waged by a small cadre of highly trained professionals, is a spectator event. And the home front looks not like wartime but like a postwar aftermath, in which the normal instincts of a nation at war—to rally round the flag and place trust in our leaders—are all too easily exploited.

Indeed, current events bear an almost eerie resemblance to the period just after World War I. John Ashcroft is re-enacting the Palmer raids, which swept up thousands of immigrants suspected of radicalism; the vast majority turned out to be innocent of any wrongdoing, and some turned out to be U.S. citizens. Executives at Enron seem to have been channeling the spirit of Charles Ponzi. And the push to open public lands to private exploitation sounds like Teapot Dome, which also involved oil drilling on public land. Presumably this time there have been no outright bribes, but the giveaways to corporations are actually much larger.

What this country needs is a return to normalcy. And I don't mean the selective normalcy the Bush administration wants, in which everyone goes shopping but the media continue to report only inspiring stories and war news. It's time to give the American people the whole picture.

# THE ROVE DOCTRINE

*June 11, 2002*

Some months ago an academic colleague—a man with strong Democratic connections—urged me to write a couple of columns praising the Bush administration. "What should I praise?" I asked.

There was a long pause—funny, isn't it, how "balance" becomes a goal in itself?—but eventually he came up with something: "How about its commitment to free trade?"

Ahem. In fact, George W. Bush has turned out to be quite protectionist. The steel tariff and the farm bill attracted the most attention, but they are part of a broader picture that includes the punitive (and almost completely unjustified) tariff on Canadian softwood lumber and the revocation of Caribbean trade privileges. When it comes to free trade, the Bush administration is all for it—unless there is some political cost, however small, to honoring its alleged principles.

Which brings me to the story that has Washington's political groupies twittering: that *Esquire* article in which the White House chief of staff, Andy Card, frets that with the moderating influence of Karen Hughes gone, the hard-liner Karl Rove will run the show. If the past 18 months have been what policy looks like with Mr. Rove only partly in control, one shudders to think what comes next.

For the most distinctive feature of Mr. Rove's modus operandi is not his conservatism; it's his view that the administration should do whatever gives it a political advantage. This includes, of course, exploiting the war on terrorism—something Mr. Rove has actually boasted about. But it also includes coddling special interests.

One of Bill Clinton's underappreciated virtues was his considerable idealism when it came to economic policy. The Berkeley economist Brad DeLong lauded Mr. Clinton's "record of being willing to take major political risks in order to do what he thinks is right for the country as far as international economic policy is concerned." What he had in mind was the way Mr. Clinton went out on a limb, defying the polls and reaching across party lines, to pass the North American Free Trade Agreement in 1993, and the even bigger risks he took to rescue Mexico from its financial crisis in 1995. Like Mr. DeLong, I know some of the key players in both of those decisions, and I'm sure that they were taken on the merits: the Clintonites really, truly believed they were doing the right thing.

That scrupulousness continued to the end. If Bill Clinton had given the steel industry the tariffs it wanted, Al Gore would probably be living in the White House. But administration officials actually worried about the consequences—for the nation, and for the world economy—of giving in to special interests.

Mr. Rove's administration has no use for such niceties. The deals don't stop with trade and farm subsidies. As analysts at the Cato Institute point out, the Bush-Cheney energy plan may have been conservative in the sense that it was anti-environmentalist, but otherwise it was stuffed full of things free-marketeers are supposed to abhor: expanded government power to seize private land (for transmission lines), large tax incentives for energy sources that don't pay their way at market prices (nuclear power, in particular). The energy plan wasn't about principles; it was about payback.

And if the administration won't take a stand on principle,

who will? I was particularly struck by a story in the newspaper *The Hill* titled "Unions taking fresh look at G.O.P." It quoted the U.A.W. spokesman saying his union was "looking beyond party labels" to where politicians stand "on certain issues." In other words, his union will go with whoever caters to its special interests.

To some extent we've been here before. Paula Stern, the former head of the International Trade Commission, matter-of-factly describes Ronald Reagan as "the most protectionist president since Herbert Hoover," and says that he "legitimized efforts by powerful industries to use political muscle—not necessarily economic merit or legal criteria" to get what they wanted. So in a way Mr. Bush is following in Mr. Reagan's footsteps.

But it seems to me that it's worse this time—that we are witnessing a race to the bottom in interest-driven politics, taking us to depths not seen since before the New Deal. And if that *Esquire* story is to be believed, it's about to get even worse. Smoot-Hawley, anyone?

## THE REALITY THING

*June 25, 2002*

You can say this about the Bush administration: where others might see problems, it sees opportunities.

A slump in the economy was an opportunity to push a tax cut that provided very little stimulus in the short run, but will place huge demands on the budget in 2010. An electricity shortage in California was an opportunity to push for drilling in Alaska, which would have produced no electricity and hardly any oil until 2013 or so. An attack by lightly armed terrorist infiltrators was an opportunity to push for lots of heavy weapons and a missile defense system, just in case Al Qaeda makes a frontal assault with tank divisions or fires an ICBM next time.

President George H. W. Bush once confessed that he was somewhat lacking in the "vision thing." His son's advisers don't have that problem: they have a powerful vision for America's future. In that future, we have recently learned, the occupant of the White House will have the right to imprison indefinitely anyone he chooses, including U.S. citizens, without any judicial process or review. But they are rather less interested in the reality thing.

For the distinctive feature of all the programs the administration has pushed in response to real problems is that they do little or nothing to address those problems. Problems are there to be used to pursue the vision. And a problem that won't serve that purpose, whether it's the collapse of confidence in corporate governance or the chaos in the Middle East, is treated as an annoyance to be ignored if possible, or at best addressed with purely cosmetic measures. Clearly, George W. Bush's people believe that real-world problems will solve themselves, or at least won't make the evening news, because by pure coincidence they will be pre-empted by terror alerts.

But real problems, if not dealt with, have a way of festering. In the last few weeks, a whole series of problems seem to have come to a head. Yesterday's speech notwithstanding, Middle East policy is obviously adrift. The dollar and the stock market are plunging, threatening an already shaky economic recovery. Amtrak has been pushed to the edge of shutdown, because it couldn't get the administration's attention. And the federal government itself is about to run out of money, because House Republicans are unwilling to face reality and increase the federal debt limit. (This avoidance thing seems to be contagious.)

So now would be a good time to do what the White House always urges its critics to do—put partisanship aside. Will Mr. Bush be willing to set aside, even for a day or two, his drive to consolidate his political base, and actually do something that wasn't part of his preconceived agenda? Oh, never mind.

I think that most commentators missed the point of the story about Mr. Bush's commencement speech at Ohio State, the one his aide said drew on the thinking of Emily Dickinson, Pope John Paul II, Aristotle and Cicero, among others. Of course the aide's remarks were silly—but they gave us an indication of the level of sycophancy that Mr. Bush apparently believes to be his due. Next thing you know we'll be told that Mr. Bush is also a master calligrapher, and routinely swims across the Yangtze River. And nobody will dare laugh: just before Mr. Bush gave his actual, Aristotle-free speech, students at Ohio State were threatened with expulsion and arrest if they heckled him, and were instructed to offer "thunderous applause" instead.

It's interesting to note that the planned Department of Homeland Security, while of dubious effectiveness in its announced purpose, will be protected against future Colleen Rowleys: the new department will be exempted from both whistle-blower protection and the Freedom of Information Act.

But back to the festering problems: on the economic side, this is starting to look like the most dangerous patch for the nation and the world since the summer of 1998. Back then, luckily, our economic policy was run by smart people who were prepared to learn from their mistakes. Can you say the same about this administration?

As I've noted before, the Bush administration has an infallibility complex: it never, ever, admits making a mistake. And that kind of arrogance tends, eventually, to bring disaster. You can read all about it in Aristotle.

# THE REAL THING

*August 20, 2002*

Don't tell, maybe they won't ask. That was the message of a July memo from an official at the Department of Veterans Affairs, posted by Joshua Marshall at talkingpointsmemo.com. Citing "conservative OMB budget guidance" for spending on veterans' health care, the memo instructed subordinates to "ensure that no marketing activities to enroll new veterans occur within your networks." Veterans are entitled to medical care; but the administration hopes that some of them don't know that, and that it can save money by leaving them ignorant.

It's not the sort of thing you'd expect from an administration that wraps itself so tightly in the flag—not, that is, unless you've been paying attention. For stories like this are popping up more and more often.

Take George W. Bush's decision last week to demonstrate his resolve by blocking $5.1 billion in homeland security spending. This turned out to be a major gaffe, because the rejected bill allocated money both to improve veterans' health care and to provide firefighters with new equipment, including communication systems that could have saved lives on Sept. 11. Recalling those scenes at ground zero that did so much to raise Mr. Bush's poll numbers, the president of the International Association of Firefighters warned, "Don't lionize our fallen brothers in one breath, then stab us in the back."

Or what about the trapped coal miners? After their rescue,

Mr. Bush made a point of congratulating them in person—and Michael Novak, writing in *National Review Online*, declared Somerset, Pa., the "conservative capital of the world."

But Mr. Novak didn't mention the crucial assistance provided by the federal government's Mine Safety and Health Administration. That would have raised some awkward questions: although the Bush administration's energy plans call for major increases in coal mining, its spending plans cut funds for mine safety. More conservative budget guidance.

The point is that there is an inexorably growing gap between the image and the reality of the Bush administration's policies.

Mr. Bush is a master of photo-op populism; his handlers seek out opportunities to show him mingling with blue-collar workers. But the reality is that this administration loves 'em while the TV crews are around, then leaves 'em when it comes to actual policy. And that reality is becoming ever harder to conceal.

The federal budget is now deep in deficit, and everyone except the administration thinks it will remain there—not because of runaway spending, but because most of last year's tax cut has yet to take effect. And as my colleague Frank Rich points out, to offset the revenue losses from his tax cut, Mr. Bush would have to veto a $5 billion spending proposal every working day for the next year. Mr. Bush can no longer pretend, as he did during the 2000 campaign, that there is enough money for everything. Now, to justify that tax cut, he must hack steadily away at programs that matter to ordinary people.

Still, don't tax cuts also matter to ordinary people? It depends. Last year's rebate went to a lot of families. But the items still in the pipeline are income tax cuts for upper brackets—especially the top bracket—and elimination of the estate tax. For a married couple, only income in excess of $297,000 falls in the top bracket, and only an estate larger than $2 million pays any inheritance tax. Firefighters and coal miners don't make that kind of money.

In other words, behind the photo-ops, the administration is busy squeezing programs that benefit firefighters, police officers, coal miners, veterans and other "humble people of America" (Mr. Novak's phrase), in order to make room for tax cuts that mainly help a handful of not at all humble people. That's not demagoguery, it's the plain truth. And it's a truth that will become ever harder to disguise.

What are the political implications? When Al Gore wrote an Op-Ed article condemning the elitist policies of the Bush administration, pundits—and many Democratic politicians, including his former running mate—jumped on him with both feet. Populism, everyone insisted, doesn't work in American politics.

Yet conservatives enthusiastically rely on populism—fake populism, based on staged shmoozing with ordinary Americans and attacks on the imagined cultural elitism of the liberal media. Why shouldn't liberals, who actually have the facts on their side, try engaging in the real thing?

# DEAD PARROT SOCIETY

*October 25, 2002*

A few days ago *The Washington Post*'s Dana Milbank wrote an article explaining that for George W. Bush, "facts are malleable." Documenting "dubious, if not wrong" statements on a variety of subjects, from Iraq's military capability to the federal budget, the White House correspondent declared that Mr. Bush's "rhetoric has taken some flights of fancy."

Also in the last few days, *The Wall Street Journal* reported that "senior officials have referred repeatedly to intelligence . . . that remains largely unverified." The C.I.A.'s former head of counterterrorism was blunter: "Basically, cooked information is working its way into high-level pronouncements." *USA Today* reports that "pressure has been building on the intelligence agencies to deliberately slant estimates to fit a political agenda."

Reading all these euphemisms, I was reminded of Monty Python's parrot: he's pushing up the daisies, his metabolic processes are history, he's joined the choir invisible. That is, he's dead.

And the Bush administration lies a lot.

Let me hasten to say that I don't blame reporters for not quite putting it that way. Mr. Milbank is a brave man, and is paying the usual price for his courage: he is now the target of a White House smear campaign.

That standard response may help you understand how Mr.

Bush retains a public image as a plain-spoken man, when in fact he is as slippery and evasive as any politician in memory. Did you notice his recent declaration that allowing Saddam Hussein to remain in power wouldn't mean backing down on "regime change," because if the Iraqi despot meets U.N. conditions, "that itself will signal that the regime has changed"?

The recent spate of articles about administration dishonesty mainly reflects the campaign to sell war with Iraq. But the habit itself goes all the way back to the 2000 campaign, and is manifest on a wide range of issues. High points would include the plan for partial privatization of Social Security, with its $2 - 1 = 4$ arithmetic; the claim that a tax cut that delivers 40 percent or more of its benefits to the richest 1 percent was aimed at the middle class; the claim that there were 60 lines of stem cells available for research; the promise to include limits on carbon dioxide in an environmental plan.

More generally, Mr. Bush ran as a moderate, a "uniter, not a divider." *The Economist* endorsed him back in 2000 because it saw him as the candidate better able to transcend partisanship; now the magazine describes him as the "partisan-in-chief."

It's tempting to view all of this merely as a question of character, but it's more than that. There's method in this administration's mendacity.

For the Bush administration is an extremely elitist clique trying to maintain a populist facade. Its domestic policies are designed to benefit a very small number of people—basically those who earn at least $300,000 a year, and really don't care about either the environment or their less fortunate compatriots. True, this base is augmented by some powerful special-interest groups, notably the Christian right and the gun lobby. But while this coalition can raise vast sums, and can mobilize operatives to stage bourgeois riots when needed, the policies themselves are inherently unpopular. Hence the need to reshape those malleable facts.

What remains puzzling is the long-term strategy. Despite Mr. Bush's control of the bully pulpit, he has had little success in changing the public's fundamental views. Before Sept. 11 the nation was growing increasingly dismayed over the administration's hard right turn. Terrorism brought Mr. Bush immense personal popularity, as the public rallied around the flag; but the helium has been steadily leaking out of that balloon.

Right now the administration is playing the war card, inventing facts as necessary, and trying to use the remnants of Mr. Bush's post–Sept. 11 popularity to gain control of all three branches of government. But then what? There is, after all, no indication that Mr. Bush ever intends to move to the center.

So the administration's inner circle must think that full control of the government can be used to lock in a permanent political advantage, even though the more the public learns about their policies, the less it likes them. The big question is whether the press, which is beginning to find its voice, will lose it again in the face of one-party government.

# THE PITT PRINCIPLE

*November 1, 2002*

So Harvey Pitt decided not to tell other members of the Securities and Exchange Commission a small detail about the man he had chosen to head a crucial new accounting oversight board, after turning his back on a far more qualified candidate. William Webster, reports Stephen Labaton of *The Times*, headed the audit committee at U.S. Technologies. Now that company is being sued by investors who claim that management defrauded them of millions.

And what did Mr. Webster's committee do after an outside auditor raised concerns about the company's financial controls? That's right: It fired the auditor.

Mr. Pitt's response when this story broke beats anything a satirist could have imagined. "Pitt seeks probe of himself," read one headline. Honest: Mr. Pitt's own agency will investigate how he chose Mr. Webster.

Meanwhile, what was Mr. Webster thinking? Nobody thinks he's corrupt; but having failed so spectacularly to police executives at a single, small company, how could he imagine himself qualified to enforce honest accounting for all of corporate America?

Yet it's no accident that Mr. Pitt picked the wrong man. Mr. Webster was chosen over better candidates precisely because accounting industry lobbyists—a group that clearly still includes Mr. Pitt—believed he would be ineffectual.

Let's call it the Pitt Principle. The famous Peter Principle said that managers fail because they rise to their level of incompetence. The Pitt Principle tells us that sometimes incompetence is exactly what the people in charge want.

In this particular case, ordinary investors demanded a crackdown on corporate malfeasance—and Mr. Pitt pretended to comply. But this administration is run by and for people who have profited handsomely from their insider connections. (Remember Harken and Halliburton? And why won't the administration come clean about that energy task force?) So he picked someone with an impressive but irrelevant background, whom he could count on not to get the job done.

This principle explains a lot. For example, the Treasury secretary's job is to pursue sound fiscal and economic policies. So if you don't want that job done, you appoint a prominent manufacturing executive with little understanding either of federal budgets or of macroeconomics. He'll be just the man to preside over a lightning-fast transition from record budget surpluses to huge deficits. He'll even cheerily declare that "the latest indicators look good" just days before consumer confidence plunges to a nine-year low.

The attorney general's job is to uphold the Constitution and enforce the rule of law. So if you don't want that job done, you pick a former senator who doesn't have much respect either for the law or for the Constitution—particularly silly stuff about due process, separation of church and state, and all that. He'll be just the man to respond to a national crisis by imprisoning more than 1,000 people without charges, while catching not a single person who has committed an act of terrorism—not even the anthrax mailer.

The same principle can be applied at lower levels. Intelligence and defense experts should realistically assess threats to national security, and the consequences of U.S. military action.

So if you don't want that job done, you place it in the hands of prominent neoconservative intellectuals, with no real-world experience. They can be counted on to perceive terrorist links where the C.I.A. says they don't exist, and to offer blithe assurances about fighting a war in a densely populated urban area when the military itself is very nervous.

But the most important application of the Pitt Principle comes at the top. The president's job is to unify the nation, and lead it through difficult times. If you don't want that job done, you appoint an affable fellow from a famous family who has led a charmed business and political life thanks to his insider advantage. He'll be the kind of guy who sees nothing wrong in seeking partisan advantage from a national crisis, even going so far as to declare that members of the other party don't care about the nation's security.

That way, a great surge of national unity and good feeling can be converted, in little more than a year, into a growing sense of dismay, with more and more Americans saying that the country is going in the wrong direction.

## VICTORS AND SPOILS

*November 19, 2002*

Rule No. 1: Always have a cover story. The ostensible purpose of the Bush administration's plan to open up 850,000 federal jobs to private competition is to promote efficiency. Competitive vigor, we're told, will end bureaucratic sloth; costs will go down, and everyone—except for a handful of overpaid union members—will be better off.

And who knows? Here and there the reform may actually save a few dollars. But I doubt that there's a single politician or journalist in Washington who believes that privatizing much of the federal government—a step that the administration says it can take without any new legislation—is really motivated by a desire to reduce costs.

After all, there's a lot of experience with privatization by governments at all levels—state, federal and local; that record doesn't support extravagant claims about improved efficiency. Sometimes there are significant cost reductions, but all too often the promised savings turn out to be a mirage. In particular, it's common for private contractors to bid low to get the business, then push their prices up once the government work force has been disbanded. Projections of a 20 or 30 percent cost saving across the board are silly—and one suspects that the officials making those projections know that.

So what's this about?

First, it's about providing political cover. In the face of budget deficits as far as the eye can see, the administration—determined to expand, not reconsider the program of tax cuts it initially justified with projections of huge surpluses—must make a show of cutting spending. Yet what can it cut? The great bulk of public spending is either for essential services like defense and the justice system, or for middle-class entitlements like Social Security and Medicare that the administration doesn't dare attack openly.

Privatizing federal jobs is a perfect answer to this dilemma. It's not a real answer—the pay of those threatened employees is only about 2 percent of the federal budget, so efficiency gains from privatization, even if they happen, will make almost no dent in overall spending. For a few years, however, talk of privatization will give the impression that the administration is doing something about the deficit.

But distracting the public from the reality of deficits is, we can be sure, just an incidental payoff. So, too, is the fact that privatization is a way to break one of the last remaining strongholds of union power. Karl Rove is after much bigger game.

A few months ago Mr. Rove compared his boss to Andrew Jackson. As some of us noted at the time, one of Jackson's key legacies was the "spoils system," under which federal jobs were reserved for political supporters. The federal civil service, with its careful protection of workers from political pressure, was created specifically to bring the spoils system to an end; but now the administration has found a way around those constraints.

We don't have to speculate about what will follow, because Jeb Bush has already blazed the trail.

Florida's governor has been an aggressive privatizer, and as *The Miami Herald* put it after a careful study of state records, "his bold experiment has been a success—at least for him and the Republican Party, records show. The policy has spawned a network of contractors who have given him, other Republican politicians and the Florida G.O.P. millions of dollars in campaign donations."

What's interesting about this network of contractors isn't just the way that big contributions are linked to big contracts; it's the end of the traditional practice in which businesses hedge their bets by giving to both parties. The big winners in Mr. Bush's Florida are companies that give little or nothing to Democrats. Strange, isn't it? It's as if firms seeking business with the state of Florida are subject to a loyalty test.

So am I saying that we are going back to the days of Boss Tweed and Mark Hanna? Gosh, no—those guys were pikers. One-party control of today's government offers opportunities to reward friends and punish enemies that the old machine politicians never dreamed of.

How far can the new spoils system be pushed? To what extent will it be used to lock in a permanent political advantage for the ruling party? Stay tuned; I'm sure we'll soon find out.

## CHAPTER 11

# A Vast Conspiracy?

## THE SMOKE MACHINE

*March 29, 2002*

In a way, it's a shame that so much of David Brock's *Blinded by the Right: The conscience of an ex-conservative* is about the private lives of our self-appointed moral guardians. Those tales will sell books, but they may obscure the important message: That the "vast right-wing conspiracy" is not an overheated metaphor but a straightforward reality, and that it works a lot like a special-interest lobby.

Modern political economy teaches us that small, well-organized groups often prevail over the broader public interest. The steel industry got the tariff it wanted, even though the losses to consumers will greatly exceed the gains of producers, because the typical steel consumer doesn't understand what's happening.

*Blinded by the Right* shows that the same logic applies to non-economic issues. The scandal machine that employed Mr. Brock was, in effect, a special-interest group financed by a handful of wealthy fanatics—men like the Rev. Sun Myung

Moon, whose cultlike Unification Church owns *The Washington Times*, and Richard Mellon Scaife, who bankrolled the scandal-mongering *American Spectator* and many other right-wing enterprises. It was effective because the typical news consumer didn't realize what was going on.

The group's efforts managed to turn Whitewater—a $200,000 money-losing investment—into a byword for scandal, even though an eight-year, $73 million investigation never did find any evidence of wrongdoing by the Clintons. Just imagine what the scandal machine could have done with more promising raw material—such as the decidedly unusual business transactions of the young George W. Bush.

But there is, of course, no comparable scandal machine on the left. Why not?

One answer is that for some reason there is a level of anger and hatred on the right that has at best a faint echo in the antiglobalization left, and none at all in mainstream liberalism. Indeed, the liberals I know generally seem unwilling to face up to the nastiness of contemporary politics.

It's also true that in the nature of things, billionaires are more likely to be right-wing than left-wing fanatics. When billionaires do support more or less liberal causes, they usually try to help the world, not take over the U.S. political system. Not to put too fine a point on it: While George Soros was spending lavishly to promote democracy abroad, Mr. Scaife was spending lavishly to undermine it at home.

And his achievement is impressive; key figures from the Scaife empire are now senior officials in the Bush administration. (And Mr. Moon's newspaper is now in effect the administration's house organ.) Clearly, scandalmongering works: the public and, less excusably, the legitimate media all too readily assume that where there's smoke there must be fire—when in reality it's just some angry rich guys who have bought themselves a smoke machine.

And the media are still amazingly easy to sucker. Just look at the way the press fell for the fraudulent tale of vandalism by departing Clinton staffers, or the more recent spread of the bogus story that Ken Lay stayed at the Clinton White House.

Regular readers of this column know that not long ago I found myself the target of a minor-league smear campaign. The pattern was typical: right-wing sources insisting that a normal business transaction (in my case consulting for Enron, back when I was a college professor, not an Op-Ed columnist, and in no position to do the company any favors) was somehow corrupt; then legitimate media picking up on the story, assuming that given all the fuss there must be something to the allegations; and no doubt a lingering impression, even though no favors were given or received, that the target must have done something wrong ("Isn't it hypocritical for him to criticize crony capitalism when he himself was on the take?"). Now that I've read Mr. Brock's book, I understand what happened.

*Slate*'s Tim Noah, whom I normally agree with, says that Mr. Brock tells us nothing new: "We know . . . that an appallingly well-financed hard right was obsessed with smearing Clinton." But who are "we"? Most people don't know that—and anyway, he shouldn't speak in the past tense; an appallingly well-financed hard right is still in the business of smearing anyone who disagrees with its agenda, and too many journalists still allow themselves to be used.

I found *Blinded by the Right* distasteful, but revelatory. So, I suspect, will many others.

# THE ANGRY PEOPLE

*April 23, 2002*

A slightly left-of-center candidate runs for president. In a rational world he would win easily. After all, his party has been running the country, with great success: unemployment is down, economic growth has accelerated, the sense of malaise that prevailed under the previous administration has evaporated.

But everything goes wrong. His moderation becomes a liability; denouncing the candidate's pro-market stance, left-wing candidates—who have no chance of winning, but are engaged in politics as theater—draw off crucial support. The candidate, though by every indication a very good human being, is not a natural campaigner; he has, say critics, "a professorial style" that seems "condescending and humorless" to many voters. Above all, there is apathy and complacency among moderates; they take it for granted that he will win, or that in any case the election will make little difference.

The result is a stunning victory for the hard right. It's by and large a tolerant, open-minded country; but there is a hard core, maybe 20 percent of the electorate, that is deeply angry even in good times. And owing to the peculiarities of the electoral system, this right-wing minority prevails even though more people actually cast their votes for the moderate left.

If all this sounds like a post-mortem on the Gore campaign in 2000, that's intentional. But I'm actually describing Sunday's shocking election in France, in which the current prime minister, Lionel Jospin, placed third, behind the rabid rightist Jean-Marie Le Pen. Until very recently, Mr. Le Pen was regarded as a spent force. Now he has scored an astonishing triumph.

As I've implicitly suggested, there are some important parallels between the earthquake in French politics and recent political events in the United States. Let me draw out those parallels, then go to the big difference.

What the French election revealed is that in France, as in the United States, there are a lot of angry people. They aren't a majority; Mr. Le Pen received about 17 percent of the vote, less than Ross Perot got here in 1992. But they are highly motivated, and can exert influence out of proportion to their numbers if moderates take a tolerant society for granted.

What are the angry people angry about? Not economics; peace and prosperity did not reconcile them to Bill Clinton or to Mr. Jospin. Instead, it seems to be about traditional values. Our angry right rails against godless liberals; France's targets immigrants. In both cases, what really seems to bother them is the loss of certainty; they want to return to a simpler time, one without that disturbing modern mix of people and ideas.

And in both cases this angry minority has had far more influence than its numbers would suggest, largely because of the fecklessness of the left and the apathy of moderates. Al Gore had Ralph Nader; Mr. Jospin had a potpourri of silly leftists (two Trotskyists took 10 percent of the vote). And both men were mocked and neglected by complacent moderates.

Now for the important difference. Mr. Le Pen is a political outsider; his showing in Sunday's election puts him into the second-round runoff, but he won't actually become France's president. So his hard-right ideas won't be put into practice anytime soon.

In the United States, by contrast, the hard right has essentially been co-opted by the Republican Party—or maybe it's the other way around. In this country people with views that are, in their way, as extreme as Mr. Le Pen's are in a position to put those views into practice.

Consider, for example, the case of Representative Tom DeLay. Last week Mr. DeLay told a group that he was on a mission from God to promote a "biblical worldview," and that he had pursued the impeachment of Bill Clinton in part because Mr. Clinton held "the wrong worldview." Well, there are strange politicians everywhere. But Mr. DeLay is the House majority whip—and, in the view of most observers, the real power behind Speaker Dennis Hastert.

And then there's John Ashcroft.

What France's election revealed is that we and the French have more in common than either country would like to admit. There as here, there turns out to be a lot of irrational anger lurking just below the surface of politics as usual. The difference is that here the angry people are already running the country.

## THE BULLY'S PULPIT

*September 6, 2002*

War is peace. Freedom is slavery. Ignorance is strength. Colin Powell and Dick Cheney are in perfect agreement. And the Bush administration won't privatize Social Security.

Ari Fleischer's insistence that Mr. Powell and Mr. Cheney have no differences over Iraq seems to have pushed some journalists into facing up, at least briefly, to the obvious. ABC's weblog *The Note* described it as a "chocolate-is-vanilla" claim, admitting that "The Bush team has always had a credibility problem with some reporters because of their insistence on saying 'up is down' and 'black is white.' "

But the administration needn't worry; if history is any guide, many reporters will soon return to their usual cringe. The next time the administration insists that chocolate is vanilla, much of the media—fearing accusations of liberal bias, trying to create the appearance of "balance"—won't report that the stuff is actually brown; at best they'll report that some Democrats claim that it's brown.

The Bush team's Orwellian propensities have long been apparent to anyone following its pronouncements on economics. Even during campaign 2000 these pronouncements relied on doublethink, the ability to believe two contradictory things at the same time. For example, George W. Bush's plan to partially privatize Social Security always depended on the assertion that $2 - 1 = 4$—that we can divert payroll taxes into high-yielding personal accounts, yet still use the same money to pay benefits to retirees.

The Orwellian tactics don't stop with doublethink; they also include newspeak, the redefinition of words to rule out disloyal thoughts. Again, Social Security is a perfect example. Republican political consultants have found that in an era of plunging stocks and corporate scandal the word "privatization" has taken on negative connotations. The answer? Deny that personal accounts constitute privatization, and bully the press into going along. A Republican National Campaign Committee memo lays out the new strategy: "It is very important that we not allow reporters to shill for Democrat demagoguery by inaccurately characterizing 'personal accounts' and 'privatization' as one and the same."

Is it inaccurate to say that personal accounts equal privatization? We could argue on the merits. Under the Bush plan, a worker's personal account reflects any gains or losses on the stocks it represents. When risks and rewards accrue entirely to the individual, isn't that privatization?

But wait, we can do better. The push to convert Social Security into a system of personal accounts has been led by the Cato Institute. The Bush plan emerged directly from Cato's project on the subject, several members of Mr. Bush's commission on Social Security reform had close Cato ties, and much of the commission's staff came straight from Cato. You can read all about Cato's role on the special Web site the institute set up, socialsecurity.org.

And what's the name of the Cato project to promote personal accounts? Why, the Project on Social Security Privatization, of course.

Which brings us back to the issue of intimidation. The R.N.C.C. doesn't really think it can convince people that privatization isn't privatization. But that's not the goal. The memo doesn't talk about how to communicate with the public; it's a list of demands to place on journalists. As Joshua Marshall put it at talkingpointsmemo.com, the goal is to "mau-mau reporters out of using the word 'privatization' in this context."

And the intimidation will probably succeed. Indeed, it's already working. As Mr. Marshall notes, in a recent interview of the House minority leader, Richard Gephardt, Judy Woodruff of CNN duly echoed the R.N.C.C.'s memo.

Unfortunately, this isn't just a question of Social Security policy. Once an administration believes that it can get away with insisting that black is white and up is down—and everything in this administration's history suggests that it believes just that—it's hard to see where the process stops. A habit of ignoring inconvenient reality, and presuming that the docile media will go along, soon infects all aspects of policy. And yes, that includes matters of war and peace.

The trouble is that eventually reality has a way of asserting itself. And in case you are wondering, ignorance isn't strength.

# FOR THE PEOPLE

*October 29, 2002*

Ghoulish but true: as Minnesota mourns the death of Senator Paul Wellstone, many of the state's residents have been receiving fliers bearing a picture of a tombstone. The fliers, sent out by a conservative business group, denounce the late senator's support for maintaining the estate tax. Under the tombstone, the text reads in part: "Paul Wellstone not only wants to tax you and your business to death . . . he wants to tax you in the hereafter."

To be fair, the people who mailed out those fliers—which are carefully worded so that the cost of the mailing doesn't officially count as a campaign contribution—didn't know how tasteless they would now appear. Yet in a sense the mass mailing is a fitting epitaph; it reminds us what Paul Wellstone stood for, and how brave he was to take that stand.

Sometimes it seems as if Americans have forgotten what courage means. Here's a hint: talking tough doesn't make you a hero; you have to take personal risks. And I'm not just talking about physical risks—though it's striking how few of our biggest flag wavers have ever put themselves in harm's way. What we should demand of our representatives in Washington is the willingness to take political risks—to make a stand on principle, even if it means taking on powerful interest groups.

Paul Wellstone took risks. He was, everyone acknowledges, a politician who truly voted his convictions, who supported what he thought was right, not what he thought would help him get re-elected. He took risky stands on many issues: agree or disagree, you have to admit that his vote against authorization for an Iraq war was a singularly brave act. Yet the most consistent theme in his record was economic—his courageous support for the interests of ordinary Americans against the growing power of our emerging plutocracy.

In our money-dominated politics, that's a dangerous position to take. When Wellstone first ran for the Senate, his opponent outspent him seven to one. According to one of his advisers, the success of that ramshackle campaign, run from a rickety green school bus, "made politics safe for populists again."

If only. Almost every politician in modern America pretends to be a populist; indeed, it's a general rule that the more slavishly a politician supports the interests of wealthy individuals and big corporations, the folksier his manner. But being a genuine populist, someone who really tries to stand up against what Wellstone called "Robin Hood in reverse" policies, isn't easy: You must face the power not just of money, but of sustained and shameless hypocrisy.

And that's why those fliers are a perfect illustration of what Paul Wellstone was fighting.

On one side, the inclusion of estate tax repeal in last year's federal tax cut is the most striking example to date of how our political system serves the interests of the wealthy. After all, the estate tax affects only a small minority of families; the bulk of the tax is paid by a tiny elite. In fact, estate tax repeal favors the wealthy to such an extent that defenders of last year's tax cut—like Senator Charles Grassley, R-Iowa, who published a misleading letter in last Friday's *Times* [October 25, 2002]—always carefully omit it from calculations of who benefits. (The letter talked only about the income tax; had he included the effects of estate tax repeal, he would have been forced to admit that more than 40 percent of the benefits of that tax cut go to the wealthiest 1 percent of the population.) To eliminate the estate tax in the face of budget deficits means making the rich richer even as we slash essential services for the middle class and the poor.

On the other side, the estate tax debate illustrates the pervasive hypocrisy of our politics. For repeal of the "death tax" has been cast, incredibly, as a populist issue. Thanks to sustained, lavishly financed propaganda—of which that anti-Wellstone flier was a classic example—millions of Americans imagine, wrongly, that the estate tax mainly affects small businesses and farms, and that its repeal will help ordinary people. And who pays for the propaganda? Guess.

It's amazing what money can buy.

In an age of fake populists, Paul Wellstone was the real thing. Now he's gone. Will others have the courage to carry on?

# IN MEDIA RES

*November 29, 2002*

This week Al Gore said the obvious. "The media is kind of weird these days on politics," he told *The New York Observer*, "and there are some major institutional voices that are, truthfully speaking, part and parcel of the Republican Party."

The reaction from most journalists in the "liberal media" was embarrassed silence. I don't quite understand why, but there are some things that you're not supposed to say, precisely because they're so clearly true.

The political agenda of Fox News, to take the most important example, is hardly obscure. Roger Ailes, the network's chairman, has been advising the Bush administration. Fox's Brit Hume even claimed credit for the midterm election. "It was because of our coverage that it happened," he told Don Imus. "People watch us and take their electoral cues from us. No one should doubt the influence of Fox News in these matters." (This remark may have been tongue in cheek, but imagine the reaction if the Democrats had won and Dan Rather, even jokingly, had later claimed credit.)

But my purpose in today's column is not to bash Fox. I want to address a broader question: Will the economic interests of the media undermine objective news coverage?

For most of the last 50 years, public policy took it for granted that media bias was a potential problem. There were, after all, only three national networks, a limited number of radio licenses and only one or two newspapers in many cities. How could those who controlled major news outlets be deterred from misusing their position?

The answer was a combination of regulation and informal guidelines. The "fairness doctrine" forced broadcast media to give comparable representation to opposing points of view. Restrictions on ownership maintained a diversity of voices. And there was a general expectation that major news outlets would stay above the fray, distinguishing clearly between opinion and news reporting. The system didn't always work, but it did set some limits.

Over the past 15 years, however, much of that system has been dismantled. The fairness doctrine was abolished in 1987. Restrictions on ownership have been steadily loosened, and it seems likely that next year the Federal Communications Commission will abolish many of the restrictions that remain—quite possibly even allowing major networks to buy each other. And the informal rule against blatantly partisan reporting has also gone away—at least as long as you are partisan in the right direction.

The F.C.C. says that the old rules are no longer necessary because the marketplace has changed. According to the official line, new media—first cable television, then the Internet—have given the public access to a diversity of news sources, eliminating the need for public guidelines.

But is this really true? Cable television has greatly expanded the range of available entertainment, but has had far less broadening effect on news coverage. There are now five major sources of TV news, rather than three, but this increase is arguably more than offset by other trends. For one thing, the influence of print news has continued its long decline; for another, all five sources of TV news are now divisions of large conglomerates—you get your news from AOLTimeWarnerGeneralElectricDisneyWestinghouseNewsCorp.

And the Internet is a fine thing for policy wonks and news junkies—anyone can now read Canadian and British newspapers, or download policy analyses from think tanks. But most people have neither the time nor the inclination. Realistically, the Net does little to reduce the influence of the big five sources.

In short, we have a situation rife with conflicts of interest. The handful of organizations that supply most people with their news have major commercial interests that inevitably tempt them to slant their coverage, and more generally to be deferential to the ruling party. There have already been some peculiar examples of news not reported. For example, last month's 100,000-strong Washington antiwar demonstration—an important event, whatever your views on the issue—was almost ignored by some key media outlets.

For the time being, blatant media bias is still limited by old rules and old norms of behavior. But soon the rules will be abolished, and the norms are eroding before our eyes.

Do the conflicts of interest of our highly concentrated media constitute a threat to democracy?

I've reported; you decide.

# DIGITAL ROBBER BARONS?

*December 6, 2002*

Bad metaphors make bad policy. Everyone talks about the "information highway." But in economic terms the telecommunications network resembles not a highway but the railroad industry of the robber-baron era—that is, before it faced effective competition from trucking. And railroads eventually faced tough regulation, for good reason: they had a lot of market power, and often abused it.

Yet the people making choices today about the future of the Internet—above all Michael Powell, chairman of the Federal Communications Commission—seem unaware of this history. They are full of enthusiasm for the wonders of deregulation, dismissive of concerns about market power. And meanwhile tomorrow's robber barons are fortifying their castles.

Until recently, the Internet seemed the very embodiment of the free-market ideal—a place where thousands of service providers competed, where anyone could visit any site. And the tech sector was a fertile breeding ground for libertarian ideology, with many techies asserting that they needed neither help nor regulation from Washington.

But the wide-open, competitive world of the dial-up Internet depended on the very government regulation so many Internet enthusiasts decried. Local phone service is a natural monopoly, and in an unregulated world local phone monopolies would probably insist that you use their dial-up service. The reason you have a choice is that they are required to act as common carriers, allowing independent service providers to use their lines.

A few years ago everyone expected the same story to unfold in broadband. The Telecommunications Act of 1996 was supposed to create a highly competitive broadband industry. But it was a botched job; the promised competition never materialized. For example, I personally have no choice at all: if I want broadband, the Internet service provided by my local cable company is it. I'm like a 19th-century farmer who had to ship his grain on the Union Pacific, or not at all. If I lived closer to a telephone exchange, or had a clear view of the Southern sky, I might have some alternatives. But there are only a few places in the U.S. where there is effective broadband competition.

And that's probably the way it will stay. The political will to fix the 1996 act, to create in broadband the kind of freewheeling environment that many Internet users still take for granted, has evaporated.

Last March the F.C.C. used linguistic trickery—defining cable Internet access as an "information service" rather than as telecommunications—to exempt cable companies from the requirement to act as common carriers. The commission will probably make a similar ruling on DSL service, which runs over lines owned by your local phone company. The result will be a system in which most families and businesses will have no more choice about how to reach cyberspace than a typical 19th-century farmer had about which railroad would carry his grain.

There were and are alternatives. We could have restored competition by breaking up the broadband industry, restricting local phone and cable companies to the business of selling space on their lines to independent Internet service providers. Or we could have accepted limited competition, and regulated Internet providers the way we used to regulate AT&T. But right now we seem to be heading for a system without either effective competition or regulation.

Worse yet, the F.C.C. has been steadily lifting restrictions on cross-ownership of media and communications companies. The day when a single conglomerate could own your local newspaper, several of your local TV channels, your cable company and your phone company—and offer your only route to the Internet—may not be far off.

The result of all this will probably be exorbitant access charges, but that's the least of it. Broadband providers that face neither effective competition nor regulation may well make it difficult for their customers to get access to sites outside their proprietary domain—ending the Internet as we know it. And there's a political dimension too. What happens when a few media conglomerates control not only what you can watch, but what you can download?

There's still time to rethink; a fair number of Congressmen, from both parties, have misgivings about Mr. Powell's current direction. But time is running out.

## BEHIND THE GREAT DIVIDE

*February 18, 2003*

There has been much speculation why Europe and the U.S. are suddenly at such odds. Is it about culture? About history? But I haven't seen much discussion of an obvious point: We have different views partly because we see different news.

Let's back up. Many Americans now blame France for the chill in U.S.-European relations. There is even talk of boycotting French products.

But France's attitude isn't exceptional. Last Saturday's huge demonstrations confirmed polls that show deep distrust of the Bush administration and skepticism about an Iraq war in all major European nations, whatever position their governments may take. In fact, the biggest demonstrations were in countries whose governments are supporting the Bush administration.

There were big demonstrations in America too. But distrust of the U.S. overseas has reached such a level, even among our British allies, that a recent British poll ranked the U.S. as the world's most dangerous nation—ahead of North Korea and Iraq.

So why don't other countries see the world the way we do? News coverage is a large part of the answer. Eric Alterman's new book, *What Liberal Media?*, doesn't stress international comparisons, but the difference between the news reports Americans and Europeans see is a stark demonstration of his point. At least compared with their foreign counterparts, the "liberal" U.S. media are strikingly conservative—and in this case hawkish.

I'm not mainly talking about the print media. There are differences, but the major national newspapers in the U.S. and the U.K. at least seem to be describing the same reality.

Most people, though, get their news from TV—and there the difference is immense. The coverage of Saturday's antiwar rallies was a reminder of the extent to which U.S. cable news, in particular, seems to be reporting about a different planet than the one covered by foreign media.

What would someone watching cable news have seen? On Saturday, news anchors on Fox described the demonstrators in New York as "the usual protesters" or "serial protesters." CNN wasn't quite so dismissive, but on Sunday morning the headline on the network's Web site read "Antiwar rallies delight Iraq," and the accompanying picture showed marchers in Baghdad, not London or New York.

This wasn't at all the way the rest of the world's media reported Saturday's events, but it wasn't out of character. For months both major U.S. cable news networks have acted as if the decision to invade Iraq has already been made, and have in effect seen it as their job to prepare the American public for the coming war.

So it's not surprising that the target audience is a bit blurry about the distinction between the Iraqi regime and Al Qaeda. Surveys show that a majority of Americans think that some or all of the Sept. 11 hijackers were Iraqi, while many believe that Saddam Hussein was involved in Sept. 11, a claim even the Bush administration has never made. And since many Americans think that the need for a war against Saddam is obvious, they think that Europeans who won't go along are cowards.

Europeans, who don't see the same things on TV, are far

more inclined to wonder why Iraq—rather than North Korea, or for that matter Al Qaeda—has become the focus of U.S. policy. That's why so many of them question American motives, suspecting that it's all about oil or that the administration is simply picking on a convenient enemy it knows it can defeat. They don't see opposition to an Iraq war as cowardice; they see it as courage, a matter of standing up to the bullying Bush administration.

There are two possible explanations for the great trans-Atlantic media divide. One is that European media have a pervasive anti-American bias that leads them to distort the news, even in countries like the U.K. where the leaders of both major parties are pro-Bush and support an attack on Iraq. The other is that some U.S. media outlets—operating in an environment in which anyone who questions the administration's foreign policy is accused of being unpatriotic—have taken it as their assignment to sell the war, not to present a mix of information that might call the justification for war into question.

So which is it? I've reported, you decide.

# CHANNELS OF INFLUENCE

*March 25, 2003*

By and large, recent pro-war rallies haven't drawn nearly as many people as antiwar rallies, but they have certainly been vehement. One of the most striking took place after Natalie Maines, lead singer for the Dixie Chicks, criticized President Bush: a crowd gathered in Louisiana to watch a 33,000-pound tractor smash a collection of Dixie Chicks CD's, tapes and other paraphernalia. To those familiar with 20th-century European history it seemed eerily reminiscent of. . . . But as Sinclair Lewis said, it can't happen here.

Who has been organizing those pro-war rallies? The answer, it turns out, is that they are being promoted by key players in the radio industry—with close links to the Bush administration.

The CD-smashing rally was organized by KRMD, part of Cumulus Media, a radio chain that has banned the Dixie Chicks from its playlists. Most of the pro-war demonstrations around the country have, however, been organized by stations owned by Clear Channel Communications, a behemoth based in San Antonio that controls more than 1,200 stations and increasingly dominates the airwaves.

The company claims that the demonstrations, which go under the name Rally for America, reflect the initiative of individual stations. But this is unlikely: according to Eric Boehlert, who has written revelatory articles about Clear Channel in *Salon*, the company is notorious—and widely hated—for its iron-fisted centralized control.

Until now, complaints about Clear Channel have focused on its business practices. Critics say it uses its power to squeeze recording companies and artists and contributes to the growing blandness of broadcast music. But now the company appears to be using its clout to help one side in a political dispute that deeply divides the nation.

Why would a media company insert itself into politics this way? It could, of course, simply be a matter of personal conviction on the part of management. But there are also good reasons for Clear Channel—which became a giant only in the last few years, after the Telecommunications Act of 1996 removed many restrictions on media ownership—to curry favor with the ruling party. On one side, Clear Channel is feeling some heat: it is being sued over allegations that it threatens to curtail the airplay of artists who don't tour with its concert division, and there are even some politicians who want to roll back the deregulation that made the company's growth possible. On the other side, the Federal Communications Commission is considering further deregulation that would allow Clear Channel to expand even further, particularly into television.

Or perhaps the quid pro quo is more narrowly focused. Experienced Bushologists let out a collective "Aha!" when Clear Channel was revealed to be behind the pro-war rallies, because the company's top management has a history with George W. Bush. The vice chairman of Clear Channel is Tom Hicks, whose name may be familiar to readers of my column. When Mr. Bush was governor of Texas, Mr. Hicks was chairman of the University of Texas Investment Management Company, called Utimco, and Clear Channel's chairman, Lowry Mays, was on its board. Under Mr. Hicks, Utimco placed much of the university's endowment under the management of companies with strong Republican Party or Bush family ties. In 1998

Mr. Hicks purchased the Texas Rangers in a deal that made Mr. Bush a multimillionaire.

There's something happening here. What it is ain't exactly clear, but a good guess is that we're now seeing the next stage in the evolution of a new American oligarchy. As Jonathan Chait has written in *The New Republic*, in the Bush administration "government and business have melded into one big 'us.'" On almost every aspect of domestic policy, business interests rule: "Scores of midlevel appointees . . . now oversee industries for which they once worked." We should have realized that this is a two-way street: if politicians are busy doing favors for businesses that support them, why shouldn't we expect businesses to reciprocate by doing favors for those politicians—by, for example, organizing "grass roots" rallies on their behalf?

What makes it all possible, of course, is the absence of effective watchdogs. In the Clinton years the merest hint of impropriety quickly blew up into a huge scandal; these days, the scandalmongers are more likely to go after journalists who raise questions. Anyway, don't you know there's a war on?

*Part Four*

# WHEN
# MARKETS
# GO BAD

PEOPLE who don't know much about economics often seem to imagine that economists fall into two camps: they are either conservative free-marketeers or liberal big-government types, and never the twain shall meet. In fact, there's a lot less disagreement among economists than legend would have it. In particular, economists with generally liberal political views, like myself, often have a strong respect for the effectiveness of free markets.

But to respect markets is not to deify them. Sometimes markets go bad—and during the last few years there have been some spectacular examples of what economists call "market failure," with very nasty consequences for the public.

Chapter 12 focuses on the California energy crisis of 2000–01, where an attempt to give market forces freer rein, by deregulating the market for electricity, turned into a disaster. The nature of that disaster was obscured by rigid free-market prejudices. It has become an article of faith among many people—certainly among the punditocracy—that markets always get it right, and that government regulation is always a bad thing. So when California suddenly faced skyrocketing prices and rolling blackouts, most commentators *knew* that it had to be the result of government mistakes, of "flawed deregulation" (though they were never very clear about what the flaw was). And they also blamed environmentalists, who supposedly had prevented the energy industry from building enough capacity.

But I approached the issue with an open mind and, better yet, enough background in economics to find some real experts and understand what they were saying. It soon became clear to me that the California disaster wasn't the result of a shortage of production capacity. It was the result of market manipulation by energy producers and traders.

At first, I was almost alone in making that case; the evidence, though compelling, was circumstantial, and ran counter to prevailing prejudices. But eventually evidence surfaced that was convincing even to non-economists: memos detailing strategies to game the markets, even recordings of traders telling power plant operators to shut down. At that point it became clear that an enormous market raid had been carried out in broad daylight—with almost nobody willing to believe what was happening.

Why were people so ready to believe that environmentalists caused the California crisis, when there was never a shred of evidence for this view? Put it down to another myth, about the incompatibility of free markets and environmental protection. Indeed, one thing radical environmentalists and radical free-marketeers have in common is the belief that good economics and environmental values don't mix. But it's not true: textbook economics gives us very good reasons to protect the environment, recognizing that environmental damage is every bit as real a cost as more conventional monetary expenses. Economists, myself included, often criticize the way our current environmental policies work, but it's a criticism of means rather than ends: smarter regulation doesn't mean less protection for the environment.

But our current political leadership, though it sometimes talks of making environmental policy smarter, mainly seems to want less regulation of any kind. In fact, the Bush administration is strikingly anti-environmentalist, perhaps because so many of its members—and so much of its campaign finance—come from extractive industries (oil, coal, lumber, etc.). Chapter 13 describes the administration's anti-environmental policies, together with the inevitable dishonesty used to cloak those policies.

The last chapter in this section is a short look at a big subject: the perceived failure of free-market policies in other countries. Fairly or unfairly, much of the world now believes that the United States pressed nations to free up their markets, then disavowed responsibility when currency speculation and other market disasters befell their economies. Here I offer a few case studies.

# CHAPTER 12

# *California Screaming*

## CALIFORNIA SCREAMING

*December 10, 2000*

California's deregulated power industry, in which producers can sell electricity for whatever the traffic will bear, was supposed to deliver cheaper, cleaner power. But instead the state faces an electricity shortage so severe that the governor has turned off the lights on the official Christmas tree—a shortage that has proved highly profitable to power companies, and raised suspicions of market manipulation.

The experience raises questions about deregulation. And more broadly, it is a warning about the dangers of placing blind faith in markets.

True, part of California's problem is an unexpected surge in electricity demand, the byproduct of a booming economy. It's possible that the crisis would have happened even without deregulation.

But probably not. In the bad old days, monopolistic power companies were guaranteed a good profit even if their industry had excess capacity. So they built more capacity than they needed, enough to meet even unexpectedly high demand. But in the deregulated market, where prices fluctuate constantly, companies knew that if they overinvested, prices and profits would plunge. So they were reluctant to build new plants—which is why unexpectedly strong demand has led to shortages and soaring prices.

Now you could say that in the long run there is nothing wrong with that. Building extra generating capacity was costly, and the costs were passed on to consumers; while prices may fluctuate in a system with less slack, on average consumers will pay less. In fact, textbook economics suggests that it's actually a good thing that electricity prices skyrocket when supply runs short: that's what gives the power companies an incentive to invest. And so you could argue that no public intervention is warranted—indeed, that the caps that still place an upper limit on electricity prices only worsen the problem, that we should rely on market competition to solve the crisis.

But how competitive is the electricity market? What makes California's power crisis politically explosive is the suspicion that it's not just about inadequate capacity, but also about artificially inflated prices.

How might market manipulation work? Suppose that it's a hot July, with air-conditioners across the state running full blast and the power industry near the limits of its capacity. If some of that capacity suddenly went off line for whatever reason, the resulting shortage would send wholesale electricity prices sky high. So a large producer could actually increase its profits by inventing technical problems that shut down some of its generators, thereby driving up the price it gets on its remaining output.

Does this really happen? A recent National Bureau of Economic Research working paper by Severin Borenstein, James

Bushnell and Frank Wolak cites evidence that exactly this kind of market manipulation took place in Britain before 1996 and in California during the summers of 1998 and 1999.

You wouldn't normally expect this to happen in colder months, when demand is lower. Still, state officials have understandably become suspicious about California's current power emergency—an emergency precipitated by the odd fact that about a quarter of the state's generating capacity is off line as the result of either scheduled repairs or breakdowns.

Maybe California power companies aren't rigging electricity prices. But they clearly have both the means and the incentive to do so—and you have to wonder why the deregulators didn't worry about this, why they didn't ask seemingly obvious questions about whether the market they proposed to create would really work as advertised.

And maybe that is the broader lesson of the debacle: Don't rush into a market solution when there are serious questions about whether the market will work. Both economic analysis and British experience should have rung warning bells about California's deregulation scheme; but those warnings were ignored—just as similar warnings are being ignored by enthusiasts for market solutions for everything from prescription drug coverage to education.

# THE UNREAL THING

*February 18, 2001*

"Treason doth never prosper: what's the reason?" asked Sir John Harrington. "Why, if it prosper, none dare call it treason." Fortunately, the stakes are lower these days. A modern version might read: "Deregulation never fails: what's the deal? That when it fails, they say it wasn't real."

On the face of it, California's electricity debacle is an object lesson in the risks of deregulation. The magic of the free market was supposed to provide abundant, cheap, clean power; instead the state faces not only shortages and skyrocketing prices but also insistent demands that it relax air-quality rules. The only bright spots—literally—are a few cities, including Los Angeles, that own their own power systems.

Nonetheless, a growing chorus denies that deregulation was at fault. According to what seems to be becoming the conventional wisdom, meddling bureaucrats prevented the state from having "real" deregulation, creating instead a neither-fish-nor-fowl system that combined the worst features of both worlds. It's a comforting view: it lets true believers in the infallibility of free markets cling to their faith, and it also lets deregulators in other states continue to claim that it can't happen here.

Alas, a close look at the claims that California's deregulation wasn't "real" suggests that while the deregulation was indeed flawed, the flaws didn't cause the catastrophe.

To understand the limits to California's deregulation, recall that it separated the power industry into two pieces. Generators, mainly owned by out-of-state companies, produce power and sell it wholesale to utilities, which then sell retail power to consumers.

One way in which California didn't fully deregulate was that while prices in the wholesale market were decontrolled, the prices charged by utilities continued to be fixed by the state. This meant that even when power shortages sent wholesale prices sky high, homes and businesses had no financial incentive to conserve electricity. The history of retail price control is a little odd; it was actually a temporary measure intended as a sweetener for the utilities, a way to let them earn some extra profits in the face of what were expected to be falling wholesale prices. As it turned out, however, the rigidity of retail prices made it harder for the state to cope with its crisis.

But would it really have made a big difference if those prices had not been fixed? All the evidence suggests that to reduce demand enough to eliminate today's shortages retail electricity prices would have to rise enormously—and that such a rise would be politically unacceptable. In fact, in San Diego the original retail price freeze ended before the crisis struck. But when prices suddenly tripled last summer, a firestorm of public outrage forced the imposition of new controls.

Another way in which deregulation was incomplete was that regulators prevented the utilities from entering into long-term contracts to buy power, forcing them instead to buy wholesale electricity in a short-term "spot" market. Soaring spot prices have bankrupted the utilities, and are forcing the state government to spend billions to keep the power flowing. If the utilities had locked in large supplies at lower prices, they would not yet be bankrupt—but they would still be hemorrhaging money.

While long-term contracts might have postponed the financial day of reckoning, would they have made more power available? Some say yes: if much of their output were under long-term contract, the generators would have less market power—that is, less incentive to restrict output in order to drive up spot prices. The generators, of course, vehemently deny that they are doing any such thing, despite circumstantial evidence that they are. If we accept their denials, long-term contracts would have done nothing to prevent the current power shortages.

And whose idea was it to prevent long-term contracts anyway? In 1999, some of the major utilities petitioned for the right to sign such contracts. Consumer groups, which initially had qualms, eventually supported the bid. But the regulators turned the request down, largely because any change in the rules to allow such contracts was fiercely opposed by, you guessed it, the generators. There's a myth in the making, one that portrays California as a victim, not of deregulation gone bad, but of quasi-socialist politicians who didn't give deregulation a chance to work. Well, that's not the way it happened. The defenders of deregulation should stop making excuses and look seriously at what went wrong.

# THE PRICE OF POWER

*March 24, 2001*

Welcome to the Cartel California. Last week a report by the Independent System Operator, which runs California's power grid, made it more or less official: the electricity crisis in the Golden State is partly the result of market manipulation by power generators. The report alleges that generators overcharged the state's utilities, which distribute power to consumers, by more than $6 billion over a 10-month period.

The report is almost certain to be ignored by federal authorities. But I'll come back to that in a minute. First, there are a couple of things I need to make clear about the report's claims.

The I.S.O. is not alleging that power generators were part of some vast conspiracy. Actually, I shouldn't have used the word "Cartel" in the opening sentence. The generators didn't have to conspire: the logic of the situation made it easy, almost irresistible, for each individual company to manipulate the market. In fact, to believe that the generators didn't engage in market manipulation, you have to believe that they are either saints or very bad businessmen, because they would have been passing up an obvious opportunity to increase their profits.

Imagine the situation: it's a hot summer, and the California electricity market is very tight. You are one of only a handful of major players selling wholesale electricity. Surely the thought has to occur to you: what would happen to prices if one of my plants just happened to go off line? And when companies act on that thought . . . well, you get the picture.

It's also important to realize that accusations that power companies were withholding electricity to drive up prices didn't emerge out of nowhere when the crisis erupted; this isn't a case of politicians suddenly looking for scapegoats. On the contrary, economists were raising red flags about the possibility of market manipulation long before California's woes hit the headlines. Indeed, some economists warned about the issue before California even deregulated: there was clear evidence that "market power" was a problem in Britain, which began experimenting with deregulation and privatization years before the movement came to America.

And the research evidence continues to pile up. Just before the I.S.O. issued its report, the economists Paul Joskow and Edward Kahn circulated a study that found strong evidence that "exercise of market power" played a large role in raising electricity prices last summer. The authors aren't leftists, or even opponents of deregulation. They were merely trying to look objectively at the evidence, which points more or less unmistakably to the conclusion that deliberate withholding of electricity to drive up prices has been an important factor in the California crisis.

Still, there is every reason to believe that Washington will turn a deaf ear to this evidence. As an article in this newspaper explained on Friday, the Federal Energy Regulatory Commission, which is supposed to act as the nation's watchdog over the energy industry, lately seems more like a lapdog. I was particularly struck with the report that FERC's staff found that California's power companies "had the potential to exercise market power," but could not conclude that they had actually used that power. As I said, those power generators must be saints, bad businessmen or both.

What should the regulators be doing? I'm skeptical about

proposals to make the generators pay big fines; it's not clear that you could figure out which company was responsible for which part of the problem, or for that matter that the companies were doing anything illegal. What FERC could do is impose a temporary cap on wholesale prices. This would limit the financial damage to California—the state government is currently spending more than a billion dollars a month to subsidize electricity purchases. And in a market where "exercise of market power" is a major factor, a wholesale price cap might actually increase supplies, because power companies would no longer have an incentive to withhold electricity to drive up its price.

But it's not going to happen. Blame knee-jerk free-market ideology, or the political influence of the power companies (many of which are based in, yes, Texas). Whatever the reason, it is hard to imagine an administration less likely to be sympathetic to California's plight than the one currently in power.

And if this indifference makes Californians angry, it should.

# THE REAL WOLF

*April 29, 2001*

Recently I received a letter from an economist I respect, chiding me for my "Naderite" columns on the California energy crisis. He just didn't believe that market manipulation by power companies could possibly be an important issue; it sounded too much to him like the sort of thing one hears from knee-jerk leftists, who blame greedy capitalists for every problem, be it third-world poverty or high apartment rents. The left has cried "Wolf!" so many times that sensible people have learned to discount such claims.

But now a bona fide wolf has arrived, whose predatory behavior is doing terrible damage to our most populous state—and nobody will believe it.

True, California would be heading for a summer of power shortages even if it had never deregulated. And even if there was workable competition in the wholesale electricity market, prices in that market would spike during periods of peak demand, transferring billions of dollars from either taxpayers or consumers to the generators.

But the evidence is now overwhelming that there isn't workable competition in California's power market, and that the actions of generators "gaming the system" have greatly magnified the crisis. The key fact is that California has somehow remained in a state of more or less continuous power shortage and very high wholesale prices regardless of the level of demand. A rash of outages has kept the electricity market conveniently—and very profitably—short of supply even during periods of low demand, when there ought to be lots of excess capacity.

As Frank Wolak, the Stanford economist who also advises the state's power grid, has pointed out, an outage at a power plant is a lot like an employee calling in sick. You can't tell directly whether he is really sick or has chosen to take the day off for other reasons, but you can look for circumstantial evidence. And such evidence has convinced Mr. Wolak that "generators use forced outages strategically to withhold capacity from the market"—a view shared by a growing number of other researchers.

Which brings us to the latest move by the Federal Energy Regulatory Commission. On Wednesday, the commission apparently decided to offer California some relief, and put new price caps in place on the California electricity market. I say "apparently" because the more you look at the plan the less likely it seems to be any help at all. Indeed, the measure was passed on a 2-to-1 vote, with William Massey—the one commissioner who has been sympathetic to calls for price controls—voting against it on the grounds that it would be ineffectual.

What's wrong with FERC's plan? First, it caps prices only in emergency conditions—ignoring the fact that electricity prices have stayed at hard-to-explain levels even when there is no emergency. In effect, the plan is laid out as if the electricity market were really competitive, in spite of all the evidence that it is not.

Second, even those emergency price caps are full of loopholes, offering extensive opportunities for what Mr. Wolak calls "megawatt laundering"—selling power to affiliated companies that for one reason or another are exempted from the price controls (for example, the controls do not apply to "imports" from neighboring states), then selling it back into the California market. Severin Borenstein of the University of California Energy Institute adds that because the allowed price depends on the cost of generation at the least efficient plant, generators will have a clear incentive to produce inefficiently: "I predict we will find some plants we never heard of before that are suddenly operating again, and they will be pretty inefficient."

The general verdict seems to be that this is not a serious plan. There are serious proposals to mitigate the crisis out there—indeed, last fall Mr. Wolak submitted a proposal that was well received by other experts—but FERC has ignored all of them.

The charitable interpretation is that FERC still doesn't get it, that it just can't bring itself to believe that this time the wolf is real. The uncharitable interpretation is that last week's action was meant to fail. *The Medley Report*, an online newsletter, calls the FERC plan "a grand exercise in posturing without substance . . . a very clever temporary move by the Bush administration to deflect any political fallout" from the looming disaster.

Whatever the explanation, the plain fact is that FERC and the administration have yet to offer California any significant relief.

# TURNING CALIFORNIA ON

*June 27, 2001*

Those wimpy Californians, with all their fuzzy talk about conservation and their hostility to Big Energy, were supposed to spend this summer sweltering in the dark. But events are not following the script. Summer has begun, yet so far power supplies have been adequate—and prices have been fairly reasonable. In fact, in the last few days wholesale electricity, which often sold for $750 per megawatt hour this time last year, has been going for less than $100, sometimes less than $50.

Everyone seems reluctant to talk about this good news, out of fear that saying anything optimistic would be a self-defeating prophecy. And it is still possible for things to go very wrong. Still, the contrast between dire expectations and the relatively benign picture so far demands an explanation.

One big reason for California's improved energy situation is conservation. Taking temperature into account, California consumers are using between 5 and 10 percent less electricity this summer than expected.

Another reason is a sharp drop in the price of natural gas, an important part of the cost of generating electricity. More on that in a minute.

The most important factor in the turnaround, however, is that the state's power plants are back on line. In March, with air-conditioners turned off, there should have been plenty of spare generating capacity. But around 15,000 megawatts, a third of the state's capacity, was mysteriously unavailable. Now the offline capacity is less than 4,000 megawatts.

Why are the state's power plants operating again? More to the point, why weren't they operating back when the state was desperately short of power, and prices were much higher than they are now?

Many economists now accept the uncomfortable answer: Generators deliberately withheld electricity from the market in order to drive high prices even higher. Until recently the evidence for this market manipulation was purely circumstantial; but it has now been reinforced by direct testimony by former employees of one generator.

So why did the market manipulation stop? Generators now sell much of their output under long-term contracts with the state, which reduces the incentive to drive up prices in the spot market. But the main answer is probably that intense public scrutiny, culminating in the recent decision by federal regulators to impose price caps, has convinced generators that they had better behave themselves. (The details of the price caps, it turns out, may be less important than the signal that the regulators are, finally, prepared to do some regulating.)

The natural gas story may be similar. Last year El Paso Natural Gas, which controls one of the crucial pipelines serving California, leased a big chunk of that pipeline's capacity to its own marketing subsidiary. That subsidiary has been widely accused of using its control of the pipeline to withhold gas from the California market, and thereby drive up prices. The company denies the accusation, and says that an internal document that talks about "ability to influence the physical market to the benefit of any financial/hedge position" wasn't saying what it seemed to be saying. But when the lease expired at the beginning of this month, gas prices in California promptly plunged 50 percent.

And so, sooner than anyone expected, it seems that the worst may be over. A drought or a heat wave could still cause rolling blackouts. But time is on California's side; some new power plants will come on line in a few weeks, and many more over the course of the next 18 months.

The big loser from all this—for somebody always gets hurt even by good news—is, of course, Dick Cheney, the architect of the Bush administration's drill-and-burn energy plan. Remember that Mr. Cheney sneeringly dismissed conservation as a mere "sign of personal virtue," and was scathing about people who thought price controls would help. Now things are suddenly looking up—partly because of conservation, and partly because price controls and the threat of further government intervention have deterred energy producers from manipulating the market.

It turns out, in other words, that Mr. Cheney—who prides himself on his tough-mindedness—was naïvely out of touch with reality. And the real realists were those silly people who thought that California could solve its crisis by saving energy and suing energy producers.

## ENRON GOES OVERBOARD

*August 17, 2001*

Whom the gods would destroy, they first put on the cover of *BusinessWeek*. When the Feb. 12 issue featured a cover photo of Jeffrey Skilling, you knew bad things were about to happen both to Enron and to its new C.E.O. Sure enough, on Tuesday Mr. Skilling resigned for "personal reasons." The next day he conceded that the most important of those personal reasons was the 50 percent drop in Enron's stock since January.

Is this just another tale of extravagant expectations disappointed, the kind of story that has become all too common lately? No; this case has wider significance. Enron, based in Houston, is in the vanguard of a powerful movement that hopes to "financialize" (Enron's term) just about everything—that is, trade almost everything as if it were stock options.

That movement is as much about politics as it is about business, and the company has not been shy about using its political connections to advance its cause. With the arrival of George W. Bush in the White House—thanks largely to Enron, a prime mover behind his campaign—the sky seemed to be the limit.

But financialization looks more and more like a movement that has overreached itself.

Enron was originally a natural gas pipeline company, swaddled like all such companies in a tight regulatory straitjacket. In the mid-1980's, however, gas markets were set free. And Kenneth Lay, who was C.E.O. at the time and is returning to succeed Mr. Skilling, saw a great opportunity.

He transformed Enron from a company that delivered B.T.U.'s to one that dealt in contracts; as *BusinessWeek* put it, the company became "more akin to Goldman Sachs than to Consolidated Edison." Enron became the lead market-maker for the new, deregulated natural gas industry; since deregulation worked well for natural gas, which increasingly became the nation's fuel of choice, Enron's new role was highly profitable.

After gas, electricity. As power deregulation became the rage across the U.S., Enron took on a key role as a broker for wholesale electricity. Soon the company was looking for new worlds to conquer: water supply, bandwidth on fiber-optic cables, data storage, even advertising space.

Then things started to go wrong. Enron abandoned its venture into water supply when it became clear that governments were reluctant to entrust so crucial a matter to the magic of the invisible hand. And skeptics found ample justification for their lack of faith when electricity deregulation, which was supposed to be a certified success story, went spectacularly astray in California.

True believers insist that the power crisis of 2000–2001, which transferred tens of billions of dollars from taxpayers to electricity-generating companies—and quite a bit to Enron too—was not a verdict on deregulation, that it was all the fault of meddling politicians who didn't let the market work. But this claim isn't particularly convincing, mainly because it isn't true. The real lesson of the California catastrophe was that the concerns that led to regulation in the first place—monopoly power and the threat of market manipulation—are still real issues today.

State and local governments, alerted by what happened in California, will henceforth be a lot more wary about deregulation. There's even a movement to reregulate electricity markets. And that means fewer opportunities for Enron, whose stock price depends on the expectation that it will keep finding new Californias to conquer.

Of course, the people Enron put in the White House are still there, and they seem to have learned nothing from California. It's true that the Bush administration sometimes compromises on its free-market principles—it believes, for example, that energy producers need huge subsidies, even though the shortages those subsidies were supposed to correct have turned out to be imaginary (a recent cover story in *Barron's* warned of "the coming energy glut").

But otherwise the administration's faith in absolutely unregulated markets is unshaken. The new head of the Federal Energy Regulatory Commission—the watchdog agency that conspicuously refused to do its job in California—is, you guessed it, a Texan with close ties to the energy industry. And the administration continues to believe that "financialization" is the way to go on just about everything, from school vouchers to Social Security.

But it's wrong. And let's hope that it doesn't take a string of catastrophes to teach us that there are limits to what markets can do.

# SMOKING FAT BOY

*May 10, 2002*

An old joke: A farmer hears suspicious noises in his henhouse. "Who's there?" he calls out. "Nobody here but us chickens," replies the thief. Satisfied, the farmer goes back to bed.

That about sums up the behavior of federal regulators during California's electricity crisis. As I've been pointing out for more than a year, there is powerful circumstantial evidence that market manipulation played a key role in that crisis. Energy companies had the motive, the means and the opportunity to drive prices sky-high. And the crisis exhibited exactly the features you would expect if market manipulation was playing a big role: much of the state's generating capacity stood idle even as wholesale electricity prices went to 50 times normal levels.

Yet federal officials, from George W. Bush on down, offered California nothing but sermons on the virtues of the free market. The Federal Energy Regulatory Commission, which is supposed to police these things, found no evidence of foul play. Essentially, FERC asked energy companies whether they were manipulating the market. "Who, us?" they replied—and that was that. My favorite FERC study found that power companies had the ability to exercise "market power," and that it would have been profitable for them to do so, but that there was no evidence that they actually had. Those power executives must be swell guys!

The significance of the "smoking-gun" Enron memos that

came to light a few days ago is that they show exactly how swell those power executives really were. It turns out that Enron was indeed rigging the markets, with schemes that had smart-alecky nicknames like Fat Boy, Death Star and Get Shorty. Who said business isn't fun?

These memos came to light despite FERC's evident determination to see no evil. (We now know that the Bush administration in effect allowed Enron to choose the commission's members.) As one California official put it: "FERC is like a parent who doesn't want to believe their teenager has gone bad. The memos are significant because they are like finding a diary in the kid's backpack saying, 'I robbed the liquor store.' "

The great risk now is that this will be treated purely as an Enron story. That's wrong; Enron was mainly a trader rather than a power producer, and as such could have only limited impact on electricity prices. The bigger story involves market manipulation by a number of producers. The circumstantial evidence for that manipulation is overwhelming. And if no smoking-gun memos have yet come to light, what do you expect? The Enron story shows just how easy it is for companies to cover their tracks, especially when the regulators are in their corner. If Enron hadn't lost its clout by going bankrupt, you can be sure that we would never have heard about Fat Boy and Death Star.

There is, however, one specific Enron angle here. I may have done Thomas White, secretary of the Army, an injustice. He ran Enron Energy Services, a division that—or so I thought—was mainly used as a way to generate phony profits, inflating Enron's stock price. But the division turns out to have had another role: to create phony energy transactions, inflating Enron's actual profits at the expense of the state of California. Why, exactly, is Mr. White still in office?

What really annoys me in this story, however, isn't the behavior of the energy companies. It isn't even the behavior of the Bush administration—though the administration not only stood idly by while California was robbed of around $30 billion, it also shamelessly exploited the state's misery to promote its own, utterly irrelevant energy plan. (Now, of course, that same energy plan is essential to the war on terrorism.)

No, what bothers me is the position taken by so many business and political commentators: that the California catastrophe says nothing about the risks of deregulation and the dangers of loving free markets too much. It was California's own fault, they say, for creating a "flawed" system—a wonderfully vague term that evades the necessity of explaining what really happened. In fact, the main flaw was that the system contained no safeguards against market-rigging.

And I'm sure that there will be a determined effort to ignore even these latest revelations. After all, why let facts get in the way of a beautiful, and politically convenient, theory?

# IN BROAD DAYLIGHT

*September 27, 2002*

"You are one of only a handful of major players selling whole-sale electricity. Surely the thought has to occur to you: what would happen to prices if one of my plants just happened to go off line? And when companies act on that thought . . . well, you get the picture."

I wrote that in March 2001, when the California electricity crisis was at its height. Even then the experts I talked to—economists who followed the situation closely, and kept an open mind—believed that energy companies were deliberately creating shortages. But only in the last few weeks, with a series of damning reports and judgments, has conventional wisdom grudgingly accepted the obvious.

And that's the real mystery of the California crisis: how could a $30 billion robbery take place in broad daylight?

True, it was always hard to pin down specific acts of market manipulation. Stanford's Frank Wolak likens energy companies to an employee who keeps calling in sick: the pattern is clear, but unless you catch him faking an ailment, it's hard to prove that he is malingering.

But the evidence is starting to pile up. First there were those Enron memos. Then the California Public Utilities Commission determined that most of the blackouts that afflicted California between November 2000 and May 2001 took place not because generating capacity was inadequate, but because the major power companies kept much of their capacity off line. Most recently, a judge for the Federal Energy Regulatory Commission has ruled that El Paso Corporation used its control over a key pipeline to create an artificial natural gas shortage.

But why did energy companies think they could get away with it?

One answer might be that the apparent malefactors are very big contributors to the Republican Party. Some analysts have suggested that energy companies felt free to manipulate markets because they believed they had bought protection from federal regulation—the conspiracy-minded point out that severe power shortages began just after the 2000 election, and ended when Democrats gained control of the Senate.

Federal regulators certainly seemed determined to see and hear no evil, and above all not to reveal evidence of evil to state officials. A previous FERC ruling on El Paso was, in the view of many observers, a whitewash. In another case, AES/Williams was accused of shutting down generating units, forcing the power system to buy power at vastly higher prices from other units of the same company. In April 2001, FERC and Williams reached a settlement in which the company repaid the extra profits, but paid no penalty—and FERC sealed the evidence. Last week CBS News reported that "federal regulators have power control room audiotapes that prove traders from Williams Energy called plant operators and told them to turn off the juice. The government sealed the tapes in a secret settlement"—the same settlement?—"and still refuses to release them."

If that's true, FERC caught at least one power company red-handed, in the middle of the crisis, at a time when state officials were begging the agency to take action—and then suppressed the evidence. Yet this story has received little national play.

For some reason it has never been cool to talk about what

was really happening in California. When the crisis was in full swing, most commentators clung to a story line that blamed meddlesome bureaucrats, not profiteering corporations. When the crisis came to an end, it suddenly became old news.

Maybe our national faith in free markets is so strong that people just don't want to talk about a case in which markets went spectacularly bad. But I'm still puzzled by the lack of attention, not just to the disaster, but to hints of a cover-up. After all, this was the most spectacular abuse of market power since the days of the robber barons—and the feds did nothing to stop it.

And if FERC was strangely ineffective during the California crisis, what can we expect from other agencies? Across the government, from the Interior Department and the Forest Service to the Environmental Protection Agency, former lobbyists for the regulated industries now hold key positions—and they show little inclination to make trouble for their once and future employers.

So we ignore California's experience at our peril. It's all too likely to be the shape of things to come.

## DELUSIONS OF POWER

*March 28, 2003*

They considered themselves tough-minded realists, and regarded doubters as fuzzy-minded whiners. They silenced those who questioned their premises, even though the skeptics included many of the government's own analysts. They were supremely confident—and yet with shocking speed everything they had said was proved awesomely wrong.

No, I'm not talking about the war; I'm talking about the energy task force that Dick Cheney led back in 2001. Yet there are some disturbing parallels. Right now, pundits are wondering how Mr. Cheney—who confidently predicted that our soldiers would be "greeted as liberators"—could have been so mistaken. But a devastating new report on the California energy crisis reminds us that Mr. Cheney has been equally confident, and equally wrong, about other issues.

In spring 2001 the lights were going out all over California. There were blackouts and brownouts, and the price of electricity was soaring. The Cheney task force was convened in the midst of that crisis. It concluded, in brief, that the energy crisis was a long-term problem caused by meddling bureaucrats and pesky environmentalists, who weren't letting big companies do what needed to be done. The solution? Scrap environmental rules, and give the energy industry multibillion-dollar subsidies.

Along the way, Mr. Cheney sneeringly dismissed energy conservation as a mere "sign of personal virtue" and scorned California officials who called for price controls and said the crisis was being exacerbated by market manipulation. To be fair, Mr. Cheney's mocking attitude on that last point was shared by almost everyone in politics and the media—and yes, I am patting myself on the back for getting it right.

For we now know that everything Mr. Cheney said was wrong.

In fact, the California energy crisis had nothing to do with environmental restrictions, and a lot to do with market manipulation. In 2001 the evidence for manipulation was basically circumstantial. But now we have a new report from the Federal Energy Regulatory Commission, which until now has discounted claims of market manipulation. No more: the new report concludes that market manipulation was pervasive, and offers a mountain of direct evidence, including phone conversations, e-mail and memos. There's no longer any doubt: California's power shortages were largely artificial, created by energy companies to drive up prices and profits.

Oh, and what ended the crisis? Key factors included energy conservation and price controls. Meanwhile, what happened to that long-term shortage of capacity, which required scrapping environmental rules and providing lots of corporate welfare? Within months after the Cheney report's release, stock analysts were downgrading energy companies because of a looming long-term-capacity glut.

In short, Mr. Cheney and his tough-minded realists were blowing smoke: their report described a fantasy world that bore no relation to reality. How did they get it so wrong?

One answer is that Mr. Cheney made sure that his task force included only like-minded men: as far as we can tell, he didn't consult with anyone except energy executives. So the task force was subject to what military types call "incestuous amplification," defined by *Jane's Defence Weekly* as "a condition in warfare where one only listens to those who are already in lock-step agreement, reinforcing set beliefs and creating a situation ripe for miscalculation."

Another answer is that Mr. Cheney basically drew his advice about how to end the energy crisis from the very companies creating the crisis, for fun and profit. But was he in on the joke?

We may never know what really went on in the energy task force since the Bush administration has gone to extraordinary lengths to keep us from finding out. At first the nonpartisan General Accounting Office, which is supposed to act as an internal watchdog, seemed determined to pursue the matter. But after the midterm election, according to the newsletter *The Hill*, Congressional Republicans approached the agency's head and threatened to slash his budget unless he backed off.

And therein lies the broader moral. In the last two years Mr. Cheney and other top officials have gotten it wrong again and again—on energy, on the economy, on the budget. But political muscle has insulated them from any adverse consequences. So they, and the country, don't learn from their mistakes—and the mistakes keep getting bigger.

## CHAPTER 13

# *Smog and Mirrors*

## THE UNREFINED TRUTH

*May 9, 2001*

Gasoline prices are rising again, and the administration is rushing to turn this into another argument for its drill-and-burn energy strategy. But a look at the causes of the current gasoline shortage actually suggests a quite different moral: namely, that conservation ought to be a major element in our energy strategy, and that lack of conservation is a large part of what we've been doing wrong.

First things first: This year's gasoline price spike has nothing to do with a shortage of crude oil. Even if we had already punched the Alaskan tundra and the ocean floor off Florida full of holes, we'd still be in the same fix. The binding constraint right now is the nation's limited capacity to refine crude oil into gasoline.

Why is refining capacity inadequate? No new refineries have been built in this country for 20 years, a point emphasized with obvious relish by Dick Cheney. His implicit subtext, of course, is that it's the fault of environmentalist types who stood in the oil industry's way. That must be the story, right?

Wrong. It's true that environmental rules have somewhat crimped the production of our existing refineries. The problem is not so much the strictness of the regulations as their lack of consistency: each region has its own rules—like the insistence of Midwestern states that gasoline include corn-derived ethanol—fragmenting the nation's production. But the reason the oil industry didn't build any new refineries for two decades was that they weren't needed. In fact, right up until last year oil refining was a persistently depressed business, plagued by overcapacity.

Here's what happened: In the wake of the energy crisis in the 1970's, ordinary people in the U.S. began conserving energy—not as a "sign of personal virtue," as Mr. Cheney sneeringly puts it, but because they wanted to save money. Cars, in particular, became much more fuel-efficient. Meanwhile the oil industry was subject to "refinery creep," the tendency of refining capacity to grow through incremental improvements even when no new refineries are built. The result was excess capacity and squeezed margins, right up to the late 1990's.

What finally brought us up against capacity constraints was a surge in demand that was partly due to the economic boom of the later Clinton years, but mainly due to the renewed enthusiasm of Americans for huge, gas-guzzling vehicles—an enthusiasm, er, fueled by cheap gas. In 1998 gasoline was cheaper compared with overall consumer prices than ever before in U.S. history—60 percent cheaper than it was in 1981. The nation rushed out to buy ever bigger S.U.V.'s—and then suddenly discovered that we had run out of refining capacity. Refiners weren't frustrated by rules that prevented them from building new facilities; they were simply caught by surprise.

You have to bear this history in mind when parsing Mr. Cheney's recent speeches. To listen to him, you would imagine that we live in a country in which powerful political forces oppose energy production and preach a return to the dark ages. "To speak exclusively of conservation," Mr. Cheney declared in one speech, "is to duck the tough issues . . . it is not a sufficient basis—all by itself—for a sound, comprehensive energy policy." In another speech he ridiculed unspecified types for "saying to the American people that you have to live in the dark, turn out all of the lights." The story according to Mr. Cheney, in other words, is that we have an energy shortage because extreme conservationists prevented us from developing the supply capacity that serious people knew we needed.

Need I point out that this, like so much of what one hears from this administration, is a cynical misrepresentation? I defy Mr. Cheney to come up with examples of influential people who "speak exclusively of conservation," let alone anyone who says to the American people that they have to live in the dark. In fact, hardly any important politicians have spoken about conservation at all—never mind exclusively—this past decade.

We will need to build more refineries—and more power plants, and pipelines, and so on. But it is ludicrous to suggest that our current energy woes are the result of too much emphasis on conservation. It would be closer to the truth to say that we are in trouble now because our politicians haven't dared even use the word.

## BURN, BABY, BURN

*May 20, 2001*

Who knew that Dick Cheney had such a sense of humor?

He had us rolling in the aisles after the famous put-down in which he dismissed energy conservation as nothing more than a "sign of personal virtue." But the joke got much better Thursday, with the release of the administration's energy plan. Just for laughs, Mr. Cheney threw in a few mock conservation measures. Topping the list was a tax credit for—get this—people who purchase hybrid gas-electric cars.

In case you don't quite get the joke: during the campaign one of George W. Bush's favorite gag lines involved making fun of Al Gore's proposal for—you guessed it—a tax credit for purchase of hybrid cars. It got big laughs because it symbolized his opponent's supposed preoccupation with trivialities. Now, in a fine satirical gesture, Mr. Cheney has made the very same proposal his lead conservation measure. Take that, you wimps!

It seems that the pundits, having misjudged Mr. Bush and Mr. Cheney during the campaign, have done it again. We now know that the moderate rhetoric Mr. Bush used during the campaign was insincere; but it turns out that the administration's libertarian rhetoric during the selling of the tax cut was equally insincere. These guys don't believe in free markets: what they're really into is heavy metal. Refineries! Pipelines! Nuclear power plants! That's the stuff!

To justify their lust for tubular steel, Mr. Cheney and his collaborators have gone to great lengths to fabricate an energy crisis—and they have also suddenly decided that free markets don't work after all. "Estimates," says the report, "indicate that over the next 20 years U.S. oil consumption will increase by 33 percent." Whose estimates? We are never told. But that's an awfully high number. In the 20 years ending in 1999, the last year for which official data are available, oil consumption rose less than 5 percent. All I can figure is that Mr. Cheney's people are extrapolating from the abrupt decline in automobile fuel efficiency over the last few years, as people have switched from ordinary cars to S.U.V.'s. And what they are saying is that we should base our energy policy on the assumption that this quite recent trend will continue unabated for decades.

This doesn't have to happen. In fact, it isn't going to happen, even in the absence of any serious conservation measures. To burn as much oil as the Cheney report says we need, everyone who still drives a mere car would have to acquire an S.U.V., and everyone who now drives an S.U.V. would have to start driving something the size of a Sherman tank.

What's behind Mr. Cheney's greasy math? It goes without saying that he wants to scare us into relaxing environmental regulation. But there's more: the Cheney plan provides an array of subsidies, explicit and implicit, for energy producers. Indeed, the libertarian Cato Institute calls the plan a "smorgasbord of handouts and subsidies for virtually every energy lobby in Washington." Strange, isn't it? If you're a low-paid worker, or an energy consumer, the free market is sacrosanct—it would be a terrible thing if government provided you with any assistance. But energy producers apparently need special encouragement to do their regular job.

In fact, of course, they don't. Mr. Cheney loves to talk about our alleged need to build a new power plant every week for the next 20 years, implying that this is a herculean task that can only be accomplished with a lot of help from Washington. But high prices have already sparked a huge construction boom in the power industry, which will add three or four plants per week for the next few years. As some wags have put it, if the power industry wants to meet Mr. Cheney's target it will have to slow down its building program.

The truth is that the administration has things exactly the wrong way around. It claims that we face a long-run energy crisis, and that there are no short-term answers. The reality is that in the long run the forces of supply and demand will take care of our energy needs, with or without Mr. Cheney's expensive new program of corporate welfare. What we need is a strategy to deal with the temporary problem of sky-high prices and huge windfall profits. But we're not going to get it, at least not from Washington.

# FEELING OPEC'S PAIN

*August 5, 2001*

George W. Bush said something interesting about economics the other day. No, really. It wasn't his usual line about how tax cuts are the answer to whatever ails you; he said something unscripted, something that reflected what he really thinks and feels. You might say that his remarks gave us a sense of his soul. And it turns out that his soul—or maybe it's just his heart—belongs to people, of whatever nationality, who sell oil.

Recently Mr. Bush was asked about the decision of the Organization of Petroleum Exporting Countries to reduce output by a million barrels a day. That's about as much as the Department of Energy's estimate of peak daily production if we drill in the Alaskan tundra—a peak that won't come until the middle of the next decade. And OPEC cut production in order to keep oil prices high despite slumping world demand, which would seem to be against U.S. interests.

Yet Mr. Bush was remarkably sympathetic to OPEC's cause; it seems that he feels the oil exporters' pain. "It's very important for there to be stability in a marketplace. I've read some comments from the OPEC ministers who said this was just a matter to make sure the market remains stable and predictable," he declared. Just in case you wonder whether this was really an endorsement of price-fixing, or whether Mr. Bush was just being polite, his spokesman, Ari Fleischer, left no doubt: "The president thinks it's important to have stability, and stability can come in the form of low prices, stability can come in the form of moderate prices."

This is the same man who boasted during last year's campaign that he would force OPEC to "open the spigot." Did OPEC take Mr. Bush's remarks as a green light for further cuts?

According to one oil analyst interviewed by Reuters, Mr. Bush's apparent expression of support for their efforts to keep prices high "excited a lot of OPEC ministers."

Funny, isn't it? When California complains about high electricity prices, it gets a lecture about how you can't defy the laws of supply and demand. But when foreign producers collude to prevent prices from falling in the face of an oil glut, the administration not only signals its approval but endorses the old, discredited theory that cartels are in consumers' interest.

This was not the only case in which the administration dropped its principles when the subject turned to oil. The energy bill the House passed last week was notable for its indifference to environmental consequences and its lack of serious conservation measures—increased fuel-efficiency standards could easily save far more oil than we'll ever get by punching holes in the tundra.

But the most amazing thing is that the bill contains more than $30 billion in subsidies and special tax breaks for energy producers. That's even more amazing given that money is looking very tight: Republicans are nervously awaiting new budget projections, which everyone in Washington expects will show that the tax cut has wiped out the non-trust-fund budget surplus for the foreseeable future.

So it seems that many of the administration's principles contain a special clause, making an exception when it comes to oil. The administration tells people that they should place their trust in the free market, and accept the fact that prices will move up and down with changes in supply and demand—unless those people happen to be selling oil. The administration tells people that they should be self-reliant, and should not expect subsidies from the federal government—unless those people happen to be selling oil. And the administration tells countries that they must expect the U.S. to stand up for its own interests, and that our government doesn't worry about offending their delicate sensibilities—unless those countries happen to be selling oil.

Mr. Bush was, needless to say, naïve in ascribing any altruistic motives to the OPEC ministers. They don't want stability, they want money—your money. And their action didn't do the world economy a favor—on the contrary, falling oil prices were one of the things that economists had hoped might reduce the risk of a global recession. So OPEC's decision to cut output, which Mr. Bush seems to condone, was bad for the world, and bad for the people of the U.S.—except, of course, for those people who happen to be selling oil.

## ERSATZ CLIMATE POLICY

*February 15, 2002*

Alert shoppers know that an extra word in a product's description can make a big difference, and rarely for the better. Apologies to connoisseurs of Velveeta, but most of us don't regard "cheese food" as a good substitute for plain ordinary cheese.

To the unwary, yesterday's pledge by the Bush administration to reduce "greenhouse gas intensity" by 18 percent may have sounded like a pledge to reduce greenhouse gases, the emissions (mainly carbon dioxide, released by burning fossil fuels) that cause global warming. In fact, that's the way it was reported in some news articles. But the extra word makes all the difference. In fact, the administration proposed to achieve almost nothing; consistent with that goal, it also announced specific policies that are trivial in scope and will have virtually no effect.

What is this thing called greenhouse gas intensity? It is the volume of greenhouse gas emissions divided by gross domestic product. The administration says that it will reduce this ratio by 18 percent over the next decade. But since most forecasts call for GDP to expand 30 percent or more over the same period, this is actually a proposal to allow a substantial increase in emissions.

Still, doesn't holding the growth of emissions to less than the growth of the economy show at least some effort to face up to climate change? No, because that would happen anyway. In fact, the administration's target for reduction in greenhouse gas intensity might well be achieved without any policy actions—which is good news, because the administration hasn't really proposed any.

The reasons greenhouse gas intensity tends to fall over time are complex, but the basic logic is simple: We are gradually becoming a post-industrial society, in which knowledge and service industries grow faster than the old smokestack sector. Because pushing bits around doesn't take as much energy as pushing around large pieces of sheet metal, a dollar of new-economy GDP generally doesn't require burning as much carbon as a dollar of old-economy GDP.

But the old economy is still there, and the new economy still uses significant amounts of energy—especially if office workers drive S.U.V.'s long distances on their way from house to mouse and back. So as the economy grows, greenhouse gas intensity may fall, but greenhouse gas emissions—which are what damages the planet—continue to rise.

So what does the Bush administration propose to do? Nothing much.

The main actual policy described yesterday was an array of tax credits for planet-friendly activities, such as installing solar power or capturing methane from landfill. It's not worth trying to analyze the specifics of this proposal, such as why tax credits should be the tool of choice. (Oh, I forgot—tax cuts are the answer to all problems.) The key point is that it's just too small to do the job. It offers $4.6 billion over the next five years. That's less than a penny a day per American. Do you really think that's enough to produce a major change in the way we use energy, or that it is an appropriate level of response to a major threat to the planet?

And that's the substantive part of the proposal. The other part is creation of a "registry": companies can, if they choose, report their emissions of greenhouse gases. If they show reductions in emissions, they will receive—well, nothing. But future administrations might be pleased.

The real question is why an administration that clearly doesn't want to do anything about climate change feels obliged to put on this show.

The answer, of course, is that on environmental issues the administration is clearly out of step with the public. Its indifference to the fate of the planet would be quite unpopular if it were generally appreciated.

To deal with this potential political threat, the Bush administration exaggerates the economic costs of environmental regulations. Last spring Dick Cheney implied, disingenuously, that environmental rules had caused a shortage of refining capacity; now George W. Bush tells us, implausibly, that the Kyoto Protocol will destroy millions of jobs.

Meanwhile the administration offers the illusion of environmentalism, by announcing policies that sound impressive but are nearly content-free.

So buyers beware. What the administration offered yesterday was processed climate-change policy food, bearing very little resemblance to the real thing.

# TWO THOUSAND ACRES

*March 1, 2002*

According to my calculations, my work space occupies only a few square inches of office floor. You may find this implausible, but I'm using a well-accepted methodology. Well accepted, that is, among supporters of oil drilling in the Arctic National Wildlife Refuge.

Last week Interior Secretary Gale Norton repeated the standard response to concerns about extensive oil development in one of America's last wild places: "The impact will be limited to just 2,000 out of 1.9 million acres of the refuge." That number comes from the House version of the Bush-Cheney energy plan, which promises that "surface acreage covered by production and support facilities" will not exceed 2,000 acres. It's a reassuring picture: a tiny enclave of development, practically lost in the Arctic vastness.

But that picture is a fraud. Development won't be limited to a small enclave: according to the U.S. Geological Survey, oil in ANWR is scattered in many separate pools, so drilling rigs would be spread all across the coastal plain. The roads linking those rigs aren't part of the 2,000 acres: they're not "production and support facilities." And "surface acreage covered" is very narrowly defined: if a pipeline snakes across the terrain on a series of posts, only the ground on which those posts rest counts; bare ground under the pipeline isn't considered "covered."

Now you see how I work in such a small space. By those definitions, my "impact" is limited to floor areas that literally have stuff resting on them: the bottoms of the legs on my desk and chair, and the soles of my shoes. The rest of my office floor is pristine wilderness.

There's a lesson here that goes well beyond the impact of oil drilling on caribou. Deceptive advertising pervades the administration's effort to sell the nation on its drill-and-burn energy strategy. In fact, those of us following this issue can't see why people made such a fuss about the Pentagon's plan to disseminate false information. How would that differ from current policy?

Remember that this latest push to open up ANWR for drilling follows on the heels of an attempt to portray a plan to do nothing much about global warming as a major policy initiative. What else has the administration said about its energy plans that isn't true?

Top of the list, surely, is the claim that drilling in ANWR is a national security issue, the key to ending our dependence on imported oil. In fact, the Energy Information Administration's preferred scenario says that even a decade after development begins, ANWR will produce only between 600,000 and 900,000 barrels of oil a day—a small fraction of the 11 million barrels we currently import.

Then there's the absurd claim that ANWR drilling will create hundreds of thousands of jobs—a claim based on a decade-old study by, you guessed it, the oil industry's trade association.

But the most nefarious aspect of the administration's energy propaganda is its persistent effort to link energy shortages to environmentalism—an effort that, it's now clear, has often been consciously dishonest.

For example, last spring Dick Cheney lamented the fact that the U.S. hadn't built any new oil refineries since the 1970's, linking that lack of construction to environmental restrictions. I wrote a column last May pointing out that environmentalism had nothing to do with it, that refineries hadn't been built because the industry had excess capacity. What I didn't know was that several weeks earlier staffers at the Environmental Protection Agency had written a scathing critique of Mr. Cheney's draft energy report, making exactly the same point. The final version of the report, by the way, doesn't say in so many words that clean-air rules cause gasoline shortages—but it conveys that impression by innuendo.

For now, it's possible for diligent citizens to cut through these deceptions—for example, you can read on the Web what the U.S. Geological Survey actually has to say about oil reserves in the Arctic. But I keep wondering when the administration will shut down those Web sites. After all, under John Ashcroft's new rules, agencies are no longer instructed to release information whenever possible; they're supposed to refuse requests to release information whenever there's a legal basis for doing so. And honest assessments of oil reserves in environmentally sensitive locations might be useful to terrorists—you never know.

# BAD AIR DAYS

*April 26, 2002*

On Earth Day George W. Bush staged a photo op in the wilderness and touted his "clear skies" initiative. Democrats jeered and called him a tool of polluting interests.

Is there anything good to say about the Bush administration's air-quality plans? The answer is yes. But—you knew there would be a "but"—the good stuff is tentative and inadequate, while the bad stuff is being instituted with alacrity and determination.

The current system for controlling air pollution badly needs an overhaul. Back in the 1970's the Clean Air Act set strict rules, but only for "new" sources of pollution. Existing power plants, factories and so on were grandfathered. The idea was that over time, old, dirty facilities would close down.

The result was predictable. Polluters kept those old facilities operating, precisely because they were exempted from the new rules. Indeed, corporations poured money into existing power plants and factories, expanding their capacity, rather than build new ones.

The Clinton administration tried to crack down on this practice, suing companies that it said were creating new pollution sources under the guise of maintaining old ones. Not surprisingly, polluters hated "new source review," and they contributed millions to Mr. Bush's campaign.

There ought to be a better way, and there is. It's called "cap and trade." Under cap and trade, existing pollution sources receive permits to emit specified amounts of pollutants—but they can sell those permits to others. This creates an incentive to reduce pollution from old facilities in order to free permits for sale. Cap and trade has already been instituted for some pollutants, notably sulfur dioxide from power plants, with great success. And by gradually reducing the number of permits, the government can use cap and trade to achieve long-term reductions in pollution.

Sure enough, the substantive part of the Bush administration's air pollution plan is a cap-and-trade system for sulfur dioxide, nitrogen oxides and mercury. So what is there to complain about? Alas, lots.

First, the plan conspicuously fails to include carbon dioxide, the main cause of global warming. Aside from violating one of Mr. Bush's campaign pledges, this omission casts a long shadow over future policy. Environmental experts tell me that it would be much cheaper to reduce carbon dioxide emissions as part of an integrated, multi-pollutant strategy than to add on carbon dioxide controls later, after key investment decisions have already been made. So by doing nothing about global warming, this administration compromises the policies of future administrations too.

Second, the Bush plan still allows twice as much pollution as experts at the Environmental Protection Agency privately think appropriate. The cost of an additional 50 percent reduction in pollution, according to internal E.P.A. documents, would be pretty small. But the administration apparently prefers not to ask industry to bear even those small costs.

Finally, and most important, so far the administration's "clear skies" initiative is pie in the sky: no legislation has been introduced, and there doesn't seem to be any urgency. Meanwhile, the administration is moving rapidly to scuttle new source review, saving its financial backers billions in cleanup costs at the expense of the environment (especially in the downwind states of the Northeast). And by scuttling new source review, the administration may well be undermining political support for its own anti-pollution initiative. As long as they were under the gun, polluting companies favored a new, less cumbersome system of pollution control. Now they, and their powerful Congressional allies, would just as soon leave things as they are.

There is evident demoralization at the E.P.A., where the hazardous-waste ombudsman recently joined a parade of officials resigning in protest. Staff members feel that they have no backing from their political superiors. Eric Schaeffer, who recently resigned as the chief of civil enforcement, put it this way: "The E.P.A. is in the back seat, or maybe even riding the bumper, and the energy industry is having a field day."

So what's actually on offer is a modest new pollution initiative, maybe, eventually, if and when the administration gets around to it. Don't you know there's a war on? And meanwhile the big polluters get what they paid for in campaign contributions: a multibillion-dollar free pass.

# BUSH ON FIRE

*August 27, 2002*

Round up the usual suspects! George W. Bush's new "Healthy Forests" plan reads like a parody of his administration's standard operating procedure. You see, environmentalists cause forest fires, and those nice corporations will solve the problem if we get out of their way.

Am I being too harsh? No, actually it's even worse than it seems. "Healthy Forests" isn't just about scrapping environmental protection; it's also about expanding corporate welfare.

Everyone agrees that the forests' prime evil is a well-meaning but counterproductive bear named Smokey. Generations of fire suppression have led to a dangerous accumulation of highly flammable small trees and underbrush. And in some—not all—of the national forests it's too late simply to reverse the policy; thanks to growing population and urban sprawl, some forests are too close to built-up areas to be allowed to burn.

Clearly, some of the excess fuel in some of the nation's forests should be removed. But how? Mr. Bush asserts that there is a free lunch: allowing more logging that thins out the national forests will both yield valuable resources and reduce fire risks.

But it turns out that the stuff that needs to be removed—small trees and bushes, in areas close to habitation—is of little commercial value. The good stuff, from the industry's point of view, consists of large, mature trees—the kind of trees that usually survive forest fires—which are often far from inhabited areas.

So the administration proposes to make deals with logging companies: in return for clearing out the stuff that should be removed, they will be granted the right to take out other stuff that probably shouldn't be removed. Notice that this means that there isn't a free lunch after all. And there are at least three severe further problems with this plan.

First, will the quid pro quo really be enforced, or will loggers simply make off with the quid and forget about the quo? The Forest Service, which would be in charge of enforcement, has repeatedly been cited by Congress's General Accounting Office for poor management and lack of accountability. And the agency, true to Bush administration form, is now run by a former industry lobbyist. (In the 2000 election cycle, the forest products industry gave 82 percent of its contributions to Republicans.) You don't have to be much of a cynic to question whether loggers will really be held to their promises.

Second, linking logging of mature trees to clearing of underbrush is a policy non sequitur. Suppose Mayor Mike Bloomberg announced that Waste Management Inc. would pick up Manhattan's trash free, in return for the right to dump toxic waste on Staten Island. Staten Island residents would protest, correctly, that if Manhattan wants its garbage picked up, it should pay for the service; if the city wants to sell companies the right to dump elsewhere, that should be treated as a separate issue. Similarly, if the federal government wants to clear underbrush near populated areas, it should pay for it; if it wants to sell the right to log mature trees elsewhere, that should be a separate decision.

And this gets us to the last point: In fact, the government doesn't make money when it sells timber rights to loggers.

According to the General Accounting Office, the Forest Service consistently spends more money arranging timber sales than it actually gets from the sales. How much money? Funny you should ask: last year the Bush administration stopped releasing that information. In any case, the measured costs of timber sales capture only a fraction of the true budgetary costs of logging in the national forests, which is supported by hundreds of millions of dollars in federal subsidies, especially for road-building. This means that, environmental issues aside, inducing logging companies to clear underbrush by letting them log elsewhere would probably end up costing taxpayers more, not less, than dealing with the problem directly.

So as in the case of the administration's energy policy, beneath the free-market rhetoric is a plan for increased subsidies to favored corporations. Surprise.

A final thought: Wouldn't it be nice if just once, on some issue, the Bush administration came up with a plan that didn't involve weakened environmental protection, financial breaks for wealthy individuals and corporations and reduced public oversight?

# CHAPTER 14

# *Foreign Disasters*

## HONG KONG'S HARD LESSON

Fortune, *September 28, 1998*

Don't tell anyone, but I've come up with a nifty financial scheme. First, a few of my billionaire speculator friends quietly take a short position in Microsoft stock. Then we spread the rumor that Bill Gates has gone Hare Krishna or some such. Microsoft's stock plunges, and doink! we make hundreds of millions.

O.K., on second thought, maybe this isn't such a great plan. For one thing, I don't actually have any billionaire speculator friends. And even if I did, there's another little problem: My scheme would lead to an interesting conversation with the Securities and Exchange Commission, ending with a polite but firm invitation to spend the next few years of my life in a minimum-security prison.

So let's revise the plan. Instead of conspiring against a corporation, let's do it to a small country. We take a short position in the country's stock market, then sell enough of its currency on the foreign-exchange market to start a general run on the currency. The country's central bank will have to raise interest rates, causing the local stock market to plunge—and we can live wealthily ever after.

Oh, there are a few pesky details. I still need some billionaire friends. The main problem, though, is that I may have come up with this idea too late. You see, it appears that some speculators have already figured out the strategy for themselves and put it into practice. Or at least so claims the Hong Kong Monetary Authority, which, as you have probably heard, has been accusing short-selling investors of a deliberate conspiracy to undermine the city-state's economy. So the Authority poured money into the Hong Kong stock market to give it a boost and squash the short-selling miscreants; then outright banned the short-selling of the largest-cap stocks, period.

Let's back up for a moment here. Hong Kong's government has long been famous for its laissez-faire attitudes. In this town, being a speculator has never meant having to say you were sorry. The Monetary Authority has been determinedly noninterventionist in its policies: By establishing a "currency board" that pegs the Hong Kong dollar rigidly to the U.S. dollar, with the local currency 100 percent backed by U.S.-dollar reserves, it has come as close as any modern central bank to recreating the gold standard. To conservatives in the U.S., Hong Kong has been a living demonstration that all a government needs to provide is sound money and secure property rights, and the private sector will do the rest.

So when Hong Kong authorities launched their war on speculators, laissez-faire-ists around the world were horrified, to say the least. What happened to the sacred principle of nonintervention?

Well, I can't confirm or deny a conspiracy of speculators against Hong Kong. However, many economists agree that there are conditions under which a currency may be subject to what are known as "self-fulfilling speculative attacks"—that is, where a potentially sound currency is forced into a devaluation by a collapse of investor confidence, a collapse that is then validated by the devaluation. Under such circumstances there are indeed potential profits for Soroi—big players who take a short position in the currency, then deliberately provoke such a self-fulfilling attack.

Hong Kong—which does not want to impair its credibility by devaluing but also does not want to raise interest rates when its economy is already suffering a deepening recession—fits the profile of a speculative victim perfectly. And while earlier Asian claims of conspiracy have come from shrill anti-Western voices like Malaysia's Mahathir, this time they come from ultra-respectable technocrats like Joseph Yam, chief executive of the Hong Kong Monetary Authority.

If Yam is so convinced there's a conspiracy afoot, why didn't he simply turn his evidence over to the regulators and have them haul in the perpetrators for questioning? The answer is, what regulators? If I conspire against the stock of a U.S. corporation, that is a violation of U.S. law. But if hedge funds in New York attack some overseas financial market, it's unclear who, if anyone, has jurisdiction. Never mind that we are a lot more likely to cry for Hong Kong or Argentina than for Microsoft: Speculative conspiracies against companies are effectively regulated; those against countries are not. And that is the real moral of the story. If there's a theme to the economic chaos of the past few years, it's this: Capital markets are global, but the institutions that support and regulate them—that allow them to work—remain national. It's hard to imagine how truly global institutions could come into existence—how we could, for example, prosecute American traders working in London for manipulating some market in China. But until we figure it out, it's going to be a very rough ride.

## CRYING WITH ARGENTINA

*January 1, 2002*

Although images of the riots in Argentina have flickered across our television screens, hardly anyone in the U.S. cares. It's just another disaster in a small, faraway country of which we know nothing—a country as remote and unlikely to affect our lives as, say, Afghanistan.

I don't make that comparison lightly. Most people here may think that this is just another run-of-the-mill Latin American crisis—hey, those people have them all the time, don't they?—but in the eyes of much of the world, Argentina's economic policies had "made in Washington" stamped all over them. The catastrophic failure of those policies is first and foremost a disaster for Argentines, but it is also a disaster for U.S. foreign policy.

Here's how the story looks to Latin Americans: Argentina, more than any other developing country, bought into the promises of U.S.-promoted "neoliberalism" (that's liberal as in free markets, not as in Ted Kennedy). Tariffs were slashed, state enterprises were privatized, multinational corporations were welcomed and the peso was pegged to the dollar. Wall Street cheered, and money poured in; for a while, free-market economics seemed vindicated, and its advocates weren't shy about claiming credit.

Then things began to fall apart. It wasn't surprising that the 1997 Asian financial crisis had repercussions in Latin America, and at first Argentina seemed less affected than its neighbors.

But while Brazil bounced back, Argentina's recession just went on and on.

I could explain at length the causes of Argentina's slump: it had more to do with monetary policy than with free markets. But Argentines, understandably, can't be bothered with such fine distinctions—especially because Wall Street and Washington told them that free markets and hard money were inseparable.

Moreover, when the economy went sour, the International Monetary Fund—which much of the world, with considerable justification, views as a branch of the U.S. Treasury Department—was utterly unhelpful. I.M.F. staffers have known for months, perhaps years, that the one-peso-one-dollar policy could not be sustained. And the I.M.F. could have offered Argentina guidance on how to escape from its monetary trap, as well as political cover for Argentina's leaders as they did what had to be done. Instead, however, I.M.F. officials—like medieval doctors who insisted on bleeding their patients, and repeated the procedure when the bleeding made them sicker—prescribed austerity and still more austerity, right to the end.

Now Argentina is in utter chaos—some observers are even likening it to the Weimar Republic. And Latin Americans do not regard the United States as an innocent bystander.

I'm not sure how many Americans, even among the policy elite, understand this. The people who encouraged Argentina in its disastrous policy course are now busily rewriting history, blaming the victims. Anyway, we are notoriously bad at seeing ourselves as others see us. A recent Pew survey of "opinion leaders" found that 52 percent of the Americans think that our country is liked because it "does a lot of good"; only 21 percent of foreigners, and 12 percent of Latin Americans, agreed.

What happens next? The best hope for an Argentine turnaround was an orderly devaluation, in which the government reduced the dollar value of the peso and at the same time converted many dollar debts into pesos. But that now seems a remote prospect.

Instead, Argentina's new government—once it has one—will probably turn back the clock. It will impose exchange controls and import quotas, turning its back on world markets; don't be surprised if it also returns to old-fashioned anti-American rhetoric.

And let me make a prediction: these retrograde policies will work, in the sense that they will produce a temporary improvement in the economic situation—just as similar policies did back in the 1930's. Turning your back on the world market is bad for long-run growth; Argentina's own history is the best proof. But as John Maynard Keynes said, in the long run we are all dead.

Back in April, George W. Bush touted the proposed Free Trade Area of the Americas as a major foreign policy goal, one that would "build an age of prosperity in a hemisphere of liberty." If that goal really was important, we have just suffered a major setback. Don't cry for Argentina; cry with it.

# LOSING LATIN AMERICA

*April 16, 2002*

Many people, myself included, would agree that Hugo Chávez is not the president Venezuela needs. He happens, however, to be the president Venezuela elected—freely, fairly and constitutionally. That's why all the democratic nations of the Western Hemisphere, however much they may dislike Mr. Chávez, denounced last week's attempted coup against him.

All the democratic nations, that is, except one.

Here's how the BBC put it: "Far from condemning the ouster of a democratically elected president, U.S. officials blamed the crisis on Mr. Chávez himself," and they were "clearly pleased with the result"—even though the new interim government proceeded to abolish the legislature, the judiciary and the Constitution. They were presumably less pleased when the coup attempt collapsed. The BBC again: "President Chávez's comeback has . . . left Washington looking rather stupid." The national security adviser, Condoleezza Rice, didn't help that impression when, incredibly, she cautioned the restored president to "respect constitutional processes."

Surely the worst thing about this episode is the betrayal of our democratic principles; "of the people, by the people, for the people" isn't supposed to be followed by the words "as long as it suits U.S. interests."

But even viewed as realpolitik, our benign attitude toward Venezuela's coup was remarkably foolish.

It is very much in our interest that Latin America break out of its traditional political cycle, in which crude populism alternated with military dictatorship. Everything that matters to the U.S.—trade, security, drugs, you name it—will be better if we have stable neighbors.

But how can such stability be achieved? In the 1990's there seemed, finally, to be a formula; call it the new world order. Economic reform would end the temptations of populism; political reform would end the risk of dictatorship. And in the 1990's, on their own initiative but with encouragement from the United States, most Latin American nations did indeed embark on a dramatic process of reform both economic and political.

The actual results have been mixed. On the economic side, where hopes were initially highest, things have not gone too well. There are no economic miracles in Latin America, and there have been some notable disasters, Argentina's crisis being the latest. The best you can say is that some of the disaster victims, notably Mexico, seem to have recovered their balance (with a lot of help, one must say, from the Clinton administration) and moved onto a path of steady, but modest, economic growth.

Yet economic disasters have not destabilized the region. Mexico's crisis in 1995, Brazil's crisis in 1999, even Argentina's current crisis did not deliver those countries into the hands either of radicals or of strongmen. The reason is that the political side has gone better than anyone might have expected. Latin America has become a region of democracies—and these democracies seem remarkably robust.

So while the U.S. may have hoped for a new Latin stability based on vibrant prosperity, what it actually got was stability despite economic woes, thanks to democracy. Things could be a lot worse.

Which brings us to Venezuela. Mr. Chávez is a populist in the traditional mold, and his policies have been incompetent and erratic. Yet he was fairly elected, in a region that has come to understand the importance of democratic legitimacy. What did the U.S. hope to gain from his overthrow? True, he has spouted a lot of anti-American rhetoric, and been a nuisance to our diplomacy. But he is not a serious threat.

Yet there we were, reminding everyone of the bad old days when any would-be right-wing dictator could count on U.S. backing.

As it happens, we aligned ourselves with a peculiarly incompetent set of plotters. Mr. Chávez has alienated a broad spectrum of his people; the demonstrations that led to his brief overthrow began with a general strike by the country's unions. But the short-lived coup-installed government included representatives of big business and the wealthy—full stop. No wonder the coup collapsed.

But even if the coup had succeeded, our behavior would have been very stupid. We had a good thing going—a new hemispheric atmosphere of trust, based on shared democratic values. How could we so casually throw it away?

# THE LOST CONTINENT

*August 9, 2002*

On Wednesday the Bush administration, which says that it is for free trade and against bailouts, once again put its money where its mouth isn't. Less than two weeks ago Treasury Secretary Paul O'Neill created a diplomatic incident and sent Brazil's currency into free fall with his remark about assistance ending up in "Swiss bank accounts." Now the International Monetary Fund, with Mr. O'Neill's blessing, has agreed to lend Brazil an unprecedented $30 billion.

I guess it's good news that our leadership finally woke up to two uncomfortable facts: A major threat to U.S. interests is developing in this hemisphere, and doing the opposite of what Bill Clinton did isn't always a wise policy. Indeed, if Brazil hadn't gotten a loan the South American financial crisis, already comparable to the one that struck Asia in 1997, might quickly have turned into something much bigger.

And yet I have a bad feeling about this. Let me make the case for the I.M.F. loan, then explain my misgivings.

The good news is that Brazil's current leadership is highly responsible. In the past, I.M.F. loans went to governments that didn't collect taxes (Russia) or were committed to an unsustainable exchange rate (Argentina). By comparison, Brazil is a model of upright behavior.

So why is there a crisis? With an election due in October, President Fernando Henrique, Cardoso's chosen successor, is running far behind two left-of-center candidates. Investors are nervous, and the result has been one of those downward spirals all too familiar from the history of currency crises. Fears that the government will default on its debt have caused the currency to plunge and interest rates to soar; since most of the debt is indexed either to the dollar or to short-term interest rates, this makes default seem even more likely.

Mr. O'Neill's remark was unforgivable because it reinforced this death spiral; the I.M.F. loan is an attempt to turn that spiral around. The end result of Mr. O'Neill's flub was probably to get Brazil an extra $10 billion.

So why am I feeling queasy? One reason is that there is some question about who, exactly, is being bailed out. Paul Erdman writes on CBSMarketWatch.com—in a column praising the administration!—that "The fact that the Brazilian bailout also gave a big boost to Citigroup and FleetBoston, which combined had close to $20 billion at risk in Brazil, will hardly go unnoticed when it comes time to raise campaign funds among the Wall Street elite."

More important, if you look beyond the question of short-term financial stabilization you have to wonder where all this is supposed to be leading. Asian economies were doing very well before their crisis, and you could think of bailouts as a way to get them back on track. But there is a reason the left is having a resurgence in Brazil and elsewhere in the region: We promised them a rose garden, but even before this latest crisis too many people got nothing but thorns.

A decade ago Washington confidently assured Latin American nations that if they opened themselves to foreign goods and capital and privatized their state enterprises they would experience a great surge of economic growth. But it hasn't happened. Argentina is a catastrophe. Both Mexico and Brazil were, a few months ago, regarded as success stories, but in both countries per capita income today is only slightly higher than it was in 1980. And because inequality has increased sharply, most people are probably worse off than they were 20 years ago. Is it any wonder that the public is weary of yet more calls for austerity and market discipline?

Why hasn't reform worked as promised? That's a difficult and disturbing question. I, too, bought into much though not all of the Washington consensus; but now it's time, as Berkeley's Brad DeLong puts it, to mark my beliefs to market. And my confidence that we've been giving good advice is way down. One has to sympathize with Latin political leaders who want to temper enthusiasm for free markets with more efforts to protect workers and the poor.

What that suggests to me is that the U.S. should be very cautious about what it expects for its money. Pulling Brazil back from the brink doesn't mean that we are once again in a position to demand that Latin Americans do things our way. The truth is that we've lost a lot of credibility with our southern neighbors. If we overplay our hand, we'll lose whatever is left.

*Part Five*

# THE WIDER
# VIEW

M OST of this book, as you've seen, is about what went wrong in the United States over the last few years. But while that's a big subject, it's only part of a bigger story. Americans are, after all, only 5 percent of the world's population, and someday the troubles of current American policy will someday recede. This section tries to step back and take a wider view.

From a human point of view, globalization—a catchall phrase for growing world trade, the growing linkages between financial markets in different countries, and the many other ways in which the world is becoming a smaller place—is *the* issue of the 21st century. It's also an issue I've worked on a lot in my academic career. The title of chapter 15 comes from my parents, who once gave me a sweatshirt with the words "Global Schmobal" across the front. When I asked why, they explained that whenever I was going to an academic conference, they would ask me what it was about, and I would reply, "Oh, global schmobal, you know." So now you know the truth about my academic life.

In general I am pro-globalization—much more so than many people I agree with when it comes to current U.S. politics.

Indeed, it was my pro-free-trade arguments that earned me the enmity of Ralph Nader and various liberal publications. I haven't changed my views on that subject: Much of chapter 15 is devoted to arguments for free trade, the benefits it brings to poor countries, and the wrong-headedness of some popular arguments against globalization. But trade is not enough: it's our human duty to provide aid to poor countries, and it's a duty that—as I explain in the chapter—we as a nation shirk.

Chapter 16 takes a wider view in a different sense. It's about economists and economics—about the people who help us make sense of the business of getting and spending, and how they do their work. These are happier essays than those in the rest of the book—even my eulogy for James Tobin is a celebration of a life well lived. My fondest hope is that someday the bad things I have had to write about will be forgotten, while the work of these economists will live on.

# CHAPTER 15

# Global Schmobal

## ENEMIES OF THE WTO: BOGUS ARGUMENTS AGAINST THE WORLD TRADE ORGANIZATION

Slate, *November 24, 1999*

If a picture is worth a thousand words, a two-page spread in the *New York Times*, featuring more than a dozen pictures, can speak volumes. And sure enough, the lavish Nov. 15 advertisement by the Turning Point Project, a coalition of activists opposed to globalization in general and the World Trade Organization in particular, said more than any merely verbal exposition about what really motivates those activists could. Indeed, it revealed quite a bit more than its sponsors intended.

The occasion for the ad was the upcoming WTO "ministerial" taking place in Seattle in a few days. The WTO has become to leftist mythology what the United Nations is to the militia movement: the center of a global conspiracy against all that is good and decent. According to the myth, the "ultrasecretive" WTO has become a sort of super-governmental body that forces nations to bow to the wishes of multinational corporations. It destroys local cultures (the headline on the ad read "Global Monoculture"); it despoils the environment; and it rides roughshod over democracy, forcing governments to remove laws that conflict with its sinister purposes.

Like most successful urban legends, this one is based on a sliver of truth. The gradual global progress toward free trade that began in the 1930s, when Franklin Roosevelt introduced the Trade Agreements Program, has always depended on international negotiations: I'll reduce my tariffs if you reduce yours. But there has always been the problem of governments that give with one hand and take away with the other, that dutifully remove tariffs and then use other excuses to keep imports out. (*Certainement*, there is free trade within the European Union, but those British cows, they are not safe.) To make agreements work there has to be some kind of quasi-judicial process that determines when ostensibly domestic measures are de facto a reimposition of trade barriers and hence a violation of treaty. Under the pre-WTO system, the General Agreement on Tariffs and Trade, this process was slow and cumbersome. It has now become swifter and more decisive. Inevitably, some of its decisions can be challenged: Was the U.S. ban on dolphin-unsafe tuna really a trade barrier in disguise? But the much-feared power of the WTO to overrule local laws is strictly limited to enforcement of the spirit of existing agreements. It cannot in any important way force countries that are skeptical about the benefits of globalization to open themselves further to foreign trade and investment. If most countries nonetheless are eager or at least willing to participate in globalization, it is because they are convinced that it is in their own interests.

And by and large they are right. The raw fact is that every successful example of economic development this past century—every case of a poor nation that worked its way up to a more or less decent, or at least dramatically better, standard of living—has taken place via globalization; that is, by producing for the world market rather than trying for self-sufficiency. Many of the workers who do that production for the global market are very badly paid by First World standards. But to claim that they have been impoverished by globalization, you have to carefully ignore comparisons across time and space—namely, you have to forget that those workers were even poorer before the new exporting jobs became available and ignore the fact that those who do not have access to the global market are far worse off than those who do. (See my old *Slate* piece "In Praise of Cheap Labor.") The financial crisis of 1997–99 temporarily gave those who claim that globalization is bad for workers everywhere a bit of ammunition, but the crisis did not go on forever, and anyway the solution to future crises surely involves some policing of short-term capital movements rather than a retreat from globalization as a whole. Even the Malaysians continue to welcome long-term foreign investors and place their faith on manufactured exports.

What about the environment? Certainly some forests have been cut down to feed global markets. But nations that are heedless of the environment are quite capable of doing immense damage without the help of multinational corporations—just ask the Eastern Europeans. For what it is worth, the most conspicuous examples of environmental pillage in the Third World today have nothing to do with the WTO. The forest fires that envelop Southeast Asia in an annual smoke cloud are set by land-hungry locals; the subsidized destruction of Amazonian rain forests began as part of a Brazilian strategy of inward-looking development. On the whole, integration of the world economy, which puts national actions under international scrutiny, is probably on balance a force toward better, not worse, environmental policies.

But anyway, these are side issues, because what that advertisement makes clear—clearer, I suspect, than its sponsors intended—is that the opposition to globalization actually has very little to do with wages or the environment. After all, leaving aside a photo of tree stumps and another of an outfall pipe, here are the horrors of globalization the Turning Point Project chose to illustrate:

A highway interchange, a parking lot filled with cars, a traffic jam, suburban tract housing, an apartment building with numerous satellite dishes, an office with many computer screens, office workers on a busy street, high-rise office buildings, a "factory farm" with many chickens, a supermarket aisle, a McDonald's arch.

Each picture was accompanied by a caption asking, "Is this Los Angeles or Cairo?" "Is this India or London?" etc.

What is so horrible about these scenes? Here's what the ad says, "A few decades ago, it was still possible to leave home and go somewhere else: The architecture was different, the landscape was different, the language, dress, and values were different. That was a time when we could speak of cultural diversity. But with economic globalization, diversity is fast disappearing."

You can't argue with that; lives there the tourist with soul so dead that he does not wish that he could visit rural France, or Mexico City, or for that matter Kansas City the way they were, rather than the way they are? But the world is not run for the edification of tourists. It is or should be run for the benefit of ordinary people in their daily lives. And that is where the indignation of the Turning Point people starts to seem rather strange.

For surely the most striking thing about the horrors of globalization illustrated in those photos is that for most of the world's people they represent aspirations, things they wish they had, rather than ominous threats. Traffic jams and ugly interchanges are annoying, but most people would gladly accept that annoyance in exchange for the freedom that comes with owning a car (and more to the point, being wealthy enough to afford one). Tract housing and apartment buildings may be ugly, but they are paradise compared with village huts or urban shanties. Wearing a suit and working at a computer in an office tower are, believe it or not, preferable to backbreaking work in a rice paddy. And nobody forces you to eat at McDonald's.

Now, of course what is good for the individual is not always good if everyone else does it too. Having a big house with a garden is nice, but seeing the countryside covered by suburban sprawl is not, and we might all be better off if we could all agree (or be convinced by tax incentives) to take up a bit less space. The same goes for cultural choices: Boston residents who indulge their taste for Canadian divas do undermine the prospects of local singer-songwriters and might be collectively better off if local radio stations had some kind of cultural content rule. But there is a very fine line between such arguments for collective action and supercilious paternalism, especially when cultural matters are concerned; are we warning societies about unintended consequences or are we simply disagreeing with individual tastes?

And it is very clear from the advertisement in the *Times* that the Turning Point Project—and the whole movement it represents—are on the supercilious side of that line. Although they talk of freedom and democracy, their key demand is that individuals be prevented from getting what they want—that governments be free, nay encouraged, to deny individuals the right to drive cars, work in offices, eat cheeseburgers, and watch satellite TV. Why? Presumably because people will really be happier if they retain their traditional "language, dress, and values." Thus, Spaniards would be happier if they still dressed in black and let narrow-minded priests run their lives, and residents of the American South would be happier if planters still sipped mint juleps, wore white suits, and accepted traditional deference from sharecroppers . . . instead of living in this "dreary" modern world in which Madrid is just like Paris and Atlanta is just like New York.

Well, somehow I suspect that the residents of Madrid and Atlanta, while they may regret some loss of tradition, prefer modernity. And you know what? I think the rest of the world has the right to make the same choice.

# SAINTS AND PROFITS

*July 23, 2000*

"Saints," wrote George Orwell, "should always be judged guilty until proved innocent." I don't think he was talking about garden-variety hypocrisy—although many supposed ascetics do turn out to have something to hide. The more important point is that there are other temptations besides those of the flesh. And those who renounce small pleasures may be all the more susceptible to monomania, to the urge to sacrifice the good in pursuit of the perfect. In other words, beware the cause of the rebel without a life.

Some commentators have made much of the secrecy shrouding the accounts of Ralph Nader's organizations, of the revelation that speaking fees and stock market investments have made him a multimillionaire, and of hints that his lifestyle might not be quite as austere as it seems. But what should worry those sympathetic to Mr. Nader are not his vices, if he has any, but his virtues—and his determination to impose those virtues on the rest of us.

Mr. Nader did not begin as an extremist. On the contrary: in the 1960's, when he made his reputation, the striking thing about Mr. Nader was his relative moderation. Fashionable radicals were preaching revolution; he was demanding safer cars. And because his radicalism was practical and realistic, it left a lasting legacy: our tradition of consumer activism, a tradition that rightly honors Mr. Nader as its founding father, makes this country a better place. One might even give Mr. Nader some credit for our current prosperity: if Japan had shared our healthy distrust of claims that what is good for General Motors is good for America, its current economic morass might have been avoided.

But somewhere along the way the practical radical disappeared. The causes that Mr. Nader and his organizations have pursued in the last couple of decades seem to have less and less to do with his original, humane goals.

Everyone knows about Mr. Nader's furious opposition to global trade agreements. But it is less well known that he was equally adamant in opposing a bill removing barriers to Africa's exports—a move that Africans themselves welcomed, but which Mr. Nader denounced because of his fear that African companies would be "run into the ground by multinational corporations moving into local economies." (Most African countries would be delighted to attract a bit of foreign investment.) Similar fears led Mr. Nader to condemn South Africa's new Constitution, the one that ended apartheid, because—like the laws of every market economy—it grants corporations some legal status as individuals.

Or consider another example, one closer to home—my home, in particular. When my arthritis stopped responding to over-the-counter remedies, I brought it back under control with a new regime that included the anti-inflammatory drug Feldene. But Mr. Nader's organization Public Citizen not only tried to block Pfizer's introduction of Feldene in the 1980's; it also tried to get it banned in 1995, despite what was by then a firm consensus among medical experts that the drug's benefits outweighed its risks.

If you look for a unifying theme in all these causes, it seems to be not consumer protection but general hostility toward corporations. Mr. Nader now apparently believes that whatever is good for General Motors, or Pfizer, or any corporation, must be bad for the world. To block opportunities for corporate profit he is quite willing to prevent desperately poor nations from selling their goods in U.S. markets, prevent patients from getting drugs that might give them a decent life and prevent a moderate who gets along with business from becoming president.

At times Mr. Nader's hostility to corporations goes completely over the edge. Newt Gingrich disgusted many people when, in his first major speech after leaving Congress, he blamed liberalism for the Columbine school shootings. But several days before Mr. Gingrich spoke, Ralph Nader published an article attributing those same shootings to—I'm serious—corporate influence.

And was I the only person who shuddered when Mr. Nader declared that if he were president, he wouldn't reappoint Alan Greenspan—he would "re-educate" him?

Many of those who are thinking about voting for Mr. Nader probably imagine that he is still the moderate, humane activist of the 1960's. They should know that whatever the reason—your amateur psychology is as good as mine—he is now a changed man.

# WORKERS VS. WORKERS

*May 21, 2000*

In the 1920's, South Africa's Communist Party campaigned under the slogan: "Workers of the world unite for a white South Africa!" This wasn't quite as incongruous as it sounds: the political movement that eventually imposed apartheid had strong populist, even socialist roots. It was sincerely concerned with improving the economic status of the Afrikaner worker, and protecting him from the depredations of international capital. Unfortunately, the movement improved the lot of white labor mainly by preventing capitalists from offering industrial jobs to nonwhites, whose intense poverty made them willing to work for less.

The U.S. labor movement is not as brutally direct in its slogans. Probably its leaders don't even admit to themselves that their increasingly vociferous opposition to imports is, in effect, an effort to improve the condition of American workers by denying opportunity to workers in the rest of the world. But when the Teamsters' president, James P. Hoffa, declares, as he did on this page not long ago, that "American workers should not be asked to compete with foreigners who are not paid a living wage," the implications are clear. Given the low productivity of workers in third-world countries, their nations' lack of infrastructure and general lag in development, to insist that such workers be paid what Americans would regard as a living wage is to insist that they price themselves out of their jobs.

And that is no accident: any policy that didn't price those workers out of the market would offer no relief to workers here.

There is a sort of tragic inevitability about the way labor has reached this moral impasse. The U.S. labor movement has every right to feel that American workers have gotten a raw deal. By standard measures, the real take-home pay of blue-collar workers is lower now than it was a quarter-century ago. You can quibble with the statistics, but without question blue-collar workers have been largely left behind by the nation's economic growth. And far from fighting this inequality in rewards, policy has in general reinforced it: taxes have become less rather than more progressive, public schools for those who can't afford to live in the right places have gotten worse, and so on.

A well-meaning economist can give you a list of things that might help America's working class: some form of national health insurance, bigger and better wage supplements along the lines of the earned-income tax credit, etc., etc. But if I were a labor leader, I would sneer at my professorial naïveté. You know and I know that such proposals are pipe dreams, that in America today the left, such as it is, has its hands full holding back efforts to tilt the tax-and-benefit system even more toward the interests of the affluent. And the labor movement—whose influence is far less today than it was even 20 years ago—is in no position to reverse the political tide.

So what's a labor leader to do? Choose a fight that he might be able to win: a fight to limit imports that compete with the workers he represents. Voters might not see protection as a direct threat to their pocketbooks (though it is). The payoff may be limited—the arithmetic suggests that even a total ban on manufactured imports from third-world countries would raise blue-collar wages no more than 3 or 4 percent—but who's counting? And if the target is unattractive enough—if it is, say, a nasty regime in China—labor's limited but not negligible lobbying power just might pull off a victory.

In other words, it's understandable that labor has decided that it must try to help American workers by denying opportunity to even needier workers abroad—while, of course, denying that it is doing any such thing. If I were a labor leader I would probably be a protectionist too. But to understand this political strategy, even to accept its inevitability, is not to approve.

Those who would like easy moral certainties—which means all of us—wish that it were simpler, that corporate greed were the only enemy, that people like Mr. Hoffa were standing up for the rights of workers everywhere. It's hard for liberals to admit that the U.S. labor movement, with its noble tradition, is now working against the interests of most of the world's poor. But it is.

# THE SCROOGE SYNDROME

*December 25, 2001*

Bah, humbug!" cried the U.S. Treasury secretary. O.K., Paul O'Neill didn't actually say, "Bah." But last week he contemptuously dismissed proposals for increased aid to poor nations. And his justification—that he "would like to see evidence of what works before making new commitments"—was pure humbug.

For the truth is that we already know what works. Nobody expects foreign aid to perform miracles, to turn Mozambique into Sweden overnight. But more modest goals, such as saving millions of people a year from diseases like malaria and tuberculosis, are quite reachable, for quite modest sums of money.

That is the message of a commission report just released by the World Health Organization, which calls on advanced countries to provide resources for a plan to "scale up the access of the world's poor to essential health services." The program would provide very basic items that many poor nations simply cannot afford: antibiotics to treat tuberculosis, insecticide-treated nets to control malaria and so on. The price tag would be about 0.1 percent of advanced countries' income. The payoff would be at least eight million lives each year.

This is not starry-eyed idealism. The report quotes Jeffrey Sachs, the Harvard professor who headed the commission: "I can be 'realistic' and 'cynical' with the best of them—giving all the reasons why things are too hard to change." Mr. Sachs knows that it will be hard to persuade advanced countries to come up with the money—and that the U.S., in particular, is likely to be highly unreceptive. But this is one of those cases in which leadership could make a tremendous difference.

Right now, the U.S. is the Scrooge of the Western world—the least generous rich nation on the planet. One of the tables in that W.H.O. report shows the share of GNP given in foreign aid by advanced countries; the United States ranks dead last, well behind far poorer countries such as Portugal and Greece. The sums proposed by the W.H.O. would double our foreign aid budget, not because those sums are large, but because we start from so low a base—about a dime a day for each U.S. citizen.

Still, doubling our foreign aid budget sounds like an impossible dream. But is it? We may be a Scrooge nation, but we are not a nation of Scrooges. Not only are Americans often generous as individuals, they are—without knowing it—apparently willing to give substantially more foreign aid than the nation actually does. When asked how much of the federal budget should be devoted to foreign aid, Americans typically come up with a number around 10 percent—about 20 times what we currently spend.

Voters are, however, misinformed: they think that the share of foreign aid in federal spending should be *cut* to 10 percent. And they wonder why foreigners don't show more gratitude for all the money we give them. Americans are, in other words, living in the past: the Marshall Plan ended more than 50 years ago, but they haven't noticed.

The point is that we like to think of ourselves as generous. This suggests that a U.S. administration that really wanted to follow the W.H.O. report's recommendations would not find it hard to build political support. All it would have to do is use the bully pulpit to inform the public of the difference between America's generous self-image and the less attractive reality.

Why bother? You might say that the U.S. has a selfish interest in helping the world's poor. The Sachs commission argues that there would be large collateral benefits from improved health care in the world's poorest nations. Disease, it argues, is a major barrier to economic growth, and economic growth in developing countries would make the world as a whole a richer and safer place.

You might also say that reducing the disconnect between America's words and its deeds would give us a better claim to the moral leadership we think we deserve.

But the key argument here is surely a moral one. A sum of money that Americans would hardly notice, a dime a day for the average citizen, would quite literally save the lives of millions. Can we really say to ourselves, this Christmas Day, that this gift is not worth giving?

# HEART OF CHEAPNESS

*May 31, 2002*

Poor Bono. He got stuck in a moment, and he couldn't get out of it.

In one of the oddest enterprises in the history of development economics, Bono—the lead singer for the rock band U2—has been touring Africa with Paul O'Neill, secretary of the Treasury. For awhile, the latent tensions between the two men were masked by Bono's courtesy; but on Monday he lost his cool.

The pair were visiting a village in Uganda, where a new well yielding clean water has radically improved the villagers' health. Mr. O'Neill's conclusion from this, as from the other development projects he saw, was that big improvements in people's lives don't require much money—and therefore that no big increase in foreign aid is required. By the way, the U.S. currently spends 0.11 percent of GDP on foreign aid; Canada and major European countries are about three times as generous. The Bush administration's proposed "Millennium Fund" will increase our aid share, but only to 0.13 percent.

Bono was furious, declaring that the projects demonstrated just the opposite, that the well was "an example of why we need big money for development. And it is absolutely not an example of why we don't. And if the secretary can't see that, we're going to have to get him a pair of glasses and a new set of ears."

Maybe the easiest way to refute Mr. O'Neill is to recall last year's proposal by the World Health Organization, which wants to provide poor countries with such basic items as antibiotics and insecticide-treated mosquito nets. If the U.S. had backed the proposed program, which the W.H.O. estimated would save eight million lives each year, America's contribution would have been about $10 billion annually—a dime a day per American, but nonetheless a doubling of our current spending on foreign aid. Saving lives—even African lives—costs money.

But is Mr. O'Neill really blind and deaf to Africa's needs? Probably not. He is caught between a rock star and a hard place: he wants to show concern about global poverty, but Washington has other priorities.

A striking demonstration of those priorities is the contrast between the Bush administration's curt dismissal of the W.H.O. proposal and the bipartisan drive to make permanent the recent repeal of the estate tax. What's notable about that drive is that opponents of the estate tax didn't even try to make a trickle-down argument, to assert that reducing taxes on wealthy heirs is good for all of us. Instead, they made an emotional appeal—they wanted us to feel the pain of those who pay the "death tax." And the sob stories worked; Congress brushed aside proposals to retain the tax, even proposals that would raise the exemption—the share of any estate that is free from tax—to $5 million.

Let's do the math here. An estate tax with an exemption of $5 million would affect only a handful of very wealthy families: in 1999 only 3,300 estates had a taxable value of more than $5 million. The average value of those estates was $16 million. If the excess over $5 million were taxed at pre-2001 rates, the average taxed family would be left with $10 million—which doesn't sound like hardship to me—and the government would collect $20 billion in revenue each year. But no; the whole tax must go.

So here are our priorities. Faced with a proposal that would save the lives of eight million people every year, many of them children, we balk at the cost. But when asked to give up revenue equal to twice that cost, in order to allow each of 3,300 lucky families to collect its full $16 million inheritance rather than a mere $10 million, we don't hesitate. Leave no heir behind!

Which brings us back to the Bono-O'Neill tour. The rock star must have hoped that top American officials are ignorant rather than callous—that they just don't realize what conditions are like in poor countries, and how foreign aid can make a difference. By showing Mr. O'Neill the realities of poverty and the benefits aid can bring, Bono hoped to find and kindle the spark of compassion that surely must lurk in the hearts of those who claim to be compassionate conservatives.

But he still hasn't found what he's looking for.

# AMERICA THE SCOFFLAW

*May 24, 2002*

Early in the Reagan administration I spent a year on the staff of the Council of Economic Advisers. While there I got a disillusioning look at how economic policy is really made. But one favorable surprise was how seriously U.S. officials took our international trade agreements.

The Reagan administration, despite its free-trade rhetoric, was quite willing to protect industries for political gain; the most notable example was the "voluntary" restraint on Japanese car exports. Still, it was a firm rule that trade interventions had to be "GATT-legal"—that is, they couldn't violate the General Agreement on Tariffs and Trade. (The GATT has since been incorporated into the rules of the World Trade Organization.) And that scrupulousness continued up to the end of the Clinton years. Everyone understood that there were certain things that you didn't do, no matter how convenient they might be in terms of short-term political advantage.

In those days, in other words, responsible people ran our international economic policy.

When the Bush administration imposed steep tariffs on imported steel, it became clear that this is no longer true. In sheer economic terms, the steel tariff is not that big a deal. But it demonstrates an unprecedented contempt for international rules.

The immediate threat is that other nations will strike back; the European Union has threatened retaliatory tariffs, and earlier this week Japan, Brazil, South Korea and China said they would follow suit. (Mr. Bush really has unified the world, at least on this issue.) But as a wise trade expert once told me, the big danger when the U.S. flouts the rules isn't retaliation, it's emulation: if we don't honor trade agreements, who will?

Why do we need trade agreements anyway? The costs that tariffs and import quotas impose on domestic consumers almost always exceed the gains they provide to domestic producers. Nonetheless, if we didn't have trade agreements, protectionism would usually win. Consumers don't realize that they are hurt by steel tariffs or sugar quotas, but the steel and sugar industries know exactly what they're getting.

The reason we manage to have fairly free trade is that the world—under U.S. leadership—has evolved a system that pits the self-interest of exporters against the power of industries that would prefer not to compete with imports. Each country agrees to accept the exports of other countries in return for access to their markets. In the language of trade negotiations, the parties to such an agreement make "concessions"; but the real purpose of those concessions is to protect ourselves from our own bad instincts.

The system depends on the proposition that a deal is a deal. A country that has, say, agreed to allow imports of steel won't renege on its promise simply because the domestic political winds have shifted. Trade agreements do include "safeguards," special circumstances under which temporary tariffs are permitted; but the conditions under which you can do that are fairly restrictive.

And the steel industry clearly didn't meet those conditions. In particular, steel imports have lately been declining, not rising. When the Bush administration nonetheless decided to give the steel industry the protection it wanted, it was in effect saying—

as it has in so many other areas—that the rules don't apply to yours truly.

The administration insists that it is simply standing up for U.S. interests. Robert Zoellick, the trade representative—who used to be a genuine free-trader, but these days sounds like a broken man—declared that "Uncle Sam is not going to be Uncle Sap for these people." But if you believe that this is about the national interest, I've got a terrorist threat against the Brooklyn Bridge you might be willing to buy.

What it's really about, of course, is raw, short-sighted politics—the same politics that has led the administration to revoke crucial trade access to Caribbean nations, with devastating prospective effects on their economies, to help out a single South Carolina congressman. In the case of steel, Karl Rove weighed three electoral votes in West Virginia against the world trading system built up over 60 years, and the answer was apparently obvious.

Mr. Bush will soon have trade promotion authority—what we used to call "fast track"—which he says he needs in order to negotiate new trade agreements. But what good are new agreements if we won't honor the old ones?

# WHITE MAN'S BURDEN

*September 24, 2002*

We should listen to Karl Rove when he lauds former presidents. For example, Mr. Rove has lately taken to saying that George W. Bush is another Andrew Jackson. As Congress considers Mr. Bush's demand that the Homeland Security Department be exempt from civil service rules, it should recall that those rules were introduced out of revulsion over the "spoils system," under which federal appointments were reserved for political loyalists—a practice begun under Jackson.

But Mr. Rove's original model was William McKinley. Until Sept. 11, we thought that Mr. Rove admired McKinley's domestic political strategy. But McKinley was also the president who acquired an overseas empire. And there's a definite whiff of imperial ambition in the air once again.

Of course the new Bush doctrine, in which the United States will seek "regime change" in nations that we judge might be future threats, is driven by high moral purpose. But McKinley-era imperialists also thought they were morally justified. The war with Spain—which ruled its colonies with great brutality, but posed no threat to us—was justified by an apparent act of terror, the sinking of the battleship *Maine*, even though no evidence ever linked that attack to Spain. And the purpose of our conquest of the Philippines was, McKinley declared, "to educate the Filipinos, and uplift and civilize and Christianize them."

Moral clarity aside, the parallel between America's pursuit of manifest destiny a century ago and its new global sense of mission has a lot to teach us.

First, the experience of the Spanish-American War should remind us that quick conventional military victory is not necessarily the end of the story. Thanks to American technological superiority, Adm. George Dewey destroyed a Spanish fleet in Manila Bay without losing a single man. But a clean, high-tech war against Spain somehow turned into an extremely dirty war against the Filipino resistance, one in which hundreds of thousands of civilians died.

Second, America's imperial venture should serve as an object warning against taking grand strategic theories too seriously. The doctrines of the day saw colonies as strategic assets. In the end, it's very doubtful whether our control of the Philippines made us stronger. Now we're assured that military action against rogue states will protect us from terrorism. But the rogue state now in our sights doesn't seem to have been involved in Sept. 11; what determines whose regime gets changed?

Finally, we should remember that the economic doctrines that were used to justify Western empire-building during the late 19th century—that colonies would provide valuable markets and sources of raw materials—turned out to be nonsense. Almost without exception, the cost of acquiring and defending a colonial empire greatly exceeded even a generous accounting of its benefits. These days, pundits tell us that a war with Iraq will drive down oil prices, and maybe even yield a financial windfall. But the effect on oil prices is anything but certain, while the heavy costs of war, occupation and rebuilding—for we won't bomb Iraq, then wash our hands of responsibility, will we?—are not in doubt. And no, the United States cannot defray the costs of war out of Iraqi oil revenue—not unless we are willing to confirm to the world that we're just old-fashioned imperialists, after all.

In the end, 19th-century imperialism was a diversion. It's hard not to suspect that the Bush doctrine is also a diversion— a diversion from the real issues of dysfunctional security agencies, a sinking economy, a devastated budget and a tattered relationship with our allies.

# CHAPTER 16

# Economics and Economists

## SUPPLY, DEMAND, AND ENGLISH FOOD

Fortune, *July 20, 1998*

We Americans like to boast about our economic turnaround in the '90s, but you could argue that England—where I've spent the past few weeks—is the real comeback story of the advanced world. When I first started going there regularly in the early '80s, London was a shabby and depressed city, and the country's old industrial regions were a *Full Monty*-esque wasteland of closing factories and unemployment lines. These days, however, London positively buzzes with prosperity and with the multilingual chatter of thousands of young Europeans—French especially—who have crossed the Channel in search of the jobs they can no longer find at home. How this turnaround was achieved is a fascinating question; whether the new Labour government can sustain it is another.

But I'm not going to try answering either question, because I've been thinking about food. Marcel Proust I'm not (what the hell is a madeleine, anyway?), but the change in English eating habits is enough to get even an economist meditating on life, the universe, and the nature of consumer society.

For someone who remembers the old days, the food is the most startling thing about modern England. English food used to be deservedly famous for its awfulness—greasy fish and chips, gelatinous pork pies, and dishwater coffee. Now it is not only easy to do much better, but traditionally terrible English meals have even become hard to find. What happened?

Maybe the first question is how English cooking got to be so bad in the first place. A good guess is that the country's early industrialization and urbanization was the culprit. Millions of people moved rapidly off the land and away from access to traditional ingredients. Worse, they did so at a time when the technology of urban food supply was still primitive: Victorian London already had well over a million people, but most of its food came in by horse-drawn barge. And so ordinary people, and even the middle classes, were forced into a cuisine based on canned goods (mushy peas!), preserved meats (hence those pies), and root vegetables that didn't need refrigeration (e.g., potatoes, which explain the chips).

But why did the food stay so bad after refrigerated railroad cars and ships, frozen foods (better than canned, anyway), and eventually air-freight deliveries of fresh fish and vegetables had become available? Now we're talking about economics— and about the limits of conventional economic theory. For the answer is surely that by the time it became possible for urban Britons to eat decently, they no longer knew the difference. The appreciation of good food is, quite literally, an acquired taste— but because your typical Englishman, circa, say, 1975, had never had a really good meal, he didn't demand one. And because consumers didn't demand good food, they didn't get it.

Even then there were surely some people who would have liked better, just not enough to provide a critical mass.

And then things changed. Partly this may have been the result of immigration. (Although earlier waves of immigrants simply adapted to English standards—I remember visiting one fairly expensive London Italian restaurant in 1983 that advised diners to call in advance if they wanted their pasta freshly cooked.) Growing affluence and the overseas vacations it made possible may have been more important—how can you keep them eating bangers once they've had foie gras? But at a certain point the process became self-reinforcing: Enough people knew what good food tasted like that stores and restaurants began providing it—and that allowed even more people to acquire civilized taste buds.

So what does all this have to do with economics? Well, the whole point of a market system is supposed to be that it serves consumers, providing us with what we want and thereby maximizing our collective welfare. But the history of English food suggests that even on so basic a matter as eating, a free-market economy can get trapped for an extended period in a bad equilibrium in which good things are not demanded because they have never been supplied, and are not supplied because not enough people demand them.

And conversely, a good equilibrium may unravel. Suppose a country with fine food is invaded by purveyors of a cheap cuisine that caters to cruder tastes. You may say that people have the right to eat what they want, but by thinning the market for traditional fare, their choices may make it harder to find—and thus harder to learn to appreciate—and everyone may end up worse off. The English are often amused by the hysteria of their nearest neighbors, who are terrified by the spread of doughnuts at the expense of croissants. Great was the mirth when the horrified French realized that McDonald's was the official food of the World Cup. But France's concern is not entirely silly. (Silly, yes, but not *entirely* so.)

Compared with ethnic cleansing in Kosovo and the plunging yen, such issues are small potatoes. But they do provide, well, *frites* for thought.

# O CANADA:

## A NEGLECTED NATION GETS ITS NOBEL

Slate, *October 19, 1999*

It's about time. Those of us who work on international monetary theory have been wondering for a decade when Robert
Mundell would get his richly deserved Nobel Memorial Prize in
Economic Sciences. Mundell's work is so central to that field,
so "seminal"—an overused term that really applies here—that
on many disputed issues his ideas are the basis for both sides of
the debate. But a layperson might be confused about exactly
what Mundell and his prize are really about.

The *Wall Street Journal* editorial page, rather pathetically,
has declared this a "supply-side" Nobel. No surprise there: Editor Robert Bartley's attempts to claim intellectual vindication
have become increasingly desperate in recent years. With eight
years and counting of Clintonian expansion making Reagan's
"seven fat years" look positively shabby, and with supply-side
heroes such as Jude Wanniski looking loonier by the day, the
*Wall Street Journal* will take anything it can get. (Since when
does Bartley care about what some Swedes think, anyway?) For
what it is worth, the citation by the Nobel committee doesn't
mention anything Mundell has written since he was adopted as
mascot by Bartley et al. some 25 years ago. It is the young
Mundell, whose theories still dominate the textbooks, who
earned the prize.

So, if it isn't a supply-side Nobel, what is it? Well, how about
regarding it as a Canadian Nobel?

I'm not sure why Canadian policy issues are universally regarded as being dull—why the winning entry in the old competition for most boring headline, "Worthwhile Canadian Initiative," still seems so funny (yes, I think it's funny, too). Maybe it has something to do with the way they talk, eh? But when it comes to international monetary matters, Canada has often been a very interesting case—the country that defies the trends, that demonstrates by example the hollowness of the conventional wisdom of the moment. Right now, for example, Canada's ability to thrive with an independent dollar is the best single argument I know against British europhiles who insist that their nation must join the European Monetary Union or die. And when the young Canadian economist Robert Mundell did his most influential work, in the early 1960s, it was arguably the Canadian difference that inspired him to think outside the box.

Here's what the world looked like in 1960: Almost all countries had fixed exchange rates with their currencies pegged to the U.S. dollar. International movements of capital were sharply limited, partly by government regulations, partly by the memory of defaults and expropriations in the '30s. And most economists who thought about the international monetary system took it for granted, explicitly or implicitly, that this was the way things would continue to work for the foreseeable future.

But Canada was different. Controlling the movement of capital across that long border with the United States had never been practical; and U.S. investors felt less nervous about putting their money in Canada than anywhere else. Given those uncontrolled movements of capital, Canada could not fix its exchange rate without giving up all control over its own monetary policy.

Unwilling to become a monetary ward of the Federal

Reserve, from 1949 to 1962 Canada made the almost unique decision to let its currency float against the U.S. dollar. These days, high capital mobility and a fluctuating exchange rate are the norm, but in those days they seemed outrageous—or would have seemed outrageous, if anyone but the Canadians had been involved.

And so perhaps it was the Canadian case that led Mundell to ask, in one of his three most famous contributions, how monetary and fiscal policy would work in an economy in which capital flowed freely in and out in response to any difference between interest rates at home and abroad. His answer was that it depended on what that country did with the exchange rate. If the country insisted on keeping the value of its currency in terms of other nations' monies constant, monetary policy would become entirely impotent. Only by letting the exchange rate float would monetary policy regain its effectiveness.

Later Mundell would broaden this initial insight by proposing the concept of the "impossible trinity": free capital movement, a fixed exchange rate, and an effective monetary policy. The point is that you can't have it all: A country must pick two out of three. It can fix its exchange rate without emasculating its central bank, but only by maintaining controls on capital flows (like China today); it can leave capital movement free but retain monetary autonomy, but only by letting the exchange rate fluctuate (like Britain—or Canada); or it can choose to leave capital free and stabilize the currency, but only by abandoning any ability to adjust interest rates to fight inflation or recession (like Argentina today, or for that matter most of Europe).

And what choice should a country such as Canada—where capital controls were not a serious option—make? Should it explicitly or implicitly give up on having its own currency and go on a U.S. dollar standard, or were the risks of a fluctuating dollar-dollar rate a price worth paying for the ability to actively stabilize the domestic economy? The debate over how to define an "optimum currency area" is an endless one, but Mundell set its terms, suggesting in particular that a key feature of such an area would typically be high internal mobility of workers, that is, the willingness and ability of workers to move from slumping to booming regions. (This is a criterion, incidentally, that Europe—whose single-currency regime Mundell now enthusiastically supports—manifestly does not satisfy.)

It's hard to appreciate today just how novel both Mundell's statement of the issues and the way he tried to resolve them were at the time. But if you look at the international monetary literature when Mundell was in his glory days, you get the impression that he was 15 or 20 years ahead of his contemporaries. They were still thinking in terms of a controlled world, a world where money moved where and when the authorities told it to move. He was thinking in terms of a world where money moved freely and massively to wherever it could earn the highest return. At the time, only Canada, thanks to its giant neighbor, lived in anything like the world he envisaged; today we all do. And if you look at any major textbook in international economics—such as the perennial best seller by Krugman and Maurice Obstfeld—you still find that the monetary half of the book is very largely based on the papers Mundell wrote in the early 1960s.

So who is this economist that the *Wall Street Journal* thinks is on its side? Well, economists do change their styles and their views as they get older; Mundell changed more than most. Those seminal early papers were crisp and minimalist; they looked forward with remarkable prescience to the wild and woolly, out-of-control world of modern international macroeconomics. By contrast, Mundell's writings since the early '70s have been discursive, one might almost say rambling, and often reveal a sort of hankering for the lost certainties of the gold standard. (And yes, he has said a few things that can, with some effort, be construed as support for supply-side economics.) The precocious theorist anticipated the 1990s; the elder statesman has hearkened back to the 1890s.

So you can take your pick as to which Mundell you prefer; but the Nobel committee basically honored Mundell the younger, the economist who was iconoclastic enough to imagine that Canada, of all places, was the economy of the future—and was right.

# WHO KNEW? THE SWEDISH MODEL IS WORKING

Fortune, *October 25, 1999*

Until recently, when people asked me what kind of a society I wanted to see, I had a stock answer: "Sweden in the summer of 1980." Why Sweden? Because I am a soggy liberal, and Sweden has traditionally been the exemplar of what used to be called the "middle way," a market economy with the rough edges smoothed by generous government programs. Why summer? Because Stockholm, arguably the world's most beautiful city on a sunny day in June, has precious little daylight in winter. And why 1980? Because by the early '90s the Swedish model was falling apart. The one-time model society had contracted Euro-sclerosis, with sagging growth and an unemployment rate of more than 8 percent. And the Swedish welfare state seemed to be going broke: In 1993 the budget deficit reached an absurd 12 percent of GDP.

The collapse of the Swedish model brought joy to conservatives. As a 1991 Cato Institute report gleefully declared, "Sweden seemed to present an intellectual challenge to those who argued that high tax rates and extensive state intervention would hamper economic growth. . . . Few would now consider the Swedish system worthy of emulation."

But have they looked at Sweden lately? On a recent visit to Stockholm, I was stunned as usual by the city's beauty but also startled by the unmistakable buzz of prosperity. First impressions are confirmed by the statistics: Since 1993 the economy has grown vigorously; most predictions are for growth of almost 4 percent this year. Unemployment has fallen steadily, with many predicting that it will drop below 5 percent next year—an achievement even more impressive given very high labor force participation rates (in Sweden, as in the U.S., about three-fourths of working-age adults are employed, compared with less than two-thirds in Continental Europe). And the budget is in surplus.

How did the Swedes manage this turnaround? Did they Reaganize their economy, adopting an American-style regime of low taxes and winner-take-all markets? In a word, nej. Oh, Sweden has scaled back its welfare state a bit and eliminated some of the truly crazy disincentives in the tax system (supposedly there used to be cases in which marginal rates really were in excess of 100 percent). But last year Sweden collected an awesome 63 percent of GDP in taxes. The Swedish welfare state remains extremely generous, its safety net remarkably far above the ground. If you believe the people who think that America's comparatively trivial tax burden—a mere 34 percent of GDP!—is an oppressive drag on the economy, you would expect to see the Swedish economy imploding instead of booming.

The Swedes themselves are not entirely sure what they have done right. But a good guess is that the formula for Sweden's "New Economy" is similar to that of America's: a culture that is receptive to modern information technology combined with a monetary policy that has let the economy take advantage of higher growth potential.

Start with the technology. Nobody is sure why Scandinavians and digital technology go together like herring and boiled potatoes, but the affinity is undeniable. Americans think they own the Net; but by most measures Finland (not technically Scandinavian but close enough), the home of Linux and Nokia, is the world's most wired nation, and Norway and Sweden aren't far behind. Some say it's the combination of highly educated, highly Anglophonic populations and low telephone charges; others, that there isn't much else to do during those long, dark winters.

But higher productivity isn't enough: There also has to be enough demand to make use of the economy's higher potential. And that's where the Swedes had a great stroke of luck. Back in the dark days of 1992, Swedish officials believed that to restore prosperity they had to be part of Europe's drive toward a unified currency. Although Sweden was not a formal member of the European Monetary System, it behaved as though it was, pegging the krona to the German mark even in the face of soaring unemployment. After all, any devaluation would be a disaster, leading to spiraling inflation, right? Then, in the aftermath of Britain's devaluation in September 1992, speculators attacked, eventually forcing Sweden to accept a devaluation of its own—just what the economy needed.

Of course, Sweden's future is by no means guaranteed. Responding both to globalization and high tax rates, some Swedish companies have moved their headquarters abroad— Ericsson, for example, now has its head office in London. But the Swedish story should prove that nice societies sometimes finish first.

# THE TWO LARRYS

*November 19, 2000*

Suppose that George W. Bush pulls it off—that he gets to the White House on the strength of chads and butterflies. Will he make good on his boast of being a "uniter, not a divider"? His behavior since election night is a bad omen; it suggests that what Mr. Bush means is that everyone should unite to give him what he wants. But there are also other, subtler indicators of how Mr. Bush might behave in office. Alas, they are no more encouraging. Consider, in particular, his revealed taste in economic advisers.

Call it the case of the two Larrys. One Larry is Lawrence Summers, secretary of the Treasury and the dominant economist of the entire Clinton administration. The other is Lawrence Lindsey, the lead economic adviser to Mr. Bush during the campaign, and widely expected to take a central role if Mr. Bush manages to reach the Oval Office.

On casual inspection the two men can seem remarkably similar. Both once taught at Harvard; both served for a time on the staff of the Reagan-era Council of Economic Advisers; both began their careers working on tax issues.

But a closer look reveals them as utterly different.

Mr. Summers had a meteoric career as an academic researcher, publishing scores of papers in professional journals and establishing himself as one of the country's leading economists, before he joined the Clinton administration. This nonpolitical career culminated in 1993 when he won the John Bates

Clark Medal, a coveted award for under-40 economists that is somewhat harder to get than a Nobel prize.

Mr. Lindsey took a different path. Although he taught at Harvard following a three-year stint in the Reagan administration, his heart doesn't seem to have been in it; he published few academic papers, instead putting out a book extolling Ronald Reagan's tax cuts. In 1989 he left academia, taking a job in the Bush White House; in 1991 he was appointed by the elder Mr. Bush to the Federal Reserve Board, to the surprise of many who had expected the appointment of a Republican economist with stronger credentials. He now works at a conservative think tank.

The point of this comparison is not that Mr. Summers is smarter than Mr. Lindsey; Mr. Summers is brilliant (ask him, he'll tell you), but Mr. Lindsey is no dummy. Nor is it merely that Mr. Lindsey is a partisan ideologue. The point is that Bill Clinton turned for advice to a strong, independent professional economist, who would have been an important player whatever his politics. Mr. Bush has turned to an economist whose career has been entirely associated with his political orientation. And more specifically, Mr. Lindsey's career has depended on the patronage of the Bush family.

So the younger Mr. Bush's decision to elevate Mr. Lindsey above the many Republican economists who do have reputations independent of their politics says something. Not, I think, that Mr. Bush is a fanatical ideologue himself—though Mr. Lindsey is much more partisan than any of Mr. Clinton's economists. Mainly, it says that Mr. Bush values loyalty above expertise, perhaps that he has a preference for advisers whose personal fortunes are almost entirely bound up with his own.

John Ellis, the political analyst now notorious for his inappropriate role at Fox News—he not only gave Mr. Bush confidential poll information, but was arguably the man behind the premature decision of the networks to call the election for Mr. Bush—once declared that "I am loyal to my cousin, Governor George Bush of Texas. I put that loyalty ahead of my loyalty to anyone else outside my immediate family." Most people would be embarrassed at that sort of declaration; Mr. Bush seems to take it as his due.

Perhaps this explains Mr. Bush's post-election willingness to let his people use any argument, exploit any political advantage to secure victory, no matter how much it might taint the prize. Who in Mr. Bush's circle would dare tell him to accept the possibility of losing?

And this suggests a terrible prospect. Soon we may have a president who lost the popular vote, who won the electoral vote only after bitter controversy, who needs to act with unprecedented humility and discretion to avoid ripping the country apart. But he will have surrounded himself with obsequious courtiers.

# MISSING JAMES TOBIN

*March 12, 2002*

James Tobin—Yale professor, Nobel laureate and adviser to John F. Kennedy—died yesterday. He was a great economist and a remarkably good man; his passing seems to me to symbolize the passing of an era, one in which economic debate was both nicer and a lot more honest than it is today.

Mr. Tobin was one of those economic theorists whose influence reaches so far that many people who have never heard of him are nonetheless his disciples. He was also, however, a public figure, for a time the most prominent advocate of an ideology we might call free-market Keynesianism—a belief that markets are fine things, but that they work best if the government stands ready to limit their excesses. In a way, Mr. Tobin was the original New Democrat; it's ironic that some of his essentially moderate ideas have lately been hijacked by extremists right and left.

Mr. Tobin was one of the economists who brought the Keynesian revolution to America. Before that revolution, there seemed to be no middle ground in economics between laissez-faire fatalism and heavy-handed government intervention—and with laissez-faire policies widely blamed for the Great Depression, it was hard to see how free-market economics could survive.

John Maynard Keynes changed all that: with judicious use of monetary and fiscal policy, he suggested, a free-market system could avoid future depressions.

What did James Tobin add? Basically, he took the crude, mechanistic Keynesianism prevalent in the 1940's and transformed it into a far more sophisticated doctrine, one that focused on the tradeoffs investors make as they balance risk, return and liquidity.

In the 1960's Mr. Tobin's sophisticated Keynesianism made him the best-known intellectual opponent of Milton Friedman, then the advocate of a rival (and rather naïve) doctrine known as monetarism. For what it's worth, Mr. Friedman's insistence that changes in the money supply explain all of the economy's ups and downs has not stood the test of time; Mr. Tobin's focus on asset prices as the driving force behind economic fluctuations has never looked better. (Mr. Friedman is himself a great economist—but his reputation now rests on other work.)

But Mr. Tobin is probably best known today for two policy ideas, both of which have been hijacked—his own word—by people whose political views he did not share.

First, Mr. Tobin was the intellectual force behind the Kennedy tax cut, which started the boom of the 1960's. The irony is that nowadays that tax cut is usually praised by hard-line conservatives, who regard such cuts as an elixir for whatever ails you. Mr. Tobin did not agree. In fact I was on a panel with him just last week, where he argued strongly that the current situation called for more domestic spending, not more tax cuts.

Second, back in 1972 Mr. Tobin proposed that governments levy a small tax on foreign exchange transactions, as a way to discourage destabilizing speculation. He thought of this tax as a way to help promote free trade, by assuring countries that they could open their markets without exposing themselves to disruptive movements of "hot money." Again, irony: the "Tobin tax" has become a favorite of hard-line opponents of free trade, especially the French group Attac. As Mr. Tobin declared, "the loudest applause is coming from the wrong side."

Why do I feel that Mr. Tobin's passing marks the end of an era? Consider that Kennedy Council of Economic Advisers, the most remarkable collection of economic talent to serve the U.S. government since Alexander Hamilton pondered alone. Mr. Tobin, incredibly, was only one of three future Nobelists then working at the council. Would such a group be possible today? I doubt it. When Mr. Tobin went to Washington, top economists weren't subject to strict political litmus tests—and it would never have occurred to them that the job description included saying things that were manifestly untrue. Need I say more?

Yesterday I spoke with William Brainard, another Yale professor who worked with Mr. Tobin, who remarked on his colleague's "faith in the power of ideas." That's a faith that grows ever harder to maintain, as bad ideas with powerful political backing dominate our discourse.

So I miss James Tobin, and I mourn not just his passing, but the passing of an era when economists of such fundamental decency could flourish, and even influence policy.

*Part Six*

# ONE YEAR LATER

THE hardcover edition was put to bed the day after Baghdad fell to U.S. forces. The next year was eventful, to say the least. This new part adds twenty-nine columns from that year.

Chapter 17 tells the increasingly disturbing story of the "war on terror." On the day Baghdad fell, almost everyone thought that whatever else you might say about George Bush, he was doing a great job protecting America. But some of us had doubts. Bush seemed both obsessed with Iraq and uninterested in dealing with more pressing threats, such as North Korea. He was almost eerily unwilling to spend money on domestic security, or to treat such spending as more than a convenient source of pork. And the administration's record in Afghanistan, where it squandered a victory by refusing to invest money, attention, and military force in postwar stabilization, was a bad omen for Iraq.

Sure enough, the worst fears of the skeptics were realized. Iraq, it turned out, posed no threat at all. And it gradually became clear that the administration had hyped the case for a glamorous war it wanted to fight, while neglecting not just domestic security but even the military pursuit of Al Qaeda.

The self-proclaimed "war president" turns out to be weak on terror.

Chapter 18 turns to more mundane matters of dollars and cents. Mainly it tells the story of the gradual unveiling of the administration's radical agenda—its pursuit of more tax cuts in the face of war and massive deficits, and the growing openness of its desire to use deficits to force cuts in social programs. The chapter also looks at two crucial issues: health care and the still incomplete economic recovery.

Finally, chapter 19 looks at the alarming abuses of power that have emerged as the right tries to establish a permanent lock on power. These range from the un-American cult of personality surrounding George Bush, to the attempts to label dissent as unpatriotic, to the ever more Orwellian attitude of the administration toward truth and history.

# CHAPTER 17

# War and Terror

## GEORGE W. QUEEG

*March 14, 2003*

Aboard the U.S.S. *Caine*, it was the business with the strawberries that finally convinced the doubters that something was amiss with the captain. Is foreign policy George W. Bush's quart of strawberries?

Over the past few weeks there has been an epidemic of epiphanies. There's a long list of pundits who previously supported Bush's policy on Iraq but have publicly changed their minds. None of them quarrel with the goal; who wouldn't want to see Saddam Hussein overthrown? But they are finally realizing that Mr. Bush is the wrong man to do the job. And more people than you would think—including a fair number of people in the Treasury Department, the State Department and, yes, the Pentagon—don't just question the competence of Mr. Bush and his inner circle; they believe that America's leadership has lost touch with reality.

If that sounds harsh, consider the debacle of recent diplomacy—a debacle brought on by awesome arrogance and a vastly inflated sense of self-importance.

Mr. Bush's inner circle seems amazed that the tactics that

work so well on journalists and Democrats don't work on the rest of the world. They've made promises, oblivious to the fact that most countries don't trust their word. They've made threats. They've done the aura-of-inevitability thing—how many times now have administration officials claimed to have lined up the necessary votes in the Security Council? They've warned other countries that if they oppose America's will they are objectively pro-terrorist. Yet still the world balks.

Wasn't someone at the State Department allowed to point out that in matters nonmilitary, the U.S. isn't all that dominant—that Russia and Turkey need the European market more than they need ours, that Europe gives more than twice as much foreign aid as we do and that in much of the world public opinion matters? Apparently not.

And to what end has Mr. Bush alienated all our most valuable allies? (And I mean all: Tony Blair may be with us, but British public opinion is now virulently anti-Bush.) The original reasons given for making Iraq an immediate priority have collapsed. No evidence has ever surfaced of the supposed link with Al Qaeda, or of an active nuclear program. And the administration's eagerness to believe that an Iraqi nuclear program does exist has led to a series of embarrassing debacles, capped by the case of the forged Niger papers, which supposedly supported that claim. At this point it is clear that deposing Saddam has become an obsession, detached from any real rationale.

What really has the insiders panicked, however, is the irresponsibility of Mr. Bush and his team, their almost childish unwillingness to face up to problems that they don't feel like dealing with right now.

I've talked in this column about the administration's eerie passivity in the face of a stalling economy and an exploding budget deficit: reality isn't allowed to intrude on the obsession with long-run tax cuts. That same "don't bother me, I'm busy" attitude is driving foreign policy experts, inside and outside the government, to despair.

Need I point out that North Korea, not Iraq, is the clear and present danger? Kim Jong Il's nuclear program isn't a rumor or a forgery; it's an incipient bomb assembly line. Yet the administration insists that it's a mere "regional" crisis, and refuses even to talk to Mr. Kim.

*The Nelson Report*, an influential foreign policy newsletter, says: "It would be difficult to exaggerate the growing mixture of anger, despair, disgust and fear actuating the foreign policy community in Washington as the attack on Iraq moves closer, and the North Korea crisis festers with no coherent U.S. policy. . . . We are at the point now where foreign policy generally, and Korea policy specifically, may become George Bush's 'Waco.' . . . This time, it's Kim Jong Il (and Saddam) playing David Koresh. . . . Sober minds wrestle with how to break into the mind of George Bush."

We all hope that the war with Iraq is a swift victory, with a minimum of civilian casualties. But more and more people now realize that even if all goes well at first, it will have been the wrong war, fought for the wrong reasons—and there will be a heavy price to pay.

Alas, the epiphanies of the pundits have almost surely come too late. The odds are that by the time you read my next column, the war will already have started.

## RED-BLUE TERROR ALERT

*April 1, 2003*

As recriminations fly over Operation Predicted Cakewalk, some commentators look back wistfully to the early post–Sept. 11 era, when—or so they imagine—the nation stood united against the terrorist threat. On my beat, that era was brief indeed: less than 48 hours after the atrocity, Congressional Republicans tried to exploit the event to pass a cut in the capital gains tax. But on national security issues, there was at first some real bipartisanship.

What happened to that bipartisanship? It fell prey to two enduring prejudices of the right: its deep hostility to nonmilitary government spending and its exaltation of the "heartland" over the great urban states.

You might have expected the events of Sept. 11 to temper the right's opposition to some kinds of domestic spending. After thousands of Americans were killed by men armed only with box cutters, surely everyone would acknowledge that national security involves more than mere military might. But you would have been wrong. In a remarkable recent article titled "The 9/10 President," Jonathan Chait of *The New Republic* documents how the Bush administration has systematically neglected homeland security since 9/11. In its effort to keep spending down, the administration has repeatedly blocked proposals to enhance security at potential domestic targets like ports and nuclear plants.

What Mr. Chait doesn't point out is the extent to which already inadequate antiterrorism spending has been focused on the parts of the country that need it least.

I've written before about the myth of the heartland—roughly speaking, the "red states," which voted for George W. Bush in the 2000 election, as opposed to the "blue states," which voted for Al Gore. The nation's interior is supposedly a place of rugged individualists, unlike the spongers and whiners along the coasts. In reality, of course, rural states are heavily subsidized by urban states. New Jersey pays about $1.50 in federal taxes for every dollar it gets in return; Montana receives about $1.75 in federal spending for every dollar it pays in taxes.

Any sensible program of spending on homeland security would at least partly redress this balance. The most natural targets for terrorism lie in or near great metropolitan areas; surely protecting those areas is the highest priority, right?

Apparently not. Even in the first months after Sept. 11, Republican lawmakers made it clear that they would not support any major effort to rebuild or even secure New York. And now that anti-urban prejudice has taken statistical form: under the formula the Department of Homeland Security has adopted for handing out money, it spends seven times as much protecting each resident of Wyoming as it does protecting each resident of New York.

Here's how it works. In its main grant programs, the department makes no attempt to assess needs. Instead, each state receives a base of 0.75 percent of the total, regardless of its population; the rest is then allocated in proportion to population. This is a very good deal for states with small populations, like Wyoming or Montana. It's a very bad deal for states like California, or New York, which receives only 4.7 percent of the money. And since New York and other big urban states remain the most likely targets of another major attack, it's a very bad deal for the country.

Why adopt such a strange formula? Well, maybe it's not that strange: what it most resembles is the Electoral College, which also gives disproportionate weight (though not that dispropor-tionate) to states with small populations. And with a few excep-tions, small-population states are red states—indeed, the small-state bias of the Electoral College is what allowed Mr. Bush to claim the White House despite losing the popular vote. It's hard not to suspect that the formula—which makes abso-lutely no sense in terms of national security—was adopted pre-cisely because it caters to that same constituency. (To be fair, there's one big "red state" loser from the formula: Texas. But one of these days, sooner than most people think, Texas may well turn blue.)

In other words, the allocation of money confirms Mr. Chait's point: even in a time of war—a war that seems oddly unrelated to the terrorist threat—the Bush administration isn't serious about protecting the homeland. Instead, it continues to subor-dinate U.S. security needs to its unchanged political agenda.

# CONQUEST AND NEGLECT

*April 11, 2003*

Credit where credit is due: the hawks were right to say that a whiff of precision-guided grapeshot would lead to the collapse of Saddam Hussein's regime. But even skeptics about this war expected a military victory. ("Of course we'll win on the battlefield, probably with ease" was the opening line of my start-of-the-war column.) Instead, we worried—and continue to worry—about what would follow. As another skeptic, Michael Kinsley of *Slate*, wrote yesterday: "I do hope to be proven wrong. But it hasn't happened yet."

Why worry? I won't pretend to have any insights into what is going on in the minds of the Iraqi people. But there is a pattern to the Bush administration's way of doing business that does not bode well for the future—a pattern of conquest followed by malign neglect.

One has to admit that the Bush people are very good at conquest, military and political. They focus all their attention on an issue; they pull out all the stops; they don't worry about breaking the rules. This technique brought them victory in the Florida recount battle, the passage of the 2001 tax cut, the fall of Kabul, victory in the midterm elections, and the fall of Baghdad.

But after the triumph, when it comes time to take care of what they've won, their attention wanders, and things go to pot.

The most obvious example is Afghanistan, the land the Bush administration forgot. Most of the country is back under the control of fundamentalist warlords; unpaid soldiers and police-men are deserting in droves. (Remember that the Bush admin-istration forgot to include any Afghan aid in its latest budget.)

President Hamid Karzai's brother, Ahmed Wali Karzai, told an Associated Press reporter: "It is like I am seeing the same movie twice and no one is trying to fix the problem. What was promised to Afghans with the collapse of the Taliban was a new life of hope and change. But what was delivered? Nothing. Everyone is back in business."

The same pattern can be seen on the economic front. Presi-dent Bush won a great triumph in 2001 when he pushed through a huge tax cut—claiming that his plan was just the medicine to cure the economy's ills. What has happened since?

The answer is that things have gradually fallen apart. There was one quarter of good growth, early in 2002—and there were cries of triumph over the policy's success. After that, however, things went steadily wrong. Growth was too slow to create jobs: at the end of 2002, after a year of "recovery," fewer people were working than at the end of 2001.

And in the last two months the situation has deteriorated rapidly. In February and March the U.S. economy lost 465,000 jobs, bringing the total job loss since the recession officially began in March 2001 to more than two million.

At this point the employment decline has been bigger, and has gone on longer, than the slump that took place during the first Bush administration. And there's no sign of an upturn: new claims for unemployment insurance are still running well above the level that would signal an improving labor market.

Some hope that the economy will turn around of its own accord—that consumers and businesses, relieved that the war has gone well, will begin spending freely. But hope is not a plan. What is the plan?

The answer seems to be that there is no plan for the economy. Instead, the White House is fixated on achieving another political triumph—the elimination of taxes on dividends—that has little or no relevance to our current economic troubles.

I could demonstrate this irrelevance by going through an economic analysis, but here's a telling political clue: *USA Today* reports that faced with concerns in Congress about budget deficits, the administration has indicated that it is willing to consider a phase-in of its dividend plan.

That is, it's willing to forgo immediate tax cuts—the one piece of its proposal that might actually help the economy now—in order to be able to pass its long-run proposal intact, and hence claim total victory.

The scary thing is that this slash-and-burn approach to governing may continue to work for Mr. Bush's people because the initial triumphs get all the headlines. Unfortunately, the rest of the world has to live in the wreckage they leave behind.

## MATTERS OF EMPHASIS

*April 29, 2003*

"We were not lying," a Bush administration official told ABC News. "But it was just a matter of emphasis." The official was referring to the way the administration hyped the threat that Saddam Hussein posed to the United States. According to the ABC report, the real reason for the war was that the administration "wanted to make a statement." And why Iraq? "Officials acknowledge that Saddam had all the requirements to make him, from their standpoint, the perfect target."

A British newspaper, *The Independent*, reports that "intelligence agencies on both sides of the Atlantic were furious that briefings they gave political leaders were distorted in the rush to war." One "high-level source" told the paper that "they ignored intelligence assessments which said Iraq was not a threat."

Sure enough, we have yet to find any weapons of mass destruction. It's hard to believe that we won't eventually find some poison gas or crude biological weapons. But those aren't true W.M.D.'s, the sort of weapons that can make a small, poor country a threat to the greatest power the world has ever known. Remember that President Bush made his case for war by warning of a "mushroom cloud." Clearly, Iraq didn't have anything like that—and Mr. Bush must have known that it didn't.

Does it matter that we were misled into war? Some people say that it doesn't: we won, and the Iraqi people have been freed. But we ought to ask some hard questions—not just about Iraq, but about ourselves.

First, why is our compassion so selective? In 2001 the World Health Organization—the same organization we now count on to protect us from SARS—called for a program to fight infectious diseases in poor countries, arguing that it would save the lives of millions of people every year. The U.S. share of the expenses would have been about $10 billion per year— a small fraction of what we will spend on war and occupation. Yet the Bush administration contemptuously dismissed the proposal.

Or consider one of America's first major postwar acts of diplomacy: blocking a plan to send U.N. peacekeepers to Ivory Coast (a former French colony) to enforce a truce in a vicious civil war. The U.S. complains that it will cost too much. And that must be true—we wouldn't let innocent people die just to spite the French, would we?

So it seems that our deep concern for the Iraqi people doesn't extend to suffering people elsewhere. I guess it's just a matter of emphasis. A cynic might point out, however, that saving lives peacefully doesn't offer any occasion to stage a victory parade.

Meanwhile, aren't the leaders of a democratic nation supposed to tell their citizens the truth?

One wonders whether most of the public will ever learn that the original case for war has turned out to be false. In fact, my guess is that most Americans believe that we have found W.M.D.'s. Each potential find gets blaring coverage on TV; how many people catch the later announcement—if it is ever announced—that it was a false alarm? It's a pattern of misinformation that recapitulates the way the war was sold in the first place. Each administration charge against Iraq received prominent coverage; the subsequent debunking did not.

Did the news media feel that it was unpatriotic to question the administration's credibility? Some strange things certainly happened. For example, in September Mr. Bush cited an International Atomic Energy Agency report that he said showed that Saddam was only months from having nuclear weapons. "I don't know what more evidence we need," he said. In fact, the report said no such thing—and for a few hours the lead story on MSNBC's Web site bore the headline "White House: Bush Misstated Report on Iraq." Then the story vanished—not just from the top of the page, but from the site.

Thanks to this pattern of loud assertions and muted or suppressed retractions, the American public probably believes that we went to war to avert an immediate threat—just as it believes that Saddam had something to do with Sept. 11.

Now it's true that the war removed an evil tyrant. But a democracy's decisions, right or wrong, are supposed to take place with the informed consent of its citizens. That didn't happen this time. And we are a democracy—aren't we?

## PATHS OF GLORY

*May 16, 2003*

The central dogma of American politics right now is that George W. Bush, whatever his other failings, has been an effective leader in the fight against terrorism. But the more you know about the state of the world, the less you believe that dogma. The Iraq war, in particular, did nothing to make America safer—in fact, it did the terrorists a favor.

How is the war on terror going? You know about the Riyadh bombings. But something else happened this week: The International Institute for Strategic Studies, a respected British think tank with no discernible anti-Bush animus, declared that Al Qaeda is "more insidious and just as dangerous" as it was before Sept. 11. So much for claims that we had terrorists on the run.

Still, isn't the Bush administration doing its best to fight terrorism? No.

The administration's antiterror campaign makes me think of the way television studios really look. The fancy set usually sits in the middle of a shabby room, full of cardboard and duct tape. Networks take great care with what viewers see on their TV screens; they spend as little as possible on anything off camera.

And so it has been with the campaign against terrorism. Mr. Bush strikes heroic poses on TV, but his administration neglects anything that isn't photogenic.

I've written before about the Bush administration's amazing refusal to pay for even minimal measures to protect the nation against future attacks—measures that would secure ports, chemical plants, nuclear facilities and so on. (But the Department of Homeland Security isn't completely ineffectual: this week it helped Texas Republicans track down their Democratic colleagues, who had staged a walkout.)

The neglect of homeland security is mirrored by the Bush administration's failure to follow through on overseas efforts once the TV-friendly part of the operation has come to an end. The overthrow of the Taliban was a real victory—arguably our only important victory against terrorism. But as soon as Kabul fell, the administration lost interest. Now most of Afghanistan is under the control of warlords, the Karzai government is barely hanging on, and the Taliban are making a comeback.

Senator Bob Graham has made an even stronger charge: that Al Qaeda was "on the ropes" a year ago, but was able to recover because the administration diverted military and intelligence resources to Iraq. As former chairman of the Senate Intelligence Committee, he's in a position to know. And before you dismiss him as a partisan Democrat, bear in mind that when he began raising this alarm last fall his Republican colleagues supported him: "He's absolutely right to be concerned," said Senator Richard Shelby, who has seen the same information.

Senator Graham also claims that a classified Congressional report reveals that "the lessons of Sept. 11 are not being applied today," and accuses the administration of a cover-up.

Still, we defeated Saddam. Doesn't that make us safer? Well, no.

Saddam wasn't a threat to America—he had no important links to terrorism, and the main U.S. team searching for weapons of mass destruction has packed up and gone home. Meanwhile, true to form, the Bush team lost focus as soon as the TV coverage slackened off. The first result was an orgy of looting—including looting of nuclear waste dumps that, incredibly, we failed to secure. Dirty bombs, anyone? Now, according to an article in *The New Republic*, armed Iraqi factions are preparing for civil war.

That leaves us facing exactly the dilemma war skeptics feared. If we leave Iraq quickly it may well turn into a bigger, more dangerous version of Afghanistan. But if we stay for an extended period we risk becoming, as one commentator put it, "an occupying power in a bitterly hostile land"—just the recruiting tool Al Qaeda needs. Who said that? President George H. W. Bush, explaining his decision not to go on to Baghdad back in 1991.

Massoud Barzani, the Kurdish leader, isn't afraid to use the "Q" word, worrying that because of America's failure to follow up, "this wonderful victory we have achieved will turn into a quagmire."

The truth is that the pursuit of televised glory—which led the Bush administration to turn its attention away from Al Qaeda, and to pick a fight with a regime that, however nasty, posed no threat—has made us much less safe than we should be.

# DERELICTION OF DUTY

*June 17, 2003*

Last Thursday a House subcommittee met to finalize next year's homeland security appropriation. The ranking Democrat announced that he would introduce an amendment adding roughly $1 billion for areas like port security and border security that, according to just about every expert, have been severely neglected since Sept. 11. He proposed to pay for the additions by slightly scaling back tax cuts for people making more than $1 million per year.

The subcommittee's chairman promptly closed the meeting to the public, citing national security—though no classified material was under discussion. And the bill that emerged from the closed meeting did not contain the extra funding.

It was a perfect symbol of the reality of the Bush administration's "war on terror." Behind the rhetoric—and behind the veil of secrecy, invoked in the name of national security but actually used to prevent public scrutiny—lies a pattern of neglect, of refusal to take crucial actions to protect us from terrorists. Actual counterterrorism, it seems, doesn't fit the administration's agenda.

Yesterday *The Washington Post* printed an interview with Rand Beers, a top White House counterterrorism adviser who resigned in March. "They're making us less secure, not more secure," he said of the Bush administration. "As an insider, I saw the things that weren't being done." Among the problem areas he cited were homeland security, where he says the administration has "only a rhetorical policy"; failure to press Saudi Arabia (the home of most of the Sept. 11 terrorists) to take action; and, of course, the way we allowed Afghanistan to relapse into chaos.

Some of this pattern of neglect involves penny-pinching. Back in February, even George W. Bush in effect admitted that not enough money had been allocated to domestic security—though (to the fury of Republican legislators) he blamed Congress. Yet according to Fred Kaplan in *Slate*, the administration's latest budget proposal for homeland security actually contains less money than was spent last year. Meanwhile, urgent priorities remain unmet. For example, port security, identified as a top concern from the very beginning, has so far received only one-tenth as much money as the Coast Guard says is needed.

But it's not just a matter of money. For one thing, it's hard to claim now that the Bush administration is trying to hold down domestic spending to make room for tax cuts. With the budget deficit projected at more than $400 billion this year, a few billion more for homeland security wouldn't make much difference to the tax-cutting agenda. Moreover, Congress isn't pinching pennies across the board: last week the Senate voted to provide $15 billion in loan guarantees for the construction of nuclear power plants.

Furthermore, even on the military front the administration has been weirdly reluctant to come to grips with terrorism. It refused to provide Afghanistan's new government with an adequate security umbrella, with the predictable result that warlords are running rampant and the Taliban are making a comeback. The squandered victory in Afghanistan was one reason people like myself had a bad feeling about the invasion of

Iraq—and sure enough, the administration was bizarrely lack-adaisical about providing postwar security. Even nuclear waste dumps were left unguarded for weeks.

So what's the explanation? The answer, one suspects, is that key figures—above all, Donald Rumsfeld—just didn't feel like dealing with the real problem. Real counterterrorism mainly involves police work and precautionary measures; it doesn't look impressive on TV, and it doesn't provide many occasions for victory celebrations.

A conventional war, on the other hand, is a lot more fun: you get stirring pictures of tanks rolling across the desert, and you get to do a victory landing on an aircraft carrier. And more and more it seems that that was what the war was all about. After all, the supposed reasons for fighting that war have turned out to be false—there were no links to Al Qaeda, there wasn't a big arsenal of W.M.D.'s.

But never mind—we won, didn't we? Maybe not. About half of the U.S. Army's combat strength is now tied down in Iraq, facing what looks increasingly like a guerrilla war—and like a perfect recruiting device for Al Qaeda. Meanwhile, the real war on terror has been neglected, and we've antagonized the allies we need to fight that war. One of these days we'll end up paying the price.

## DENIAL AND DECEPTION

*June 24, 2003*

Politics is full of ironies. On the White House Web site, George W. Bush's speech from Oct. 7, 2002—in which he made the case for war with Iraq—bears the headline "Denial and Deception." Indeed.

There is no longer any serious doubt that Bush administration officials deceived us into war. The key question now is why so many influential people are in denial, unwilling to admit the obvious.

About the deception: Leaks from professional intelligence analysts, who are furious over the way their work was abused, have given us a far more complete picture of how America went to war. Thanks to reporting by my colleague Nicholas Kristof, other reports in *The New York Times* and *The Washington Post*, and a magisterial article by John Judis and Spencer Ackerman in *The New Republic*, we now know that top officials, including Mr. Bush, sought to convey an impression about the Iraqi threat that was not supported by actual intelligence reports.

In particular, there was never any evidence linking Saddam Hussein to Al Qaeda; yet administration officials repeatedly suggested the existence of a link. Supposed evidence of an active Iraqi nuclear program was thoroughly debunked by the administration's own experts; yet administration officials continued to cite that evidence and warn of Iraq's nuclear threat.

And yet the political and media establishment is in denial,

finding excuses for the administration's efforts to mislead both Congress and the public.

For example, some commentators have suggested that Mr. Bush should be let off the hook as long as there is some interpretation of his prewar statements that is technically true. Really? We're not talking about a business dispute that hinges on the fine print of the contract; we're talking about the most solemn decision a nation can make. If Mr. Bush's speeches gave the nation a misleading impression about the case for war, close textual analysis showing that he didn't literally say what he seemed to be saying is no excuse. On the contrary, it suggests that he knew that his case couldn't stand close scrutiny.

Consider, for example, what Mr. Bush said in his "denial and deception" speech about the supposed Saddam-Osama link: that there were "high-level contacts that go back a decade." In fact, intelligence agencies knew of tentative contacts between Saddam and an infant Al Qaeda in the early 1990's, but found no good evidence of a continuing relationship. So Mr. Bush made what sounded like an assertion of an ongoing relationship between Iraq and Al Qaeda, but phrased it cagily—suggesting that he or his speechwriter knew full well that his case was shaky.

Other commentators suggest that Mr. Bush may have sincerely believed, despite the lack of evidence, that Saddam was working with Osama and developing nuclear weapons. Actually, that's unlikely: why did he use such evasive wording if he didn't know that he was improving on the truth? In any case, however, somebody was at fault. If top administration officials somehow failed to apprise Mr. Bush of intelligence reports refuting key pieces of his case against Iraq, they weren't doing their jobs. And Mr. Bush should be the first person to demand their resignations.

So why are so many people making excuses for Mr. Bush and his officials?

Part of the answer, of course, is raw partisanship. One important difference between our current scandal and the Watergate affair is that it's almost impossible now to imagine a Republican senator asking, "What did the president know, and when did he know it?"

But even people who aren't partisan Republicans shy away from confronting the administration's dishonest case for war, because they don't want to face the implications.

After all, suppose that a politician—or a journalist—admits to himself that Mr. Bush bamboozled the nation into war. Well, launching a war on false pretenses is, to say the least, a breach of trust. So if you admit to yourself that such a thing happened, you have a moral obligation to demand accountability—and to do so not only in the face of a powerful, ruthless political machine but in the face of a country not yet ready to believe that its leaders have exploited 9/11 for political gain. It's a scary prospect.

Yet if we can't find people willing to take the risk—to face the truth and act on it—what will happen to our democracy?

# WHO'S UNPATRIOTIC NOW?

*July 22, 2003*

Some nonrevisionist history: On Oct. 8, 2002, Knight Ridder newspapers reported on intelligence officials who "charge that the administration squelches dissenting views, and that intelligence analysts are under intense pressure to produce reports supporting the White House's argument that Saddam poses such an immediate threat to the United States that pre-emptive military action is necessary." One official accused the administration of pressuring analysts to "cook the intelligence books"; none of the dozen other officials the reporters spoke to disagreed.

The skepticism of these officials has been vindicated. So have the concerns expressed before the war by military professionals like Gen. Eric Shinseki, the Army chief of staff, about the resources required for postwar occupation. But as the bad news comes in, those who promoted this war have responded with a concerted effort to smear the messengers.

Issues of principle aside, the invasion of a country that hadn't attacked us and didn't pose an imminent threat has seriously weakened our military position. Of the Army's 33 combat brigades, 16 are in Iraq; this leaves us ill prepared to cope with genuine threats. Moreover, military experts say that with almost two-thirds of its brigades deployed overseas, mainly in Iraq, the Army's readiness is eroding: normal doctrine calls for only one brigade in three to be deployed abroad, while the other two retrain and refit.

And the war will have devastating effects on future recruiting by the reserves. A widely circulated photo from Iraq shows a sign in the windshield of a military truck that reads: "One weekend a month, my ass."

To top it all off, our insistence on launching a war without U.N. approval has deprived us of useful allies. George Bush claims to have a "huge coalition," but only 7 percent of the coalition soldiers in Iraq are non-American—and administration pleas for more help are sounding increasingly plaintive.

How serious is the strain on our military? The Brookings Institution military analyst Michael O'Hanlon, who describes our volunteer military as "one of the best military institutions in human history," warns that "the Bush administration will risk destroying that accomplishment if they keep on the current path."

But instead of explaining what happened to the Al Qaeda link and the nuclear program, in the last few days a series of hawkish pundits have accused those who ask such questions of aiding the enemy. Here's Frank Gaffney Jr. in *The National Post*: "Somewhere, probably in Iraq, Saddam Hussein is gloating. He can only be gratified by the feeding frenzy of recriminations, second-guessing and political power plays. . . . Signs of declining popular appreciation of the legitimacy and necessity of the efforts of America's armed forces will erode their morale. Similarly, the enemy will be encouraged."

Well, if we're going to talk about aiding the enemy: By cooking intelligence to promote a war that wasn't urgent, the administration has squandered our military strength. This provides a lot of aid and comfort to Osama bin Laden—who really did attack America—and Kim Jong Il—who really is building nukes.

And while we're on the subject of patriotism, let's talk about the affair of Joseph Wilson's wife. Mr. Wilson is the former ambassador who was sent to Niger by the C.I.A. to investigate reports of attempted Iraqi uranium purchases and who recently went public with his findings. Since then administration allies have sought to discredit him—it's unpleasant stuff. But here's the kicker: both the columnist Robert Novak and *Time* magazine say that administration officials told them that they believed that Mr. Wilson had been chosen through the influence of his wife, whom they identified as a C.I.A. operative.

Think about that: if their characterization of Mr. Wilson's wife is true (he refuses to confirm or deny it), Bush administration officials have exposed the identity of a covert operative. That happens to be a criminal act; it's also definitely unpatriotic.

So why would they do such a thing? Partly, perhaps, to punish Mr. Wilson, but also to send a message.

And that should alarm us. We've just seen how politicized, cooked intelligence can damage our national interest. Yet the Wilson affair suggests that the administration intends to continue pressuring analysts to tell it what it wants to hear.

# WHO'S SORDID NOW?

*September 30, 2003*

It's official: the administration that once scorned nation-building now says that it's engaged in a modern version of the Marshall Plan. But Iraq isn't postwar Europe, and George W. Bush definitely isn't Harry Truman. Indeed, while Truman led this country in what Churchill called the "most unsordid act in history," the stories about Iraqi reconstruction keep getting more sordid. And the sordidness isn't, as some would have you believe, a minor blemish on an otherwise noble enterprise.

Cronyism is an important factor in our Iraqi debacle. It's not just that reconstruction is much more expensive than it should be. The really important thing is that cronyism is warping policy: by treating contracts as prizes to be handed to their friends, administration officials are delaying Iraq's recovery, with potentially catastrophic consequences.

It's rarely mentioned nowadays, but at the time of the Marshall Plan, Americans were very concerned about profiteering in the name of patriotism. To get Congressional approval, Truman had to provide assurances that the plan would not become a boondoggle. Funds were administered by an agency independent of the White House, and Marshall promised that priorities would be determined by Europeans, not Americans.

Fortunately, Truman's assurances were credible. Although he is now honored for his postwar leadership, Truman initially rose to prominence as a fierce crusader against war profiteering, which he considered treason.

Iraq's reconstruction, by contrast, remains firmly under White House control. And this is an administration of, by and for crony capitalists; to match this White House's blithe lack of concern about conflicts of interest, you have to go back to the Harding administration. That giant, no-bid contract given to Halliburton, the company that made Dick Cheney rich, was just what you'd expect.

And even as the situation in Iraq slides downhill, and the Iraqi Governing Council demands more autonomy and control, American officials continue to block local initiatives, and are still trying to keep the big contracts in the hands of you-know-who.

For example, in July two enterprising Middle Eastern firms started offering cellphone service in Baghdad, setting up jury-rigged systems compatible with those of neighboring countries. Since the collapse of Baghdad's phone system has been a major source of postwar problems, coalition authorities should have been pleased.

But no: the authorities promptly shut down the services. Cell service, they said, could be offered only by the winners in a bidding process—one whose rules, revealed on July 31, seemed carefully designed to shut out any non-American companies. (In the face of strenuous protests the rules were revised, but still seem to favor the usual suspects.) Oddly, the announcement of the winners, originally scheduled for Sept. 5, keeps being delayed. Meanwhile, only Paul Bremer and his people have cellphones—and, thanks to the baffling decision to give that contract to MCI, even those phones don't work very well. (Aside from the fact that its management perpetrated history's biggest accounting fraud, MCI has no experience in building cell networks.)

Then there's electricity. One reason Iraq still faces blackouts is that local experts and institutions were excluded from the repair business. Instead, the exclusive contract was given to Bechtel, whose Republican ties are almost as strong as Halliburton's. And if a recent story in *The Washington Post* is accurate, Bechtel continues to ignore pleas by Iraqi engineers for essential spare parts.

Meanwhile, several companies with close personal ties to top administration officials have begun brazenly offering their services as facilitators for companies seeking Iraqi business. The former law firm of Douglas Feith, the Pentagon undersecretary who oversees Iraq reconstruction, has hung out its shingle. So has another company headed by Joe Allbaugh, who ran the Bush-Cheney campaign in 2000 and ran FEMA until a few months ago. And a third entrant is run by Ahmad Chalabi's nephew.

There's a moral here: optimists who expect the administration to get its Iraq policy on track are kidding themselves. Think about it: the cost of the occupation is exploding, and military experts warn that our army is dangerously overcommitted. Yet officials are still allowing Iraqi reconstruction to languish, and the disaffection of the Iraqi public to grow, while they steer choice contracts to their friends. What makes you think they will ever change their ways?

*Correction: Friday, October 3, 2003*
Correction: Many people, including Paul Bremer in recent testimony and myself in my Sept. 30 column, have linked Churchill's remark about the "most unsordid act" to the Marshall Plan. In fact, Churchill was referring to an earlier program, Lend-Lease. But one suspects that he wouldn't have minded the confusion.

# WEAK ON TERROR

*March 16, 2004*

"My most immediate priority," Spain's new leader, José Luís Rodríguez Zapatero, declared yesterday, "will be to fight terrorism." But he and the voters who gave his party a stunning upset victory last Sunday don't believe the war in Iraq is part of that fight. And the Spanish public was also outraged by what it perceived as the Aznar government's attempt to spin last week's terrorist attack for political purposes.

The Bush administration, which baffled the world when it used an attack by Islamic fundamentalists to justify the overthrow of a brutal but secular regime, and which has been utterly ruthless in its political exploitation of 9/11, must be very, very afraid.

Polls suggest that a reputation for being tough on terror is just about the only remaining political strength George Bush has. Yet this reputation is based on image, not reality. The truth is that Mr. Bush, while eager to invoke 9/11 on behalf of an unrelated war, has shown consistent reluctance to focus on the terrorists who actually attacked America, or their backers in Saudi Arabia and Pakistan.

This reluctance dates back to Mr. Bush's first months in office. Why, after all, has his inner circle tried so hard to prevent a serious investigation of what happened on 9/11? There has been much speculation about whether officials ignored specific intelligence warnings, but what we know for sure is that the administration disregarded urgent pleas by departing Clinton officials to focus on the threat from Al Qaeda.

After 9/11, terrorism could no longer be ignored, and the military conducted a successful campaign against Al Qaeda's Taliban hosts. But the failure to commit sufficient U.S. forces allowed Osama bin Laden to escape. After that, the administration appeared to lose interest in Al Qaeda; by the summer of 2002, bin Laden's name had disappeared from Mr. Bush's speeches. It was all Saddam, all the time.

This wasn't just a rhetorical switch; crucial resources were pulled off the hunt for Al Qaeda, which had attacked America, to prepare for the overthrow of Saddam, who hadn't. If you want confirmation that this seriously impeded the fight against terror, just look at reports about the all-out effort to capture Osama that started, finally, just a few days ago. Why didn't this happen last year, or the year before? According to *The New York Times*, last year many of the needed forces were tied up in Iraq.

It's now clear that by shifting his focus to Iraq, Mr. Bush did Al Qaeda a huge favor. The terrorists and their Taliban allies were given time to regroup; the resurgent Taliban once again control almost a third of Afghanistan, and Al Qaeda has regained the ability to carry out large-scale atrocities.

But Mr. Bush's lapses in the struggle against terrorism extend beyond his decision to give Al Qaeda a breather. His administration has also run interference for Saudi Arabia—the home of most of the 9/11 hijackers, and the main financier of Islamic extremism—and Pakistan, which created the Taliban and has actively engaged in nuclear proliferation.

Some of the administration's actions have been so strange that those who reported them were initially accused of being nutty conspiracy theorists. For example, what are we to make of the post–9/11 Saudi airlift? Just days after the attack, at a time when private air travel was banned, the administration gave special clearance to flights that gathered up Saudi nationals, including a number of members of the bin Laden family, who were in the U.S. at the time. These Saudis were then allowed to leave the country, after at best cursory interviews with the F.B.I.

And the administration is still covering up for Pakistan, whose government recently made the absurd claim that large-scale shipments of nuclear technology and material to rogue states—including North Korea, according to a new C.I.A. report—were the work of one man, who was promptly pardoned by President Pervez Musharraf. Mr. Bush has allowed this farce to go unquestioned.

So when the Bush campaign boasts of the president's record in fighting terrorism and accuses John Kerry of being weak on the issue, when Republican congressmen suggest that a vote for Mr. Kerry is a vote for Osama, remember this: the administration's actual record is one of indulgence toward regimes that are strongly implicated in terrorism, and of focusing on actual terrorist threats only when forced to by events.

# CHAPTER 18

# Dollars and Cents

## ROADS NOT TAKEN

*April 25, 2003*

Congressman Richard Gephardt's new proposal—to scrap the 2001 tax cut and use the reclaimed revenue to provide health benefits to the uninsured—has been widely dismissed as unrealistic. And in political terms that's probably true. After all, these days it's considered "moderate" to support an irresponsible tax cut that is merely large, as opposed to gigantic.

But today I'd like to take a holiday from political realism, and ask a naïve question: Why shouldn't the American people favor a proposal like Mr. Gephardt's? Never mind the details; why shouldn't the typical citizen, faced with a choice between Bush-style tax cuts and a plan to provide health insurance to most of the uninsured, choose the latter?

Of course, originally tax cuts weren't supposed to require sacrificing something else. In the 2000 campaign, and up through the passage of the 2001 tax cut, George Bush insisted that there was plenty of money for everything. But there wasn't—and now, having returned to an era of deficits, we are told that social programs must be shrunk even as taxes are cut further. Why not choose a different road?

Most Americans were never going to get much of a tax cut, anyway. If all the Bush tax cuts—those actually passed in 2001, and those the administration is now pushing—were fully in effect, they would reduce annual taxes collected per family by about $2,500. But averages can be deeply misleading. When Bill Gates enters a bar, the average net worth of the patrons soars, but that doesn't make everyone in the bar a billionaire.

So it is with the tax cuts, which bestow most of their benefits on the very, very affluent. Most families, as best I can estimate, will see their taxes fall by less than $800—in many cases, much less. Meanwhile, a handful of people will benefit hugely: the top 1 percent of families, with incomes averaging more than $1 million, will get tax breaks to the tune of $80,000 each.

On the other hand, ordinary families would benefit greatly from a plan that provided health insurance to those now uninsured.

It's true that at any given moment most middle-income families have insurance. But people lose their jobs, companies go bankrupt, and benefits get suddenly slashed. Over any given two-year period, roughly a third of Americans spend some time without health insurance; over longer periods, the risk of losing health insurance is very significant for most families.

Would ending that risk be worth several hundred dollars a year to the typical family? (It doesn't have to be worth $800: Mr. Gephardt's plan, which would provide increased tax credits to employers, would also lead to higher wages, offsetting some of the tax-cut reversal.) Yes, without question.

When a family without health insurance suffers illness, the results are often catastrophic—either serious conditions go untreated or the family faces financial ruin. Our inadequate insurance system is one important reason why America, the richest country in the world, has lower life expectancy and higher child mortality than most other advanced nations.

So why should tax cuts take priority over health care? I know the party line: tax cuts for high earners are the key to economic growth, and a rising tide lifts all boats. But there's not a shred of evidence supporting that claim. More than two decades after the supply-siders launched their tax-cut crusade, ordinary workers have yet to see a rising tide. The median real wage is only 7 percent higher now than it was in 1979, with all of that increase achieved after Bill Clinton raised taxes for the top bracket.

If American families knew what was good for them, then most of them—all but a small, affluent minority—would cheerfully give up their tax cuts in return for a guarantee that health care would be there when needed. And even the affluent might prefer to live in a society where no sick child was left behind.

O.K., back to political reality. Nothing like Mr. Gephardt's plan is going to become law anytime soon. On the contrary, the right is likely to ram through even more tax cuts, while using deficits as an excuse for not helping the uninsured. But we have the right to ask why. And claiming that those who don't support tax cuts are somehow unpatriotic is not an answer.

# STATING THE OBVIOUS

*May 27, 2003*

"The lunatics are now in charge of the asylum." So wrote the normally staid *Financial Times*, traditionally the voice of solid British business opinion, when surveying last week's tax bill. Indeed, the legislation is doubly absurd: the gimmicks used to make an $800-billion-plus tax cut carry an official price tag of only $320 billion are a joke, yet the cost without the gimmicks is so large that the nation can't possibly afford it while keeping its other promises.

But then maybe that's the point. *The Financial Times* suggests that "more extreme Republicans" actually want a fiscal train wreck: "Proposing to slash federal spending, particularly on social programs, is a tricky electoral proposition, but a fiscal crisis offers the tantalizing prospect of forcing such cuts through the back door."

Good for *The Financial Times*. It seems that stating the obvious has now, finally, become respectable.

It's no secret that right-wing ideologues want to abolish programs Americans take for granted. But not long ago, to suggest that the Bush administration's policies might actually be driven by those ideologues—that the administration was deliberately setting the country up for a fiscal crisis in which popular social programs could be sharply cut—was to be accused of spouting conspiracy theories.

Yet by pushing through another huge tax cut in the face of record deficits, the administration clearly demonstrates either that it is completely feckless, or that it actually wants a fiscal crisis. (Or maybe both.)

Here's one way to look at the situation: Although you wouldn't know it from the rhetoric, federal taxes are already historically low as a share of G.D.P. Once the new round of cuts takes effect, federal taxes will be lower than their average during the Eisenhower administration. How, then, can the government pay for Medicare and Medicaid—which didn't exist in the 1950's—and Social Security, which will become far more expensive as the population ages? (Defense spending has fallen compared with the economy, but not that much, and it's on the rise again.)

The answer is that it can't. The government can borrow to make up the difference as long as investors remain in denial, unable to believe that the world's only superpower is turning into a banana republic. But at some point bond markets will balk—they won't lend money to a government, even that of the United States, if that government's debt is growing faster than its revenues and there is no plausible story about how the budget will eventually come under control.

At that point, either taxes will go up again, or programs that have become fundamental to the American way of life will be gutted. We can be sure that the right will do whatever it takes to preserve the Bush tax cuts—right now the administration is even skimping on homeland security to save a few dollars here and there. But balancing the books without tax increases will require deep cuts where the money is: that is, in Medicaid, Medicare and Social Security.

The pain of these benefit cuts will fall on the middle class and the poor, while the tax cuts overwhelmingly favor the rich. For example, the tax cut passed last week will raise the after-tax income of most people by less than 1 percent—not nearly enough to compensate them for the loss of benefits. But people with incomes over $1 million per year will, on average, see their after-tax income rise 4.4 percent.

*The Financial Times* suggests this is deliberate (and I agree): "For them," it says of those extreme Republicans, "undermining the multilateral international order is not enough; long-held views on income distribution also require radical revision."

How can this be happening? Most people, even most liberals, are complacent. They don't realize how dire the fiscal outlook really is, and they don't read what the ideologues write. They imagine that the Bush administration, like the Reagan administration, will modify our system only at the edges, that it won't destroy the social safety net built up over the past 70 years.

But the people now running America aren't conservatives: they're radicals who want to do away with the social and economic system we have, and the fiscal crisis they are concocting may give them the excuse they need. *The Financial Times*, it seems, now understands what's going on, but when will the public wake up?

# THE TROJAN HORSE

*November 14, 2003*

What are we going to do about Medicare? That should be the subject of an open national debate. But right now Congressional leaders are trying to settle the question by stealth, with legislation that purports to be doing something else.

An aging population and rising medical costs will eventually require the nation to provide Medicare with more money or to cut benefits, or both. Meanwhile, there are demands for a new benefit: a gradual shift away from hospital treatment and toward the use of drugs has turned the program's failure to cover prescription drugs into a gaping hole.

A Congressional conference is now trying to agree on prescription drug legislation. But beware of politicians bearing gifts—the bill will contain measures that have nothing to do with prescription drugs, and a lot to do with hostility to Medicare as we know it. Indeed, it may turn out to be a Trojan horse that finally allows conservative ideologues, who have unsuccessfully laid siege to Medicare since the days of Barry Goldwater, to breach its political defenses.

Some background: originally, Medicare provided only hospital insurance, paid for with a special tax on wages—and this tax, according to estimates from the trustees, will be enough to cover hospital insurance costs for at least 20 more years. Medicare now also includes additional benefits, but the costs of these benefits have always been covered out of general revenue—that is, money raised by other taxes.

But one of the proposals being negotiated behind closed doors—misleadingly described as "cost containment"—would set a limit on Medicare's use of general revenue, and would require action seven years before projections say that limit will be breached. This rule is reinforced with a peculiar new definition of "general revenue" that includes interest on the Medicare trust fund, accumulated out of past payroll taxes. The effect would be to force the government to declare a Medicare crisis in 2010 or 2011.

You might say it's a good idea to face up to Medicare's problems early. But the legislation would allow only two responses: either an increase in the payroll tax (a regressive tax that bears more heavily on middle-class families than on the wealthy) or benefit cuts. Other possibilities, like increases in other taxes or other spending cuts, would be ruled out. In short, this is an attempt to pre-empt discussion of how we want to deal with Medicare's future and impose a solution reflecting a particular ideology.

Meanwhile, another proposal—to force Medicare to compete with private insurers—seems intended to undermine the whole system.

This proposal goes under the name of "premium support." Medicare would no longer cover whatever medical costs an individual faced; instead, retirees would receive a lump sum to buy private insurance. (Those who opted to remain with the traditional system would have to pay extra premiums.) The ostensible rationale for this change is the claim that private insurers can provide better, cheaper medical care.

But many studies predict that private insurers would cherry-pick the best (healthiest) prospects, leaving traditional Medicare with retirees who are likely to have high medical costs. These higher costs would then be reflected in the extra payments required to stay in traditional fee-for-service coverage. The effect would be to put health care out of reach for many older Americans. As a 2002 study by the Kaiser Family Foundation judiciously put it, "Difficulties in adjusting for beneficiary health status . . . could make the traditional Medicare FFS program unaffordable to a large portion of beneficiaries."

What's going on? Why, bait and switch, of course. Few politicians want to be seen opposing a bill that finally provides retirees with prescription drug coverage. That makes a prescription drug bill a perfect vehicle for smuggling in provisions that sound as if they have something to do with improving Medicare, yet are actually designed to undermine it.

Faced with adamant opposition from Democrats who understand exactly what's going on, like Senator Edward Kennedy, the Republicans are reported to have retreated a bit. The consequences of the crunch planned for 2011 will apparently be less drastic, and premium support will be introduced as an experiment—albeit one involving millions of people—rather than all at once. But this bill is still a Trojan horse.

# OUR SO-CALLED BOOM

*December 30, 2003*

It was a merry Christmas for Sharper Image and Neiman Marcus, which reported big sales increases over last year's holiday season. It was considerably less cheery at Wal-Mart and other low-priced chains. We don't know the final sales figures yet, but it's clear that high-end stores did very well, while stores catering to middle- and low-income families achieved only modest gains.

Based on these reports, you may be tempted to speculate that the economic recovery is an exclusive party, and most people weren't invited. You'd be right.

Commerce Department figures reveal a startling disconnect between overall economic growth, which has been impressive since last spring, and the incomes of a great majority of Americans. In the third quarter of 2003, as everyone knows, real G.D.P. rose at an annual rate of 8.2 percent. But wage and salary income, adjusted for inflation, rose at an annual rate of only 0.8 percent. More recent data don't change the picture: in the six months that ended in November, income from wages rose only 0.65 percent after inflation.

Why aren't workers sharing in the so-called boom? Start with jobs.

Payroll employment began rising in August, but the pace of job growth remains modest, averaging less than 90,000 per month. That's well short of the 225,000 jobs added per month during the

Clinton years; it's even below the roughly 150,000 jobs needed to keep up with a growing working-age population.

But if the number of jobs isn't rising much, aren't workers at least earning more? You may have thought so. After all, companies have been able to increase output without hiring more workers, thanks to the rapidly rising output per worker. (Yes, that's a tautology.) Historically, higher productivity has translated into rising wages. But not this time: thanks to a weak labor market, employers have felt no pressure to share productivity gains. Calculations by the Economic Policy Institute show real wages for most workers flat or falling even as the economy expands.

An aside: how weak is the labor market? The measured unemployment rate of 5.9 percent isn't that high by historical standards, but there's something funny about that number. An unusually large number of people have given up looking for work, so they are no longer counted as unemployed, and many of those who say they have jobs seem to be only marginally employed. Such measures as the length of time it takes laid-off workers to get new jobs continue to indicate the worst job market in 20 years.

So, if jobs are scarce and wages are flat, who's benefiting from the economy's expansion? The direct gains are going largely to corporate profits, which rose at an annual rate of more than 40 percent in the third quarter. Indirectly, that means that gains are going to stockholders, who are the ultimate owners of corporate profits. (That is, if the gains don't go to self-dealing executives, but let's save that topic for another day.)

Well, so what? Aren't we well on our way toward becoming what the administration and its reliable defenders call an "ownership society," in which everyone shares in stock market gains? Um, no. It's true that slightly more than half of American families participate in the stock market, either directly or through investment accounts. But most families own at most a few thousand dollars' worth of stocks.

A good indicator of the share of increased profits that goes to different income groups is the Congressional Budget Office's estimate of the share of the corporate profits tax that falls, indirectly, on those groups. According to the most recent estimate, only 8 percent of corporate taxes were paid by the poorest 60 percent of families, while 67 percent were paid by the richest 5 percent, and 49 percent by the richest 1 percent. ("Class warfare!" the right shouts.) So a recovery that boosts profits but not wages delivers the bulk of its benefits to a small, affluent minority.

The bottom line, then, is that for most Americans, current economic growth is a form of reality TV, something interesting that is, however, happening to other people. This may change if serious job creation ever kicks in, but it hasn't so far.

The big question is whether a recovery that does so little for most Americans can really be sustained. Can an economy thrive on sales of luxury goods alone? We may soon find out.

# RED INK REALITIES

*January 27, 2004*

Even conservatives are starting to admit that George Bush isn't serious when he claims to be doing something about the exploding budget deficit. At best—to borrow the already classic language of the State of the Union address—his administration is engaged in deficit reduction–related program activities.

But these admissions have been accompanied by an urban legend about what went wrong. According to cleverly misleading reports from the Heritage Foundation and other like-minded sources, the deficit is growing because Mr. Bush isn't sufficiently conservative: he's allowing runaway growth in domestic spending. This myth is intended to divert attention from the real culprit: sharply reduced tax collections, mainly from corporations and the wealthy.

Is domestic spending really exploding? Think about it: farm subsidies aside, which domestic programs have received lavish budget increases over the last three years? Education? Don't be silly: No Child Left Behind is rapidly turning into a sick joke.

In fact, many government agencies are severely underfinanced. For example, last month the head of the National Park Service's police admitted to reporters that her force faced serious budget and staff shortages, and was promptly suspended.

A recent study by the Center on Budget and Policy Priorities does the math. While overall government spending has risen rapidly since 2001, the great bulk of that increase can be attributed either to outlays on defense and homeland security, or to types of government spending, like unemployment insurance, that automatically rise when the economy is depressed.

Why, then, do we face the prospect of huge deficits as far as the eye can see? Part of the answer is the surge in defense and homeland security spending. The main reason for deficits, however, is that revenues have plunged. Federal tax receipts as a share of national income are now at their lowest level since 1950.

Of course, most people don't feel that their taxes have fallen sharply. And they're right: taxes that fall mainly on middle-income Americans, like the payroll tax, are still near historic highs. The decline in revenue has come almost entirely from taxes that are mostly paid by the richest 5 percent of families: the personal income tax and the corporate profits tax. These taxes combined now take a smaller share of national income than in any year since World War II.

This decline in tax collections from the wealthy is partly the result of the Bush tax cuts, which account for more than half of this year's projected deficit. But it also probably reflects an epidemic of tax avoidance and evasion. Everyone who wants to understand what's happening to the tax system should read *Perfectly Legal*, the new book by David Cay Johnston, *The Times*'s tax reporter, who shows how ideologues have made America safe for wealthy people who don't feel like paying taxes.

I was particularly struck by Mr. Johnston's description of the carefully staged Senate Finance Committee hearings in 1997–1998. Senators Trent Lott and Frank Murkowski accused the I.R.S. of "Gestapo"-like tactics, and Congress passed new rules that severely restricted the I.R.S.'s ability to investigate suspected tax evaders. Only later, when the cameras were no longer rolling, did it become clear that the whole thing was a con. Most of the charges weren't true, and there was good reason to believe that the star witness, who dramatically described how I.R.S. agents had humiliated him, really was engaged in major-league tax evasion (he eventually paid $23 million, still insisting he had done no wrong).

And this was part of a larger con. What's playing out in America right now is the bait-and-switch strategy known on the right as "starve the beast." The ultimate goal is to slash government programs that help the poor and the middle class, and use the savings to cut taxes for the rich. But the public would never vote for that.

So the right has used deceptive salesmanship to undermine tax enforcement and push through upper-income tax cuts. And now that deficits have emerged, the right insists that they are the result of runaway spending, which must be curbed.

While this strategy has been remarkably successful so far, it also offers a big opportunity to the opposition. So here's a test for the Democratic contenders: details of your proposals aside, which of you can do the best job explaining the ongoing budget con to the American people?

# THE HEALTH OF NATIONS

*February 17, 2004*

The Economic Report of the President, released last week, has drawn criticism on several fronts. Let me open a new one: the report's discussion of health care, which shows a remarkable indifference to the concerns of ordinary Americans—and suggests a major political opening for the Democrats.

According to a recent Gallup poll, 82 percent of Americans rank health care among their top issues. People are happy with the quality of health care, if they can afford it, but they're afraid that they might not be able to afford it. Unlike other wealthy countries, America doesn't have universal health insurance, and it's all too easy to fall through the cracks in our system. When I saw that the president's economic report devoted a whole chapter to health care, I assumed that it would make some attempt to address these public concerns.

Instead, the report pooh-poohs the problem. Although more than 40 million people lack health insurance, this doesn't matter too much because "the uninsured are a diverse and perpetually changing group." This is good news? At any given time about one in seven Americans is uninsured, which is bad enough. Because the uninsured are a "perpetually changing group," however, a much larger fraction of the population suffers periodic, terrifying spells of being uninsured, and an even larger fraction lives with the fear of losing insurance if anything goes wrong at work or at home.

The report also seems to have missed the point of health

insurance. It argues that it would be a good thing if insurance companies had more information about the health prospects of clients so "policies could be tailored to different types and priced accordingly." So if insurance companies develop a new way to identify people who are likely to have kidney problems later in life, and use this information to deny such people policies that cover dialysis, that's a positive step?

Having brushed off the plight of those who, for economic or health reasons, cannot get insurance, the report turns to a criticism of health insurance in general, which it blames for excessive health care spending.

Is this really the crucial issue? It's true that the U.S. spends far more on health care than any other country, but this wouldn't be a bad thing if the spending got results. The real question is why, despite all that spending, many Americans aren't assured of the health care they need, and American life expectancy is near the bottom for advanced countries.

Where is the money going? A lot of it goes to overhead. A recent study found that private insurance companies spend 11.7 cents of every health care dollar on administrative costs, mainly advertising and underwriting, compared with 3.6 cents for Medicare and 1.3 cents for Canada's government-run system. Also, our system is very generous to drug companies and other medical suppliers, because—unlike other countries' systems—it doesn't bargain for lower prices.

The result is that American health care, which at its best is the best in the world, offers much of the population a worst-of-all-worlds combination of insecurity and high costs. And that combination is getting worse: insurance premiums are rising, and companies are becoming increasingly unwilling to offer insurance to their employees.

What would an answer to the growing health care crisis look

like? It would surely involve extending coverage to those now uninsured. To keep costs down, it would crack down both on drug prices and on administrative costs. And it might well cut private insurance companies out of the loop for some, if not all, coverage.

But the administration can't offer such an answer, both because of its ideological blinders and because of its special interest ties. The Economic Report of the President has only negative things to say about efforts to hold down drug prices. It talks at length about insurance reform, but it mainly complains that we rely too much on insurance; it says nothing about either expanding coverage or reducing insurance-company overhead. Its main concrete policy suggestion is a plan for tax-deductible health savings accounts, which would be worth little or nothing to a vast majority of the uninsured.

I'll talk more about alternatives for health care in future columns. But for now, let's just note that this is an issue the public cares about—an issue the administration can't address, but a bold Democrat can.

# MAESTRO OF CHUTZPAH

*March 2, 2004*

The traditional definition of chutzpah says it's when you murder your parents, then plead for clemency because you're an orphan. Alan Greenspan has chutzpah.

Last week Mr. Greenspan warned of the dangers posed by budget deficits. But even though the main cause of deficits is plunging revenue—the federal government's tax take is now at its lowest level as a share of the economy since 1950—he opposes any effort to restore recent revenue losses. Instead, he supports the Bush administration's plan to make its tax cuts permanent, and calls for cuts in Social Security benefits.

Yet three years ago Mr. Greenspan urged Congress to cut taxes, warning that otherwise the federal government would run excessive surpluses. He assured Congress that those tax cuts would not endanger future Social Security benefits. And last year he declined to stand in the way of another round of deficit-creating tax cuts.

But wait—it gets worse.

You see, although the rest of the government is running huge deficits—and never did run much of a surplus—the Social Security system is currently taking in much more money than it spends. Thanks to those surpluses, the program is fully financed at least through 2042. The cost of securing the program's future for many decades after that would be modest—a small fraction of the revenue that will be lost if the Bush tax cuts are made permanent.

And the reason Social Security is in fairly good shape is that during the 1980's the Greenspan commission persuaded Congress to increase the payroll tax, which supports the program.

The payroll tax is regressive: it falls much more heavily on middle- and lower-income families than it does on the rich. In fact, according to Congressional Budget Office estimates, families near the middle of the income distribution pay almost twice as much in payroll taxes as in income taxes. Yet people were willing to accept a regressive tax increase to sustain Social Security.

Now the joke's on them. Mr. Greenspan pushed through an increase in taxes on working Americans, generating a Social Security surplus. Then he used that surplus to argue for tax cuts that deliver very little relief to most people, but are worth a lot to those making more than $300,000 a year. And now that those tax cuts have contributed to a soaring deficit, he wants to cut Social Security benefits.

The point, of course, is that if anyone had tried to sell this package honestly—"Let's raise taxes and cut benefits for working families so we can give big tax cuts to the rich!"—voters would have been outraged. So the class warriors of the right engaged in bait-and-switch.

There are three lessons in this tale.

First, "starving the beast" is no longer a hypothetical scenario—it's happening as we speak. For decades, conservatives have sought tax cuts, not because they're affordable, but because they aren't. Tax cuts lead to budget deficits, and deficits offer an excuse to squeeze government spending.

Second, squeezing spending doesn't mean cutting back on wasteful programs nobody wants. Social Security and Medicare are the targets because that's where the money is. We might add that ideologues on the right have never given up on their hope of doing away with Social Security altogether. If Mr. Bush wins in November, we can be sure that they will move forward on privatization—the creation of personal retirement accounts. These will be sold as a way to "save" Social Security (from a nonexistent crisis), but will, in fact, undermine its finances. And that, of course, is the point.

Finally, the right-wing corruption of our government system—the partisan takeover of institutions that are supposed to be nonpolitical—continues, and even extends to the Federal Reserve.

The Bush White House has made it clear that it will destroy the careers of scientists, budget experts, intelligence operatives and even military officers who don't toe the line. But Mr. Greenspan should have been immune to such pressures, and he should have understood that the peculiarity of his position— as an unelected official who wields immense power—carries with it an obligation to stand above the fray. By using his office to promote a partisan agenda, he has betrayed his institution, and the nation.

# PROMISES, PROMISES

*March 9, 2004*

Despite a string of dismal employment reports, the administration insists that its economic program, which has relied entirely on tax cuts focused on the affluent, will produce big job gains any day now. Should we believe these promises?

Each February, the Economic Report of the President forecasts nonfarm payroll employment—generally considered the best measure of job growth—for the next several years. The black line in the chart on page 465 (inspired by a joint report from the Economic Policy Institute and the Center on Budget and Policy Priorities) shows the actual performance of employment [in the millions], both before and after its peak in March 2001. The gray lines show the forecasts in the 2002, 2003 and 2004 reports. Notice that the February 2004 forecast, which, as in previous years, is based on data only through the preceding October, is already 900,000 jobs too high.

Economic forecasting isn't an exact science, but wishful thinking on this scale is unprecedented. Nor can the administration use its all-purpose excuse: all of these forecasts date from after 9/11. What you see in this chart is the signature of a corrupted policy process, in which political propaganda takes the place of professional analysis.

## Wishful Thinking on Jobs

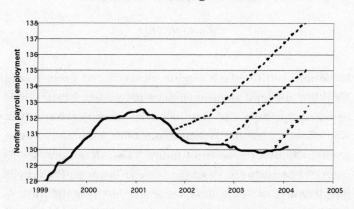

The Bush administration has consistently
overpredicted future job growth.

(*Sources*: Bureau of Labor Statistics; Economic Reports of the
President, 2002, 2003 and 2004)

# THE MEDICARE MUDDLE

*March 26, 2004*

In advance of Tuesday's reports by the Social Security and Medicare trustees, some credulous journalists wrote stories based on tips from advocates of Social Security privatization, who claimed that the report would offer a radically downgraded vision of the system's future. False alarm: projections for Social Security are about the same as last year. Projections for Medicare, however, have worsened: last year the trustees predicted that the hospital insurance trust fund would last until 2026, and now they've moved it back to 2019.

How should we react to this news?

It has become standard practice among privatizers to talk as if there is some program called Socialsecurityandmedicare. They hope to use scary numbers about future medical costs to panic us into abandoning a retirement program that's actually in pretty good shape. But the deteriorated outlook for Medicare says nothing, one way or another, about either the sustainability of Social Security (no problem) or the desirability of private retirement accounts (a lousy idea).

Even on Medicare, don't panic. It's not like a private health plan that will go belly up when it runs out of money; it's just a government program, albeit one supported by a dedicated tax. Nobody thinks America's highways will be doomed if the gasoline tax, which currently pays for highway maintenance, falls short of the system's needs—if politicians want to sustain the system, they will. The same is true of Medicare. Rising medical costs are a very big budget issue, but 2019 isn't a drop-dead date.

The trustees' report does, however, give one more reason to hate the prescription drug bill the administration rammed through Congress last year. If deception, intimidation, abuse of power and giveaways to drug companies aren't enough, it turns out that the bill also squanders taxpayer money on H.M.O.'s.

A little background: conservatives have never mounted an attack on Medicare as systematic as their effort to bully the public into privatizing Social Security. They do, however, often talk about Medicare "reform." What this amounts to, in practice, is a drive to replace the traditional system, in which Medicare pays doctors and hospitals directly, with a system in which Medicare subcontracts that role to private H.M.O.'s.

In 1997 Congress tried to take a big step in that direction, requiring Medicare to pay per-person fees to private health plans that accepted Medicare recipients. There was much talk about the magic of the marketplace: private plans, so the theory went, would be far more efficient than government bureaucrats, offering better health care at lower cost.

What actually happened was that private plans skimmed the cream, accepting only relatively healthy retirees. Yet Medicare paid them slightly more per retiree than it spent on traditional benefits. In other words, instead of saving money by subcontracting its role to private plans, Medicare was in effect required to pay H.M.O.'s a hefty subsidy.

The only thing that kept this "reform" from being a fiscal disaster was the fact that after an initial rush into the Medicare business, many H.M.O.'s pulled out again. It turns out that private plans are much less efficient than the government at providing health insurance because they have much higher over-head. Even with a heavy subsidy, they can't compete with tra-ditional Medicare.

There's a lesson in this experience. Sometimes there's no magic in the free market—in fact, it can be a hindrance. Health insurance is one place where government agencies consis-tently do a better job than private companies. I'll have more to say about this when I write about the general issue of health care reform (soon, I promise!).

But whether because of ideology or because of H.M.O. cam-paign contributions, the people now running the country refuse to learn that lesson. As part of last year's prescription drug bill, they tried again, offering an even bigger subsidy to private plans.

And that turns out to be an important reason for the deterio-ration in Medicare's prospects: of the seven years lopped off the life of the trust fund, two are the result of increased subsidies mandated by last year's law, mainly in the form of higher pay-ments to H.M.O.'s.

So what did we learn this week? Social Security is in decent shape. Medicare has problems, but ill-conceived "reform" has only made those problems worse. And let's rip up that awful prescription drug bill and start over.

# CHAPTER 19

# *Abuses of Power*

## MAN ON HORSEBACK

*May 6, 2003*

Gen. Georges Boulanger cut a fine figure; he looked splendid in uniform, and magnificent on horseback. So his handlers made sure that he appeared in uniform, astride a horse, as often as possible.

It worked: Boulanger became immensely popular. If he hadn't lost his nerve on the night of the attempted putsch, French democracy might have ended in 1889.

We do things differently here—or we used to. Has "man on horseback" politics come to America?

Some background: the Constitution declares the president commander in chief of the armed forces to make it clear that civilians, not the military, hold ultimate authority. That's why American presidents traditionally make a point of avoiding military affectations. Dwight Eisenhower was a victorious general and John Kennedy a genuine war hero, but while in office neither wore anything that resembled military garb.

Given that history, George Bush's "Top Gun" act aboard the

U.S.S. *Abraham Lincoln*—c'mon, guys, it wasn't about honoring the troops, it was about showing the president in a flight suit— was as scary as it was funny.

Mind you, it was funny. At first the White House claimed the dramatic tail-hook landing was necessary because the carrier was too far out to use a helicopter. In fact, the ship was so close to shore that, according to The Associated Press, administration officials "acknowledged positioning the massive ship to provide the best TV angle for Bush's speech, with the sea as his back-ground instead of the San Diego coastline."

A U.S.-based British journalist told me that he and his col-leagues had laughed through the whole scene. If Tony Blair had tried such a stunt, he said, the press would have demanded to know how many hospital beds could have been provided for the cost of the jet fuel.

But U.S. television coverage ranged from respectful to gush-ing. Nobody pointed out that Mr. Bush was breaking an impor-tant tradition. And nobody seemed bothered that Mr. Bush, who appears to have skipped more than a year of the National Guard service that kept him out of Vietnam, is now emphasiz-ing his flying experience. (Spare me the hate mail. An exhaus-tive study by *The Boston Globe* found no evidence that Mr. Bush fulfilled any of his duties during that missing year. And since Mr. Bush has chosen to play up his National Guard career, this can't be shrugged off as old news.)

Anyway, it was quite a show. Luckily for Mr. Bush, the frus-trating search for Osama bin Laden somehow morphed into a good old-fashioned war, the kind where you seize the enemy's capital and get to declare victory after a cheering crowd pulls down the tyrant's statue. (It wasn't much of a crowd, and Amer-ican soldiers actually brought down the statue, but it looked great on TV.)

Let me be frank. Why is the failure to find any evidence of an active Iraqi nuclear weapons program, or vast quantities of chemical and biological weapons (a few drums don't qualify—though we haven't found even that) a big deal? Mainly because it feeds suspicions that the war wasn't waged to eliminate real threats. This suspicion is further fed by the administration's lackadaisical attitude toward those supposed threats once Baghdad fell. For example, Iraq's main nuclear waste dump wasn't secured until a few days ago, by which time it had been thoroughly looted. So was it all about the photo-ops?

Well, Mr. Bush got to pose in his flight suit. And given the absence of awkward questions, his handlers surely feel empowered to make even more brazen use of the national security issue in future.

Next year—in early September—the Republican party will hold its nominating convention in New York. The party will exploit the time and location to the fullest. How many people will dare question the propriety of the proceedings?

And who will ask why, if the administration is so proud of its response to Sept. 11, it has gone to such lengths to prevent a thorough, independent inquiry into what actually happened? (An independent study commission wasn't created until after the 2002 election, and it has been given little time and a ludicrously tiny budget.)

There was a time when patriotic Americans from both parties would have denounced any president who tried to take political advantage of his role as commander in chief. But that, it seems, was another country.

## THE CHINA SYNDROME

*May 13, 2003*

A funny thing happened during the Iraq war: many Americans turned to the BBC for their TV news. They were looking for an alternative point of view—something they couldn't find on domestic networks, which, in the words of the BBC's director general, "wrapped themselves in the American flag and substituted patriotism for impartiality."

Leave aside the rights and wrongs of the war itself, and consider the paradox. The BBC is owned by the British government, and one might have expected it to support that government's policies. In fact, however, it tried hard—too hard, its critics say— to stay impartial. America's TV networks are privately owned, yet they behaved like state-run media.

What explains this paradox? It may have something to do with the China syndrome. No, not the one involving nuclear reactors—the one exhibited by Rupert Murdoch's News Corporation when dealing with the government of the People's Republic.

In the United States, Mr. Murdoch's media empire—which includes Fox News and *The New York Post*—is known for its flag-waving patriotism. But all that patriotism didn't stop him from, as a *Fortune* article put it, "pandering to China's repressive regime to get his programming into that vast market." The pandering included dropping the BBC's World Service—which reports news China's government doesn't want disseminated—

from his satellite programming, and having his publishing company cancel the publication of a book critical of the Chinese regime.

Can something like that happen in this country? Of course it can. Through its policy decisions—especially, though not only, decisions involving media regulation—the U.S. government can reward media companies that please it, punish those that don't. This gives private networks an incentive to curry favor with those in power. Yet because the networks aren't government-owned, they aren't subject to the kind of scrutiny faced by the BBC, which must take care not to seem like a tool of the ruling party. So we shouldn't be surprised if America's "independent" television is far more deferential to those in power than the state-run systems in Britain or—for another example—Israel.

A recent report by Stephen Labaton of *The Times* contained a nice illustration of the U.S. government's ability to reward media companies that do what it wants. The issue was a proposal by Michael Powell, chairman of the Federal Communications Commission, to relax regulations on media ownership. The proposal, formally presented yesterday, may be summarized as a plan to let the bigger fish eat more of the smaller fish. Big media companies will be allowed to have a larger share of the national market and own more TV stations in any given local market, and many restrictions on "cross-ownership"—owning radio stations, TV stations and newspapers in the same local market—will be lifted.

The plan's defects aside—it will further reduce the diversity of news available to most people—what struck me was the horse-trading involved. One media group wrote to Mr. Powell, dropping its opposition to part of his plan "in return for favorable commission action" on another matter. That was indiscreet, but you'd have to be very naïve not to imagine that there are a lot of implicit quid pro quos out there.

And the implicit trading surely extends to news content. Imagine a TV news executive considering whether to run a major story that might damage the Bush administration—say, a follow-up on Senator Bob Graham's charge that a Congressional report on Sept. 11 has been kept classified because it would raise embarrassing questions about the administration's performance. Surely it would occur to that executive that the administration could punish any network running that story.

Meanwhile, both the formal rules and the codes of ethics that formerly prevented blatant partisanship are gone or ignored. Neil Cavuto of Fox News is an anchor, not a commentator. Yet after Baghdad's fall he told "those who opposed the liberation of Iraq"—a large minority—that "you were sickening then; you are sickening now." Fair and balanced.

We don't have censorship in this country; it's still possible to find different points of view. But we do have a system in which the major media companies have strong incentives to present the news in a way that pleases the party in power, and no incentive not to.

## TOWARD ONE-PARTY RULE

*June 27, 2003*

In principle, Mexico's 1917 Constitution established a democratic political system. In practice, until very recently Mexico was a one-party state. While the ruling party employed intimidation and electoral fraud when necessary, mainly it kept control through patronage, cronyism and corruption. All powerful interest groups, including the media, were effectively part of the party's political machine.

Such systems aren't unknown here—think of Richard J. Daley's Chicago. But can it happen to the United States as a whole? A forthcoming article in *The Washington Monthly* shows that the foundations for one-party rule are being laid right now.

In "Welcome to the Machine," Nicholas Confessore draws together stories usually reported in isolation—from the drive to privatize Medicare, to the pro-tax-cut fliers General Motors and Verizon recently included with the dividend checks mailed to shareholders, to the pro-war rallies organized by Clear Channel radio stations. As he points out, these are symptoms of the emergence of an unprecedented national political machine, one that is well on track to establishing one-party rule in America.

Mr. Confessore starts by describing the weekly meetings in which Senator Rick Santorum vets the hiring decisions of major lobbyists. These meetings are the culmination of Grover Norquist's "K Street Project," which places Republican activists in high-level corporate and industry lobbyist jobs—and excludes Democrats. According to yesterday's *Washington Post*, a Republican National Committee official recently boasted that "33 of 36 top-level Washington positions he is monitoring went to Republicans."

Of course, interest groups want to curry favor with the party that controls Congress and the White House; but as *The Washington Post* explains, Mr. Santorum's colleagues have also used "intimidation and private threats" to bully lobbyists who try to maintain good relations with both parties. "If you want to play in our revolution," Tom DeLay, the House majority leader, once declared, "you have to live by our rules."

Lobbying jobs are a major source of patronage—a reward for the loyal. More important, however, many lobbyists now owe their primary loyalty to the party, rather than to the industries they represent. So corporate cash, once split more or less evenly between the parties, increasingly flows in only one direction.

And corporations themselves are also increasingly part of the party machine. They are rewarded with policies that increase their profits: deregulation, privatization of government services, elimination of environmental rules. In return, like G.M. and Verizon, they use their influence to support the ruling party's agenda.

As a result, campaign finance is only the tip of the iceberg. Next year, George W. Bush will spend two or three times as much money as his opponent; but he will also benefit hugely from the indirect support that corporate interests—very much including media companies—will provide for his political message.

Naturally, Republican politicians deny the existence of their burgeoning machine. "It never ceases to amaze me that people are so cynical they want to tie money to issues, money to bills, money to amendments," says Mr. DeLay. And Ari Fleischer says that "I think that the amount of money that candidates raise in our democracy is a reflection of the amount of support they have around the country." Enough said.

Mr. Confessore suggests that we may be heading for a replay of the McKinley era, in which the nation was governed by and for big business. I think he's actually understating his case: like Mr. DeLay, Republican leaders often talk of "revolution," and we should take them at their word.

Why isn't the ongoing transformation of U.S. politics—which may well put an end to serious two-party competition—getting more attention? Most pundits, to the extent they acknowledge that anything is happening, downplay its importance. For example, last year an article in *BusinessWeek* titled "The GOP's Wacky War on Dem Lobbyists" dismissed the K Street Project as "silly—and downright futile." In fact, the project is well on the way to achieving its goals.

Whatever the reason, there's a strange disconnect between most political commentary and the reality of the 2004 election. As in 2000, pundits focus mainly on images—John Kerry's furrowed brow, Mr. Bush in a flight suit—or on supposed personality traits. But it's the nexus of money and patronage that may well make the election a foregone conclusion.

## EXPLOITING THE ATROCITY

*September 12, 2003*

In my first column after 9/11, I mentioned something everyone with contacts on Capitol Hill already knew: that just days after the event, the exploitation of the atrocity for partisan political gain had already begun.

In response, I received a torrent of outraged mail. At a time when the nation was shocked and terrified, the thought that our leaders might be that cynical was too much to bear. "How can I say that to my young son?" asked one furious e-mailer.

I wonder what that correspondent thinks now. Is the public—and the news media—finally prepared to cry foul when cynicism comes wrapped in the flag? America's political future may rest on the answer.

The press has become a lot less shy about pointing out the administration's exploitation of 9/11, partly because that exploitation has become so crushingly obvious. As *The Washington Post* pointed out yesterday, in the past six weeks President Bush has invoked 9/11 not just to defend Iraq policy and argue for oil drilling in the Arctic, but in response to questions about tax cuts, unemployment, budget deficits and even campaign finance. Meanwhile, the crudity of the administration's recent propaganda efforts, from dressing the president up in a flight suit to orchestrating the ludicrously glamorized TV movie about Mr. Bush on 9/11, have set even supporters' teeth on edge.

And some stunts no longer seem feasible. Maybe it was the pressure of other commitments that kept Mr. Bush from visiting New York yesterday; but one suspects that his aides no longer think of the Big Apple as a politically safe place to visit.

Yet it's almost certainly wrong to think that the political exploitation of 9/11 and, more broadly, the administration's campaign to label critics as unpatriotic are past their peak. It may be harder for the administration to wrap itself in the flag, but it has more incentive to do so now than ever before. Where once the administration was motivated by greed, now it's driven by fear.

In the first months after 9/11, the administration's ruthless exploitation of the atrocity was a choice, not a necessity. The natural instinct of the nation to rally around its leader in times of crisis had pushed Mr. Bush into the polling stratosphere, and his re-election seemed secure. He could have governed as the uniter he claimed to be, and would probably still be wildly popular.

But Mr. Bush's advisers were greedy; they saw 9/11 as an opportunity to get everything they wanted, from another round of tax cuts, to a major weakening of the Clean Air Act, to an invasion of Iraq. And so they wrapped as much as they could in the flag.

Now it has all gone wrong. The deficit is about to go above half a trillion dollars, the economy is still losing jobs, the triumph in Iraq has turned to dust and ashes, and Mr. Bush's poll numbers are at or below their pre-9/11 levels.

Nor can the members of this administration simply lose like gentlemen. For one thing, that's not how they operate. Furthermore, everything suggests that there are major scandals—involving energy policy, environmental policy, Iraq contracts and cooked intelligence—that would burst into the light of day if the current management lost its grip on power. So these people must win, at any cost.

The result, clearly, will be an ugly, bitter campaign—probably the nastiest of modern American history. Four months ago it seemed that the 2004 campaign would be all slow-mo films of Mr. Bush in his flight suit. But at this point, it's likely to be pictures of Howard Dean or Wesley Clark that morph into Saddam Hussein. And Donald Rumsfeld has already rolled out the stab-in-the-back argument: if you criticize the administration, you're lending aid and comfort to the enemy.

This political ugliness will take its toll on policy, too. The administration's infallibility complex—its inability to admit ever making a mistake—will get even worse. And I disagree with those who think the administration can claim infallibility even while practicing policy flexibility: on major issues, such as taxes or Iraq, any sensible policy would too obviously be an implicit admission that previous policies had failed.

In other words, if you thought the last two years were bad, just wait: it's about to get worse. A lot worse.

# LESSONS IN CIVILITY

*October 10, 2003*

It's the season of the angry liberal. Books like Al Franken's *Lies and the Lying Liars Who Tell Them*, Joe Conason's *Big Lies* and Molly Ivins's *Bushwhacked* have become best sellers. (Yes, I've got one out there, too.) But conservatives are distressed because those liberals are so angry and rude. O.K., they admit, they themselves were a bit rude during the Clinton years—that seven-year, $70 million investigation of a tiny money-losing land deal, all that fuss about the president's private life—but they're sorry, and now it's time for everyone to be civil.

Indeed, angry liberals can take some lessons in civility from today's right.

Consider, for example, Fox News's genteel response to Christiane Amanpour, the CNN correspondent. Ms. Amanpour recently expressed some regret over CNN's prewar reporting: "Perhaps, to a certain extent, my station was intimidated by the administration and its foot soldiers at Fox News." A Fox spokeswoman replied, "It's better to be viewed as a foot soldier for Bush than as a spokeswoman for Al Qaeda."

And liberal pundits who may be tempted to cast personal aspersions can take lessons in courtesy from conservatives like Charles Krauthammer, who last December reminded TV viewers of his previous career as a psychiatrist, then said of Al Gore, "He could use a little help."

What's really important, of course, is that political figures stick to the issues, like the Bush adviser who told *The New York*

*Times* that the problem with Senator John Kerry is that "he looks French."

Some say that the right, having engaged in name-calling and smear tactics when Bill Clinton was president, now wants to change the rules so such behavior is no longer allowed. In fact, the right is still calling names and smearing; it wants to prohibit rude behavior only by liberals.

But there's more going on than a simple attempt to impose a double standard. All this fuss about the rudeness of the Bush administration's critics is an attempt to preclude serious discussion of that administration's policies. For there is no way to be both honest and polite about what has happened in these past three years.

On the fiscal front, this administration has used deceptive accounting to ram through repeated long-run tax cuts in the face of mounting deficits. And it continues to push for more tax cuts, when even the most sober observers now talk starkly about the risk to our solvency. It's impolite to say that George W. Bush is the most fiscally irresponsible president in American history, but it would be dishonest to pretend otherwise.

On the foreign policy front, this administration hyped the threat from Iraq, ignoring warnings from military professionals that a prolonged postwar occupation would tie down much of our Army and undermine our military readiness. (Joseph Galloway, co-author of *We Were Soldiers Once . . . and Young*, says that "we have perhaps the finest Army in history," but that "Donald H. Rumsfeld and his civilian aides have done just about everything they could to destroy that Army.") It's impolite to say that Mr. Bush has damaged our national security with his military adventurism, but it would be dishonest to pretend otherwise.

Still, some would say that criticism should focus only on Mr.

Bush's policies, not on his person. But no administration in memory has made paeans to the president's character—his "honor and integrity"—so central to its political strategy. Nor has any previous administration been so determined to portray the president as a hero, going so far as to pose him in line with the heads on Mount Rushmore, or arrange that landing on the aircraft carrier. Surely, then, Mr. Bush's critics have the right to point out that the life story of the man inside the flight suit isn't particularly heroic—that he has never taken a risk or made a sacrifice for the sake of his country, and that his business career is a story of murky deals and insider privilege.

In the months after 9/11, a shocked nation wanted to believe the best of its leader, and Mr. Bush was treated with reverence. But he abused the trust placed in him, pushing a partisan agenda that has left the nation weakened and divided. Yes, I know that's a rude thing to say. But it's also the truth.

# HACK THE VOTE

*December 2, 2003*

Inviting Bush supporters to a fund-raiser, the host wrote, "I am committed to helping Ohio deliver its electoral votes to the president next year." No surprise there. But Walden O'Dell—who says that he wasn't talking about his business operations—happens to be the chief executive of Diebold Inc., whose touch-screen voting machines are in increasingly widespread use across the United States.

For example, Georgia—where Republicans scored spectacular upset victories in the 2002 midterm elections—relies exclusively on Diebold machines. To be clear, though there were many anomalies in that 2002 vote, there is no evidence that the machines miscounted. But there is also no evidence that the machines counted correctly. You see, Diebold machines leave no paper trail.

Representative Rush Holt of New Jersey, who has introduced a bill requiring that digital voting machines leave a paper trail and that their software be available for public inspection, is occasionally told that systems lacking these safeguards haven't caused problems. "How do you know?" he asks.

What we do know about Diebold does not inspire confidence. The details are technical, but they add up to a picture of a company that was, at the very least, extremely sloppy about security, and may have been trying to cover up product defects.

Early this year Bev Harris, who is writing a book on voting

machines, found Diebold software—which the company refuses to make available for public inspection, on the grounds that it's proprietary—on an unprotected server, where anyone could download it. (The software was in a folder titled "rob-Georgia.zip.") The server was used by employees of Diebold Election Systems to update software on its machines. This in itself was an incredible breach of security, offering someone who wanted to hack into the machines both the information and the opportunity to do so.

An analysis of Diebold software by researchers at Johns Hopkins and Rice Universities found it both unreliable and subject to abuse. A later report commissioned by the state of Maryland apparently reached similar conclusions. (It's hard to be sure because the state released only a heavily redacted version.)

Meanwhile, leaked internal Diebold e-mail suggests that corporate officials knew their system was flawed, and circumvented tests that would have revealed these problems. The company hasn't contested the authenticity of these documents; instead, it has engaged in legal actions to prevent their dissemination.

Why isn't this front-page news? In October, a British newspaper, *The Independent*, ran a hair-raising investigative report on U.S. touch-screen voting. But while the mainstream press has reported the basics, the Diebold affair has been treated as a technology or business story—not as a potential political scandal.

This diffidence recalls the treatment of other voting issues, like the Florida "felon purge" that inappropriately prevented many citizens from voting in the 2000 presidential election. The attitude seems to be that questions about the integrity of vote counts are divisive at best, paranoid at worst. Even reform advocates like Mr. Holt make a point of dissociating themselves from "conspiracy theories." Instead, they focus on legislation to prevent future abuses.

But there's nothing paranoid about suggesting that political operatives, given the opportunity, might engage in dirty tricks. Indeed, given the intensity of partisanship these days, one suspects that small dirty tricks are common. For example, Orrin Hatch, the chairman of the Senate Judiciary Committee, recently announced that one of his aides had improperly accessed sensitive Democratic computer files that were leaked to the press.

This admission—contradicting an earlier declaration by Senator Hatch that his staff had been cleared of culpability—came on the same day that the Senate police announced that they were hiring a counterespionage expert to investigate the theft. Republican members of the committee have demanded that the expert investigate only how those specific documents were leaked, not whether any other breaches took place. I wonder why.

The point is that you don't have to believe in a central conspiracy to worry that partisans will take advantage of an insecure, unverifiable voting system to manipulate election results. Why expose them to temptation?

I'll discuss what to do in a future column. But let's be clear: the credibility of U.S. democracy may be at stake.

# DEMOCRACY AT RISK

*January 23, 2004*

The disputed election of 2000 left a lasting scar on the nation's psyche. A recent Zogby poll found that even in red states, which voted for George W. Bush, 32 percent of the public believes that the election was stolen. In blue states, the fraction is 44 percent.

Now imagine this: in November the candidate trailing in the polls wins an upset victory—but all of the districts where he does much better than expected use touch-screen voting machines. Meanwhile, leaked internal e-mail from the companies that make these machines suggests widespread error, and possibly fraud. What would this do to the nation?

Unfortunately, this story is completely plausible. (In fact, you can tell a similar story about some of the results in the 2002 midterm elections, especially in Georgia.) *Fortune* magazine rightly declared paperless voting the worst technology of 2003, but it's not just a bad technology—it's a threat to the republic.

First of all, the technology has simply failed in several recent elections. In a special election in Broward County, Fla., 134 voters were disenfranchised because the electronic voting machines showed no votes, and there was no way to determine those voters' intent. (The election was decided by only 12 votes.) In Fairfax County, Va., electronic machines crashed repeatedly and balked at registering votes. In the 2002 primary, machines in several Florida districts reported no votes for governor.

And how many failures weren't caught? Internal e-mail from

Diebold, the most prominent maker of electronic voting machines (though not those in the Florida and Virginia debacles), reveals that programmers were frantic over the system's unreliability. One reads, "I have been waiting for someone to give me an explanation as to why Precinct 216 gave Al Gore a minus 16022 when it was uploaded." Another reads, "For a demonstration I suggest you fake it."

Computer experts say that software at Diebold and other manufacturers is full of security flaws, which would easily allow an insider to rig an election. But the people at voting machine companies wouldn't do that, would they? Let's ask Jeffrey Dean, a programmer who was senior vice president of a voting machine company, Global Election Systems, before Diebold acquired it in 2002. Bev Harris, author of *Black Box Voting* (www.blackboxvoting.com), told The A.P. that Mr. Dean, before taking that job, spent time in a Washington correctional facility for stealing money and tampering with computer files.

Questionable programmers aside, even a cursory look at the behavior of the major voting machine companies reveals systematic flouting of the rules intended to ensure voting security. Software was modified without government oversight; machine components were replaced without being rechecked. And here's the crucial point: even if there are strong reasons to suspect that electronic machines miscounted votes, nothing can be done about it. There is no paper trail; there is nothing to recount.

So what should be done? Representative Rush Holt has introduced a bill calling for each machine to produce a paper record that the voter verifies. The paper record would then be secured for any future audit. The bill requires that such verified voting be ready in time for the 2004 election—and that districts that can't meet the deadline use paper ballots instead. And it also requires surprise audits in each state.

I can't see any possible objection to this bill. Ignore the inevitable charges of "conspiracy theory." (Although some conspiracies are real: as yesterday's *Boston Globe* reports, "Republican staff members of the U.S. Senate Judiciary Committee infiltrated opposition computer files for a year, monitoring secret strategy memos and periodically passing on copies to the media.") To support verified voting, you don't personally have to believe that voting machine manufacturers have tampered or will tamper with elections. How can anyone object to measures that will place the vote above suspicion?

What about the expense? Let's put it this way: we're spending at least $150 billion to promote democracy in Iraq. That's about $1,500 for each vote cast in the 2000 election. How can we balk at spending a small fraction of that sum to secure the credibility of democracy at home?

## GET ME REWRITE!

*February 6, 2004*

Right now America is going through an Orwellian moment. On both the foreign policy and the fiscal fronts, the Bush administration is trying to rewrite history, to explain away its current embarrassments.

Let's start with the case of the missing W.M.D. Do you remember when the C.I.A. was reviled by hawks because its analysts were reluctant to present a sufficiently alarming picture of the Iraqi threat? Your memories are no longer operative. On or about last Saturday, history was revised: see, it's the C.I.A.'s fault that the threat was overstated. Given its warnings, the administration had no choice but to invade.

A tip from Joshua Marshall, of www.talkingpointsmemo. com, led me to a stark reminder of how different the story line used to be. Last year Laurie Mylroie published a book titled *Bush vs. the Beltway: How the C.I.A. and the State Department Tried to Stop the War on Terror.* Ms. Mylroie's book came with an encomium from Richard Perle; she's known to be close to Paul Wolfowitz and to Dick Cheney's chief of staff. According to the jacket copy, "Mylroie describes how the C.I.A. and the State Department have systematically discredited critical intelligence about Saddam's regime, including indisputable evidence of its possession of weapons of mass destruction."

Currently serving intelligence officials may deny that they faced any pressure—after what happened to Valerie Plame, what would you do in their place?—but former officials tell a different story. The latest revelation is from Britain. Brian Jones, who was the Ministry of Defence's top W.M.D. analyst when Tony Blair assembled his case for war, says that the crucial dossier used to make that case didn't reflect the views of the professionals: "The expert intelligence experts of the D.I.S. [Defense Intelligence Staff] were overruled." All the experts agreed that the dossier's claims should have been "carefully caveated"; they weren't.

And don't forget the Pentagon's Office of Special Plans, created specifically to offer a more alarming picture of the Iraq threat than the intelligence professionals were willing to provide.

Can all these awkward facts be whited out of the historical record? Probably. Almost surely, President Bush's handpicked "independent" commission won't investigate the Office of Special Plans. Like Lord Hutton in Britain—who chose to disregard Mr. Jones's testimony—it will brush aside evidence that intelligence professionals were pressured. It will focus only on intelligence mistakes, not on the fact that the experts, while wrong, weren't nearly wrong enough to satisfy their political masters. (Among those mentioned as possible members of the commission is James Woolsey, who wrote one of the blurbs for Ms. Mylroie's book.)

And if top political figures have their way, there will be further rewriting to come. You may remember that Saddam gave in to U.N. demands that he allow inspectors to roam Iraq, looking for banned weapons. But your memories may soon be invalid. Recently Mr. Bush said that war had been justified because Saddam "did not let us in." And this claim was repeated by Senator Pat Roberts, chairman of the Senate Intelligence Committee: "Why on earth didn't [Saddam] let the inspectors in and avoid the war?"

Now let's turn to the administration's other big embarrassment, the budget deficit.

The fiscal 2005 budget report admits that this year's expected $521 billion deficit belies the rosy forecasts of 2001. But the report offers an explanation: stuff happens. "Today's budget deficits are the unavoidable result of the revenue erosion from the stock market collapse that began in early 2000, an economy recovering from recession and a nation confronting serious security threats." Sure, the administration was wrong—but so was everyone.

The trouble is that accepting that excuse requires forgetting a lot of recent history. By February 2002, when the administration released its fiscal 2003 budget, all of the bad news—the bursting of the bubble, the recession, and, yes, 9/11—had already happened. Yet that budget projected only a $14 billion deficit this year, and a return to surpluses next year. Why did that forecast turn out so wrong? Because administration officials fudged the facts, as usual.

I'd like to think that the administration's crass efforts to rewrite history will backfire, that the media and the informed public won't let officials get away with this. Have we finally had enough?

# THE REAL MAN

*February 13, 2004*

To understand why questions about George Bush's time in the National Guard are legitimate, all you have to do is look at the federal budget published last week. No, not the lies, damned lies and statistics—the pictures.

By my count, this year's budget contains 27 glossy photos of Mr. Bush. We see the president in front of a giant American flag, in front of the Washington Monument, comforting an elderly woman in a wheelchair, helping a small child with his reading assignment, building a trail through the wilderness and, of course, eating turkey with the troops in Iraq. Somehow the art director neglected to include a photo of the president swimming across the Yangtze River.

It was not ever thus. Bill Clinton's budgets were illustrated with tables and charts, not with worshipful photos of the president being presidential.

The issue here goes beyond using the Government Printing Office to publish campaign brochures. In this budget, as in almost everything it does, the Bush administration tries to blur the line between reverence for the office of president and reverence for the person who currently holds that office.

Operation Flight Suit was only slightly more over the top than other Bush photo-ops, like the carefully staged picture that placed Mr. Bush's head in line with the stone faces on Mount Rushmore. The goal is to suggest that it's unpatriotic to criticize the president, and to use his heroic image to block any substantive discussion of his policies.

In fact, those 27 photos grace one of the four most dishonest budgets in the nation's history—the other three are the budgets released in 2001, 2002 and 2003. Just to give you a taste: remember how last year's budget contained no money for post-war Iraq—and how administration officials waited until after the tax cut had been passed to mention the small matter of $87 billion in extra costs? Well, they've done it again: earlier this week the Army's chief of staff testified that the Iraq funds in the budget would cover expenses only through September.

But when administration officials are challenged about the blatant deceptions in their budgets—or, for that matter, about the use of prewar intelligence—their response, almost always, is to fall back on the president's character. How dare you question Mr. Bush's honesty, they ask, when he is a man of such unimpeachable integrity? And that leaves critics with no choice: they must point out that the man inside the flight suit bears little resemblance to the official image.

There is, as far as I can tell, no positive evidence that Mr. Bush is a man of exceptional uprightness. When has he even accepted responsibility for something that went wrong? On the other hand, there is plenty of evidence that he is willing to cut corners when it's to his personal advantage. His business career was full of questionable deals, and whatever the full truth about his National Guard service, it was certainly not glorious.

Old history, you may say, and irrelevant to the present. And perhaps that would be true if Mr. Bush was prepared to come clean about his past. Instead, he remains evasive. On "Meet the Press" he promised to release all his records—and promptly broke that promise.

I don't know what he's hiding. But I do think he has forfeited any right to cite his character to turn away charges that his administration is lying about its policies. And that is the point: Mr. Bush may not be a particularly bad man, but he isn't the paragon his handlers portray.

Some of his critics hope that the AWOL issue will demolish the Bush myth, all at once. They're probably too optimistic—if it were that easy, the tale of Harken Energy would have already done the trick. The sad truth is that people who have been taken in by a cult of personality—a group that in this case includes a good fraction of the American people, and a considerably higher fraction of the punditocracy—are very reluctant to give up their illusions. If nothing else, that would mean admitting that they had been played for fools.

Still, we may be on our way to an election in which Mr. Bush is judged on his record, not his legend. And that, of course, is what the White House fears.

# THIS ISN'T AMERICA

*March 30, 2004*

Last week an opinion piece in the Israeli newspaper *Haaretz* about the killing of Sheik Ahmed Yassin said, "This isn't America; the government did not invent intelligence material nor exaggerate the description of the threat to justify their attack."

So even in Israel, George Bush's America has become a byword for deception and abuse of power. And the administration's reaction to Richard Clarke's *Against All Enemies* provides more evidence of something rotten in the state of our government.

The truth is that among experts, what Mr. Clarke says about Mr. Bush's terrorism policy isn't controversial. The facts that terrorism was placed on the back burner before 9/11 and that Mr. Bush blamed Iraq despite the lack of evidence are confirmed by many sources—including *Bush at War*, by Bob Woodward.

And new evidence keeps emerging for Mr. Clarke's main charge, that the Iraq obsession undermined the pursuit of Al Qaeda. From yesterday's *USA Today*: "In 2002, troops from the Fifth Special Forces Group who specialize in the Middle East were pulled out of the hunt for Osama bin Laden to prepare for their next assignment: Iraq. Their replacements were troops with expertise in Spanish cultures."

That's why the administration responded to Mr. Clarke the way it responds to anyone who reveals inconvenient facts: with a campaign of character assassination.

Some journalists seem, finally, to have caught on. Last week an Associated Press news analysis noted that such personal attacks were "standard operating procedure" for this administration and cited "a behind-the-scenes campaign to discredit Richard Foster," the Medicare actuary who revealed how the administration had deceived Congress about the cost of its prescription drug bill.

But other journalists apparently remain ready to be used. On CNN, Wolf Blitzer told his viewers that unnamed officials were saying that Mr. Clarke "wants to make a few bucks, and that [in] his own personal life, they're also suggesting that there are some weird aspects in his life as well."

This administration's reliance on smear tactics is unprecedented in modern U.S. politics—even compared with Nixon's. Even more disturbing is its readiness to abuse power—to use its control of the government to intimidate potential critics.

To be fair, Senator Bill Frist's suggestion that Mr. Clarke might be charged with perjury may have been his own idea. But his move reminded everyone of the White House's reaction to revelations by the former Treasury Secretary Paul O'Neill: an immediate investigation into whether he had revealed classified information. The alacrity with which this investigation was opened was, of course, in sharp contrast with the administration's evident lack of interest in finding out who leaked the identity of the C.I.A. operative Valerie Plame to Bob Novak.

And there are many other cases of apparent abuse of power by the administration and its Congressional allies. A few examples: according to The Hill, Republican lawmakers threatened to cut off funds for the General Accounting Office unless it dropped its lawsuit against Dick Cheney. *The Washington Post* says Representative Michael Oxley told lobbyists that "a Congressional probe might ease if it replaced its Democratic lobbyist with a Republican." Tom DeLay used the Homeland Security Department to track down Democrats trying to prevent redistricting in Texas. And Medicare is spending millions of dollars on misleading ads for the new drug benefit—ads that look like news reports and also serve as commercials for the Bush campaign.

On the terrorism front, here's one story that deserves special mention. One of the few successful post–9/11 terror prosecutions—a case in Detroit—seems to be unraveling. The government withheld information from the defense, and witnesses unfavorable to the prosecution were deported (by accident, the government says). After the former lead prosecutor complained about the Justice Department's handling of the case, he suddenly found himself facing an internal investigation—and someone leaked the fact that he was under investigation to the press.

Where will it end? In his new book, *Worse Than Watergate*, John Dean, of Watergate fame, says, "I've been watching all the elements fall into place for two possible political catastrophes, one that will take the air out of the Bush-Cheney balloon and the other, far more disquieting, that will take the air out of democracy."

# Index

# PENGUIN ECONOMICS

### THE RETURN OF DEPRESSION ECONOMICS
PAUL KRUGMAN

'Essential reading' *Economist*

At the end of the 1990s, seven economies experienced slumps eerily reminiscent of the Great Depression. A botched devaluation in Thailand set off ripples all the way from Indonesia to South Korea. Russian debt default triggered disaster in Brazil. Hedge funds seemingly unaccountable to any government nearly succeeded in their aim of forcing up interest rates in Hong Kong. And almost no one had predicted these developments. Perhaps, argues Paul Krugman in his dazzling polemic, that is because we are trapped by a cosy free-market orthodoxy which cannot accept that 'bad things happen to good economies'. Yet if we truly hope to confront the immense challenges which lie ahead, we had better start facing up to reality right now.

'A lucid and punchy analysis of the dangers posed by global financial markets and a wake-up call for complacent or economically ignorant policymakers' *Economist*

'One of the world's most talented economists ... his combination of wit and clarity makes him a true heir to Keynes' *Independent*

'An account of the Asian crisis that is unlikely to be rivalled in its lucidity ... a rattling good read' *Financial Times*

# Online access to the facts, figures and faces behind the headlines.

**The Financial Times is giving Penguin readers the chance to SAVE OVER 40% on subscription to FT.com – the world's leading business website.**

Subscribe today and benefit from:

- **Instant access:** Search the entire FT archive, plus in-depth company information, with a tool that gives you relevant results fast.

- **Instant updates:** Give us any company names or topics and we'll email you relevant news as soon as it's published.

- **Instant analysis:** Get behind the headlines to the real story with the FT's informed, rapid-response analysis.

You'll also gain access to the full library of FT reports, an overnight preview of tomorrow's FT newspaper, sections devoted to industries, and access to our PDA service.

Claim your special Penguin price today and become an instant expert with the world's leading business website.

**Visit www.ft.com/penguinreader**

FT **.com**

FINANCIAL TIMES